AVONCLIFF

The Secret History
of an Industrial
Hamlet in War and Peace

AVONCLIFF

The Secret History
of an Industrial
Hamlet in War and Peace

by

Nick McCamley

FOLLY BOOKS

First published 2004 by Ex Libris Press, Bradford-on-Avon

This revised and extended edition published in 2018 by
Folly Books Ltd
Monkton Farleigh
BA15 2QP
www.follybooks.co.uk

A catalogue record for this book is available from the British Library.

ISBN 978-0-9928554-9-9

Designed and Typeset by Vicky

Printed and bound in India by Replika Press Pvt Ltd.

CONTENTS

ABOUT THE AUTHOR

Born in Bradford-on-Avon in November 1950, educated in the physical sciences at Bath Technical School, the historical sciences at Trowbridge College and the social sciences at Nottingham University, I finally entered the adult world totally devoid of all ambition or direction in life.

After marrying Vicky in 1973 I chose the self-employed route (for no-one else would have me) and, applying a little of everything I previously learned, I took up the restoration of antique clocks and electrical telegraph instruments while publishing an advertising magazine for collectors of railway antiquities. (I guess that had I simultaneously done voluntary work for the Citizen's Advice Bureau I would have fully engaged all three faculties).

Always passionately interested in industrial archaeology and underground engineering, I had the opportunity in 1984 to acquire the immensely sophisticated, eighty-acre underground ammunition depot at Monkton Farleigh which became the subject of an arduous ten-year restoration project.

In more recent years I became involved in the programming of air traffic control radar simulators for Bailbrook College in Bath, which in the 1990s was the world's foremost ATC training centre. Most of my time now, though, is occupied in research, writing and lecturing (principally for the University of Bristol) on a wide range of subjects based broadly upon military history and industrial archaeology.

Major publications to date are:

Secret Underground Cities (Pen & Sword, 1998)
Cold War Secret Nuclear Bunkers (Pen & Sword, 2000)
Saving Britain's Art Treasures (Pen & Sword, 2002)
Disasters Underground (Pen & Sword, 2004)
The Secret History of Chemical Warfare (Pen & Sword, 2006)
Second World War Secret Bunkers (Folly Books, 2010)
The Fauld Disaster (Folly Books 2015)

FOREWORD

Even the least observant reader might ask how I could have written such a big book about such a small place as Avoncliff. The answer is, of course, that the book, unlike the hamlet itself, actually has elastic boundaries that stretch from time to time, allowing us to wander off into more distant regions in order to place in context the events that shaped its history.

During the industrial revolution of the eighteenth and nineteenth centuries Avoncliff was, in microcosm, a reflection of everything that was going on in the larger world around it. But this brief buoyancy did not last long and, with Britain's fleeting industrial supremacy fading fast, Avoncliff teetered into obscurity during the first half of the twentieth century. Suddenly, a year into the Second World War and with a German invasion imminent, it took on a highly secret role of vital national importance that brought it once more to prominence, but by 1950, with the war five years in the past, Avoncliff had sunk back once again into obscurity and quiet decay. The restoration of the canal during the latter part of the twentieth century has given Avoncliff a new lease of life and the hamlet is probably now busier and more prosperous than it has ever been. Nothing, though, is now quite what it might appear in Avoncliff, as I will explain in the final chapter.

Readers might also notice that this book is surprisingly short of the stock-in-trade of most local histories, namely personal reminiscences and anecdotes (except for my own, of which, without wanting to seem hypocritical, I am minded to make an exception). It is not that I have any objection to reminiscences *per se*, but more that, over forty years of historical research, I have found that they are all too often completely wrong in matters of fact; not because there is amongst the contributors a willful wish to deceive but because, as all of us who were forced to study Shakespeare at school know:

> 'Old men forget; yet all shall be forgot,
> But he'll remember, with advantages,
> What feats he did that day.'

Also, it is all too easy for the researcher to misinterpret personal memories through not knowing the whole story, as the following tale, which is included to explain why this book was written and to give due acknowledgement to all those who, over the decades, have guided me on my way, might explain.

A large part of this book is concerned, directly or indirectly, with the history of the woollen industry in Bradford-on-Avon and of the great clothiers and entrepreneurs who guided its development. They, and the great houses in Bradford-on-Avon in which they lived, have fascinated me since early childhood and, indeed, two of those great houses had a predominant influence over my earliest childhood years. I was born in Bearfield House, the former home of Ezekiel Edmonds, one of Bradford's wealthiest and most successful nineteenth century mill owners. After a short labour which took everyone by surprise I was, so I have been told, delivered by my mother's sister, my Aunt Molly, who later described me as 'an ugly thin child, like a piece of string with a knot in the end.' My first Christmas, although I cannot remember it, was spent in Bearfield House. The earliest, most magical Christmases that I can remember clearly were spent in Woolley Grange, the glorious seventeenth century mansion built for the Quaker clothier John Baskerville where my Aunt Molly once lived. Although very young I vividly remember the ornate carving above the fire in the drawing room and the enormous Christmas tree lit each year with real candles. More than a decade later, I recall, rather nostalgically, some of the happiest days of my teenage years spent in the company of a close group of very special friends at the Grange.

Now, as an anecdote in isolation the foregoing might suggest a decadent and privileged upbringing, but such is far from the case. On the day that I was born, Bearfield House was the Bradford Maternity Hospital and my Aunt Molly was a ward sister. It is true that through most of the 1950s Molly lived in Woolley Grange, but for all that period the house was used as a nurses' hostel by the hospital authority and the stables were used as ambulance garages. My real privilege was the truly exceptional circle of friends I had about me during my later teenage years. Included amongst these was a lovely young girl named Anne Sheppard, whose family, by a happy coincidence, owned Woolley Grange and who always made us truly welcome there. My own family, by contrast, lived in a prefab in Ashley Close. My father was the son of a second generation Liverpool-Irish dock worker and my mother was a member of the Doel family of Wine Street who, if the archives of The *Wiltshire Times* are to be believed, were once rather notorious at the end of the nineteenth century when Wine Street and the adjoining area of Newtown were no-go areas of Bradford-on-Avon, where the rule of law and the normal conventions of social intercourse did not run.

My Aunt, whom some members of the family thought had 'Ideas Above Her Station', adopted something of a proprietorial attitude towards the two houses where she worked and lodged, an attitude which, inexplicably, her employers seemed either to encourage or turn a blind eye to. For me this had the happy consequence that by the age of five I, as her favourite nephew, had a free run of both houses to explore at will. There seemed to me to be something absolutely right about those big old houses; a sort of architectural perfection that affected me even at such a young age. An appreciation of what is right and wrong in the built world has stayed with me ever since.

Above: This image brings to mind Thomas Hood's '*I remember, I remember the house where I was born*', but unfortunately this is not the family's ancestral home; by 1950 Bearfield House had become the Bradford Maternity Hospital.

Left: The Bath Road entrance to Bearfield House. To those who didn't know, it was a mystery how more Bradfordonians came out through these gates than ever went in.

Below: Woolley Grange shortly after the end of the Second World War, when it was used as a nurse's hostel and home to my Aunt Molly.

Aunt Molly, also unwittingly, introduced me to two other features of the local landscape that would evolve into lifelong passions. One day when I was about four years old I went with her to a house adjacent to my grandmother's home in Wine Street Terrace. The house was then a rather ramshackle bungalow called 'White Horse View' and may have belonged to a distant relative. At the end of the long garden were two very old and long-abandoned underground stone quarries. I was given a torch and told to go off and explore them on my own while the adults went back to the house to chatter interminably over tea about the boring things that old people of that generation seemed to find interesting. I found the mines, and the whole business of being underground, absolutely awe-inspiring, though in fact, in comparison to the vast underground workings I was to be involved with in later life, they were not really very large at all. The smaller of the two tunnels was filled with military memorabilia, relics of the First World War collected by a previous owner, which made the whole adventure even more exciting.

A few days later I was taken by my aunt for a late autumn afternoon walk to Avoncliff where, purely by chance, I saw the very last boat pass over the aqueduct before the embankment, weakened by decades of neglect, finally collapsed at Murhill, leading to the drainage and abandonment of that section of the canal for the next thirty years. I was absolutely captivated by everything I saw; bathed in golden afternoon sunlight Avoncliff looked like a village misplaced in time, as though time there had stood still while the world evolved around it.

That was my first and last visit until the day, nearly two years later, when I was given my first bicycle. Flagrantly ignoring all my parents' dire warnings about going no further than the end of Ashley Lane (and all the not-so-veiled threats as to what was likely to happen to me if I did) I set off once again for Avoncliff. The trouble was that I really didn't know where Avoncliff was, but after a more-or-less accidental and utterly hair-raising, white-knuckle descent of Wine Street, I found myself on Belcombe Road and within an hour I was beside the canal which, to my absolute dismay, was completely devoid of water west of the aqueduct. More than a little disappointed, I cycled along the dry canal bed towards Murhill and just as I turned the first sharp right-hand corner I came across the enormous stranded hulks of the two boats I had seen crossing the aqueduct two years earlier. This was rather thrilling, made even more so by the fact that nearby on the canal bank and apparently standing sentinel over the abandoned boats was a somewhat sinister wartime pillbox. Later in the day I crept around the disused mill before returning home, far too late, to face the wrath of my parents. What I learned that day was a fact that I couldn't at first understand but which is, of course, the basis of industrial archaeology: namely that, irrespective of the initial capital investment, industrial assets of a dead industry have no value at all and are oft times just abandoned to nature.

So, those were the stages of my introduction to Avoncliff, architecture and Industrial archaeology. In 1961 I won a place at the Bath School of Art in Sydney Buildings but my father, who was an engineer, wanted me to be an engineer too, so I was packed off to the City of Bath Technical School, which I loathed with all my heart. There could not have been a more resolutely unimaginative school regime in the West Country than the one that held sway in the Technical School in Brougham Hayes during the 1960s. Its academic horizon reached no higher or wider than the Rugby pitch and its staff, with one or two celestial exceptions, was lacklustre, oppressive and punitive. The outstanding exception was Peter Coard, my art master whose specialism was the history of English vernacular architecture. His pencil records of the destruction of Georgian Bath in the 1960s are now world renowned and date for the most part from the period when I was his student. Peter transferred his concerns and enthusiasm to myself and my friend Tony Raddon. We were, I think, his favourite pupils and most devoted disciples and we copied his drawing techniques slavishly – Tony much better than me. The study of architectural history under Peter Coard formalized the rather woolly conceptions of building form and function that I had already unconsciously assimilated.

A rebellious boy, I made a premature and dramatic departure from the Technical School to continue my education at Trowbridge College, which at that time was as buoyant and progressive as the Tech had been reactionary and oppressive. At Trowbridge I studied Economic and Social History under Ken Wood, who was a truly remarkable lecturer and a lovely man who, for me, brought history to life. Much of this book is the result of the thorough grounding in social history that I learned from him, and for that I am grateful beyond measure. At the same time I was surrounded by a group of exceptional and rather talented friends (most much more talented than me) several of whom, in very different ways, have unconsciously contributed to this book. Amongst these is my old friend Graham with whom I discovered the recently abandoned underground ammunition depot at Monkton Farleigh in 1967 which, nearly twenty years later, my wife and I were able to acquire for restoration. That project, which lasted from 1984 until 1990, was both financially and physically exhausting and gave new meaning to the phrase 'money-pit'. Two other friends also deserve special mention; first, my long-lost friend Elizabeth who opened my eyes to the power of the written word, a gentle enlightenment which thirty years later brought about my career as a writer, and secondly, Geoffrey Holstead, with whom I shared so many common interests. Geoff and I seemed to spend much of our time at Avoncliff, either poking around in the mills or else drinking ourselves into a state of raucous stupidity at the Cross Guns. In 1967 Geoff passed his driving test and acquired a car which widened our sphere of investigative activity enormously. I don't think I ever contributed a penny towards the fuel used in those trips, so I hope an acknowledgement of that fact here might serve as an act of public contrition. As a final act of teenage perversity I went off to university at Nottingham to read psychology instead of history, a mistake I was to bitterly regret. To make amends I attended a series of extramural lectures given by Professor Asa Briggs whose book *The Making of Modern England* I had just read, and was enthralled. Professor Briggs joins Peter Coard and Ken Wood as the great and lasting influences on my subsequent interpretation of modern history.

So much for those friends and others from long ago who unknowingly guided me along the path that was to lead to this book – but what about the present? First I have to thank my poor wife, Vicky. By allowing me the freedom to chase my dreams for the past thirty years she has lived, with the greatest of fortitude, an exciting but precarious lifestyle of highs and lows that has been, I hope, less humdrum than it might otherwise have been. A more ordinary woman would have left me years ago for the security of an accountant, or a civil servant or a systems analyst. Her input in terms of research and proof-reading has been immense and in utter exasperation she continues to correct my worst grammatical excesses. Week after week I've dragged her off on interminably long Sunday afternoon walks around Avoncliff 'just to check another detail' for this book. She seems to have trekked along with remarkable good grace and enthusiasm, but perhaps I have misread the subliminal messages.

From the many archives that I have plundered for this book I have to offer especial thanks to the staff of the Wiltshire County Records Office in Trowbridge, to the Public Records Office (now the National Archives) at Kew and to Wiltshire Local Studies Library for permission to reproduce two pictures from their archive; also Christopher Date and Garry Thorn from the British Museum and Christopher Marsden, the archivist at the Victoria and Albert Museum for information regarding the evacuation of the treasures there to Westwood Quarry. As so often in the past, the late David Pollard provided a wealth of information about the stone quarrying industry. David and I followed vaguely similar research paths but for every crumb of new information I can offer him he returned a banquet. Finally, I offer my grateful thanks to Anthony Dunsdon and Peter Harford for allowing me to invade the privacy of their homes in pursuit of illustrations for this book.

1

INTRODUCTION

Avoncliff today looks little different from the Avoncliff of 1850 and, indeed, a visitor from the mid-nineteenth century would still discern all its main features. A few buildings have gone; rather fewer new ones have appeared and some of those older structures that remain are, through the ravages of fire and time, smaller than they once were. And, of course, except at weekends, it is much less busy than it was a century and a half ago. Go back another sixty years however, to 1790, and the terrain would be unrecognizable. Although there were mills beside the weir since at least the early sixteenth century, Avoncliff is essentially a child of the Industrial Revolution, born in 1796 with the coming of the Kennet and Avon Canal, fed by the quarries beneath the Westwood hillside and the mills on each bank of the river, and reaching its maturity in 1857 with the passage of the first train on the long delayed Wilts, Somerset and Weymouth Railway.

During this sixty year period of rapid development the whole orientation of the hamlet changed. Like countless other small enclaves in the river valleys of north Wiltshire and north-east Somerset, Avoncliff provided a source of water power to drive the mills and a river crossing, linking otherwise isolated hilltop settlements. Steep, direct tracks led from the hilltops to the valley bottoms providing routes not only for the pack-horses carrying produce to and from the mills but also joining the high winter pastures to the summer meadows in the river's flood plain. Less important trackways often ran parallel to the river, a low track close to the river's edge used when its waters were important for summer grazing cattle and a second, higher up the hillside, for winter when the water meadows flooded. Such tracks were important only within the parish, or between a pair of parishes, for, more often than not, the adjacent hamlet was the limit of the common man's horizon. By the middle of the nineteenth century this arrangement of narrow, lateral routes crossing the valleys from hilltop to hilltop had been largely replaced by revolutionary new, long-distance routes that swept down the lengths of the valleys, stimulating the growth of the riverside towns and often leading to the stultification of the hilltop settlements. Before we look in detail at the development of Avoncliff's transport links to the wider world it would, perhaps, be worthwhile to study in more general terms the pattern of pre-industrial revolution roadways and tracks that had developed around the Avon and Frome valleys since medieval times.

A pattern of isolated valley settlements, mills and steep hillside tracks can be seen all along the valleys of the Avon and Frome, their place names often give away their origin: Tellisford, Stowford, Farleigh Hungerford, Iford and Freshford on the River Frome; Bradford and Stokeford (at Limpley Stoke), to name just two, on the River Avon. The Avon was also crossed by a second ford at Freshford which is hardly discernible today, while other crossing points on the Avon are less easily identifiable by name, like Warleigh, Staverton and, of course, Avoncliff.

The beginnings of industrialization in the late eighteenth and early nineteenth centuries created an enormous demographic change. The rise of the great industrial cities and the drift of labour from the countryside to those cities is well known, but it is often forgotten that similar changes in working patterns happened in the more rural areas too. Once-small country towns grew important on the backs of the industries that thrived in them. Frome grew to be the second largest town in Somerset while Trowbridge – once called The Manchester of the South – became the most important industrial centre in Wiltshire with Bradford-on-Avon not far behind. Links between these newly enlarged towns and the outlying villages became more important than the tracks that joined parish to parish.

A key early response to the need for better transport over longer distances was the development of the network of straight, self-financing turnpike roads, one of the best examples of which in the immediate vicinity of our area of interest is the current A36. This road, which is now one of the country's most important north-south trunk routes, began as a turnpike road built by the Black Dog Turnpike Trust (named after the public house between Frome and Warminster where the trustees first met) and was intended as an outlet for the fast-growing industries of Frome. Started in 1752 and at first going no further than Warminster it was then extended to Woolverton in 1817 where it stalled for a further ten years. Frome's only outlet to the sea was via the Avon Navigation at Bath to the port of Bristol, but from Woolverton the steep climb through Midford or over Brassknocker Hill to Combe Down, followed by the precipitous descent into Bath, was backbreaking and it was imperative that an easier, if longer, route be found. The answer was the heavily engineered section of the A36, the Black Dog Turnpike Trust extension of 1830, that threads its way along the hillside through Limpley Stoke and Claverton before turning west at the Dry Arch towards the City of Bath. Driving along the A36 today one gets the impression that there are numerous small side roads that seem to have been laid as feeders to the little villages along the way, but this is not the case at all. It is no coincidence that they invariably take the form of crossroads because these little side-roads are, in fact, the ancient hilltop-to-valley-bottom tracks, bisected by the newer road that runs at a right angle to them along the length of the valley rather than across it.

Amongst the old tracks that were cut by the Black Dog Turnpike Trust were the lanes from Westwood to Norton St Phillip via Iford, Farleigh Hungerford to Hinton Charterhouse, Bath to Bradford-on-Avon via Limpley Stoke and Winsley, Bath to Bradford-on-Avon via Claverton and Warleigh, Midford to Freshford via both Midford Lane and Pipehouse Lane (now no more than an ill-defined pathway through a field for much of its length), and from Hinton Charterhouse to Freshford. This latter track once joined the Priory at Hinton Charterhouse to the ford at Freshford. It is no longer easily seen and must not be confused with the modern, straight road from Hinton Charterhouse village. The old track is now just a little-used footpath that passes beneath the A36 by means of an attractive gothic-arched bridge invisible from the road.

So, some of these early tracks have survived in the form of modern byways still used by road traffic today while others have become mere footpaths marked only by stiles at opposite sides of a field or wood. At Tellisford the old, narrow lane, impassable except on foot or horseback, must be unique. Unchanged, it still provides the only route to Tellisford from Wingfield, descending the steep hillside to cross the Frome by an ancient packhorse bridge much as it did five hundred years ago.

The construction of the Kennet and Avon Canal in the decade from 1795 and of the Wilts, Somerset and Weymouth Railway fifty years later produced even more fundamental and permanent changes in the topography of the Avon valley. Being intolerant of any incline the railway and canal were compelled wherever possible to run the lengths of the valleys through which they passed, adhering to the contours and even more ruthlessly cutting across the early tracks and lanes and packhorse ways. So complete was the transformation caused by these two new modes of transport that it is fair to say that the fifty years between 1796, when work started on the construction of the canal aqueduct, and 1846 when the first earthworks were begun for the Wilts, Somerset and Weymouth Railway, mark the change between the feudal Avoncliff that had existed for perhaps eight hundred years or more and the modern Avoncliff we see today.

A vivid picture of eighteenth century Avoncliff can be gleaned from the engineer's surveys for the Kennet and Avon Canal prepared in 1794. On these plans we see the weir with its mill buildings on each bank, served by a prominent packhorse-way that descends the hillside from Winsley via Turleigh then fords the river one hundred feet downstream of the weir before climbing again to Westwood. A series of less important tracks run parallel to the river. On the north bank a track ran westwards to meet another important lane that descends from Turleigh to cross the river to Freshford. The higher stretches of the lane from Turleigh are quite evident today, and in 1796 its traffic was sufficient to warrant the construction of a bridge over the newly constructed canal. Beyond the canal, across the water meadow, the route is less well defined and there is no longer any visible evidence of the ford. Across the river in the parish of Freshford the route is unmarked except for an accommodation bridge underneath the railway embankment which indicates that it was perhaps still used in 1846 when work on the line began.

To the east of Avoncliff a narrow track, clinging close to the riverbank, threaded its way to Bradford-on-Avon through Belcombe. This route must have been of some importance to Avoncliff's economy because when the railway line was built over much of its course in the mid-nineteenth century the Wilts, Somerset and Weymouth Railway defrayed the cost of widening and realigning it. The course of the old road can be seen on the Parliamentary Plans of the railway deposited in 1846.

On the Westwood side of the river the layout of the ancient trackways is more difficult to define due to the dramatic change in the profile of the hillside towards Bradford-on-Avon caused by the construction of the canal embankment. Three tracks once headed east towards Bradford-on-Avon. The high, winter lane from Westwood through Leigh Green is still in use today for motor traffic while the middle track from the quarries at Westwood that passed through Becky Addy Woods towards the present-day sewage works is now just a footpath. Short lengths, however, are still recognizable as the remnants of a once important route and can be seen as broad, roughly cobbled causeways rising a foot or two above the surrounding ground. The low track, a short section of which still exists today as a metalled road running from the former workhouse (now Ancliff Square), underneath the aqueduct and on past the Cross Guns inn towards the small complex of mill buildings, once extended from the ford across the River Frome at Freshford, along the riverbank to Avoncliff and thence to Barton Farm in Bradford-on-Avon. Much of the eastern course of this lane was destroyed when the canal was built.

By far the most important of these tracks, up until the beginning of the nineteenth century, was that which came down the hillside via Turleigh and crossed the ford before climbing again to Westwood. On the Turleigh side the route is still quite obvious from Winsley to the point where it crosses the lane to the bridge over the canal near Murhill. To that point it is a wide, well-used footpath bounded by walls and hedges but south of Turleigh it almost disappears and becomes an indistinct footpath running along the edge of the field. If one looks carefully, however, one can see the edging stones of the old road and some remnants of cobbling, and further down the hillside on the east side of the track there is a long length of substantial retaining wall that forms a raised causeway across the falling land. Towards the bottom of the hillside the pathway now veers to the west, towards the aqueduct, but until 1800-1803 it would have continued in a straight line to the ford. Around 1803 the Kennet and Avon Canal Company began quarrying stone for the repair of the already crumbling aqueduct from the plot of land that is now the site of the old waterworks pump-

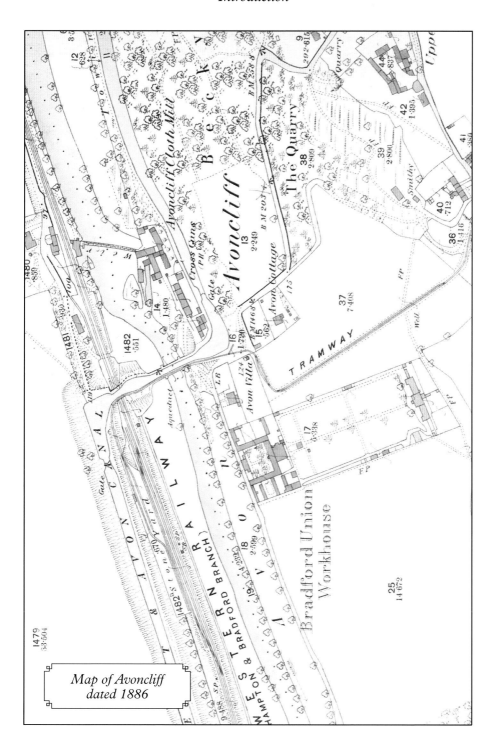

Map of Avoncliff
dated 1886

house opposite Mill House, the company having purchased the quarry-ground and a strip of land connecting it to the canal basin a few years earlier. The quarry was on the direct line of the track from Turleigh and it was for this reason that it was diverted. Obviously, however, the old, steep incline was proving impassable to the increasingly heavy traffic of the district and by the time the railway was built forty-five years later a new, much more gently graded road wide enough to take horse-drawn traffic had been built to join the lane to Belcombe a short distance to the east of Avoncliff.

Despite the enormous changes in ground levels and all the demolition and reconstruction that resulted from the building of the railway in the mid-nineteenth century, the location of the ford is still easily discernable. Before the railway was built there was a separate grist mill on the north bank of the river between the existing fulling mill and the cottage now known as Mill House. The lane from Belcombe ran between the grist mill and the cottage which at that time had its main frontage upon the lane, facing the grist mill. When the mill was demolished to make way for the railway the cottage was completely reorientated with an entrance elevation built facing the new road as we see it today. Just beyond Mill House Belcombe Lane joined the track from Turleigh and swept in a curve that is now incorporated in the long, thin garden of Mill House, down to the river. The substantial stone retaining walls that held up the embankments on either side of the approach to the ford can still be seen in the garden, cut short by the railway embankment as they turn south towards the river.

The railway company carried their rails over the approach to the ford on a small girder bridge under which the road level was lowered by approximately six feet. The bridge is still visible in photographs taken in 1906 when the new Avoncliff Halt was opened but it was removed shortly afterwards and the cutting filled in, blocking access to the ford. Vestiges of the bridge abutments can still be seen on the river side of the station, where a short length of buttress standing out at a right angle to the embankment retaining wall, now partially hidden by undergrowth, marks the position of the bridge. The lane was subsequently extended a little to the west and a level crossing laid across the line at a point close to the aqueduct. Although taken out of use some forty years ago and the gate on the river side of the rails replaced by fencing, the position of the crossing is still quite obvious.

The ford crossed the river diagonally, parallel to the weir, making landfall on the Westwood bank of the river in front of the Cross Guns public house. The route then continued diagonally on the line of the present pathway in the private section of the Cross Guns' riverside garden. The course of the road immediately above the public house has been lost due to the building of the canal but higher up the hillside the original formation remains remarkably intact in the form of the partly-walled footpath that zigzags down from Upper Westwood. The

Above: Avoncliff Halt during the early inter-war years. The bridge carrying the railway over the approach road to the ford is easily identifiable in the middle of the picture. This was infilled at the start of the Second World War as part of the anti-invasion defences. The tall chimney of the waterworks boilerhouse is just visible behind the dark trees to the left of the photograph.

present Avoncliff Lane, which takes a much longer route from Westwood, was built to replace the old track in the nineteenth century to provide an easier grade for wagons hauling heavy blocks of stone down from the quarries to the canal wharf.

2

WESTWOOD QUARRIES
IN WAR AND PEACE

Throughout most of the nineteenth century quarrying of oolitic limestone for building purposes was, apart from agriculture, the predominant employer in north-west Wiltshire. Stone has been quarried on a fairly large scale since the medieval period, although the process has only been conducted on a truly industrial basis since the latter part of the eighteenth century. The industry came to prominence at that time due, in part at least, to the architectural renaissance that was the springboard for the building of Georgian Bath, then found wider markets as a result of the relative ease and cheapness of transport via the recently opened Avon Navigation and the Kennet and Avon Canal, and caught the first glimpse of its true potential in the 1840s following the completion of the Great Western Railway. Not only did the railway, whose main line ran through the very heart of the quarrying region, further reduce transport costs to the point where Bath stone could be delivered economically to all parts of the kingdom, but it also, during the excavation of Box Tunnel, revealed vast and hitherto unknown reserves of the very best building stone below the villages of Box and Corsham.

Medieval quarrying was generally undertaken in a somewhat haphazard, *ad hoc* manner. There was little or no knowledge of geology or stratigraphy; stone was simply extracted, usually from surface outcrops on hillside edges, as near as possible to where it was needed. By far the greatest demand for stone during the medieval period was for ecclesiastical building and the first extensive quarries tended to be developed on the ecclesiastical estates. Although there was very limited private enterprise at the turn of the fifteenth century, it was not until the dissolution of the monasteries in the middle of the following century – an event that coincided with and must have been a causative factor in the rise of the entrepreneur and the commercial ethic in England, that the granting of quarry leases to private individuals became relatively commonplace. This sudden phenomenon of the lust for money and personal gain that became widespread in the 1540s applied to almost every sphere of human activity from mines and mills to drainage schemes and textiles as well as a host of other infant industries. A further two hundred years were to pass, however, before quarrying on a truly commercial, speculative basis became the norm. Until the mid-eighteenth century the extraction of building stone was usually undertaken for a specific project: quarries were opened on the large estates when a great house needed to be built or extended, were worked for a while and then closed down either temporarily or permanently. From about 1790, with the flexibility and economic benefits offered by the new forms of inland transport then evolving, speculative quarrymen could actively market and advertise their products and in this way the growth of the industry was further stimulated.

Although records indicate that there were active quarries on the hillside above Avoncliff as early as 1405 the first indications of a substantial industry occur in 1649 and relate to open quarries, evidence of which still exist today, to the south of the track that joins the old and new roadways that ascend the hillside from Avoncliff to Westwood. Long abandoned, these old workings are now partially obscured by modern bungalows. It would appear that they continued to be sporadically worked for over two hundred years but by 1795 must have been of very little consequence as they were completely disregarded in that year, when surveyors from the Kennet and Avon Canal Company were searching for a source of stone for the construction of Avoncliff aqueduct. The canal company's surveyors were as ignorant as their predecessors of the varying qualities of the local limestone and chose to quarry building material for the aqueduct from locations whose only merit was their close proximity to the building site with little regard for the strength or weathering capability of the stone.

Some years before the turn of the century the Godwin family had established themselves as quarry masters on a respectable scale at Westwood and by 1804 had begun to extract stone of an excellent quality from an underground adit rather than from surface outcrops. The original entrance to Godwin's underground quarry, now secured behind a substantial pallisade fence, can still be seen at the end of a shallow cutting adjacent to the track leading west from the first of the sharp bends near the top of Avoncliff lane. Throughout the early decades of the nineteenth century only limited inroads were made underground but by the 1850s the quality of stone from this source had become widely esteemed and over the next fifty years output increased at a prodigious rate. Some time shortly before 1882 Godwin was able to lease a further reserve of stone of similar quality lying beneath fields to the south of his existing workings and to access these reserves an inclined shaft was sunk beside the lane connecting Upper and Lower Westwood. Having been blocked for decades, this slope shaft, now hidden from view behind a rather sinister sheet steel gate beside the road, has recently been cleared and reconstructed to form an airway and emergency exit for Hanson Mineral current stone quarry.

It is probable that the success of the Godwin enterprise at Westwood attracted the attention of the larger quarrying concerns that had become established in the Corsham area, for in 1875 Randell, Saunders and Company, one of the major players in the industry, opened their own quarry in the village. This wholly

Above: Randell and Saunders' entrance to Westwood quarry in 1898.

underground quarry, known locally as 'The Tump', is situated a few hundred yards to the west of Godwin's workings and is accessed via a horizontal adit in the hillside. The arrival of Randell and Saunders effectively broke Godwin's monopoly of Westwood stone and in the longer term marked the beginning of the slow decline of the Godwin family fortunes. Their business had always been held back, to some extent, by the fact that virtually all their output was despatched by road wagon to the canal wharf at Avoncliff and thence by boat or barge to its ultimate destination. Although alterations had been made to the course of the lane from Westwood to Avoncliff to ease the gradient and make haulage a little easier and safer, the transport of Godwin's stone remained an inefficient and relatively expensive process.

With much greater resources at their disposal Randell and Saunders were able to overcome the transport problem by the application of capital and technology. From the outset the company intended to despatch the greater part of their output by rail. After a prolonged gestation and a difficult birth the Wilts, Somerset and Weymouth Railway line between Bathampton Junction and Bradford Junction was finally opened on 2nd February 1857. The Wilts, Somerset and Weymouth had been absorbed by the Great Western Railway in March 1850 and during 1875 Randell and Saunders opened negotiations with the Great Western Railway for the establishment of a private siding at

Avoncliff. Randell and Saunders also acquired from the railway company a one-acre plot of land beside the railway upon which to build a cutting yard and loading bay beside the main line where the rough hewn blocks of stone would be prepared to customers' specifications prior to despatch. Revenue from this small and otherwise sterile plot of land, sandwiched between the railway line, the aqueduct and the steep canal embankment, must have been something of an unexpected bonus for the Great Western Railway. The opening of the railway resulted in the almost immediate loss of all the Kennet and Avon Canal Company's most lucrative freight traffic and, faced with the inevitable alternative of bankruptcy, the canal company offered itself to the Great Western and was purchased by the railway company in 1854. As a consequence of this purchase the Great Western found itself in possession of the canal, the towpath and the aqueduct at Avoncliff along with numerous sundry chunks of land there, including roads and quarries that had been acquired by the canal company at the time of construction and had remained on its asset register.

To transport the huge blocks of rough cut stone from the quarry to the trackside cutting yard, Randell and Saunders proposed to construct a narrow-gauge railway that descended the steep hillside from the quarry mouth, crossed the Avon and the Great Western line on the canal aqueduct towpath and finally made a steep descent into the yard following the incline of the railway arch. The route of the tramway can be clearly seen on the plan. The single track from the quarry became double on the long incline to a point immediately behind the workhouse where it became a single track to make a ninety-degree turn, doubled again for a short, very slight incline along the contour before reverting to a single track to cross the aqueduct. A short spur on the Westwood side of the aqueduct served a canal loading wharf. Both double-track inclines were worked on the rope-hauled, self-acting principle and relied on the fact that the load descending wagons were always heavier than the empty wagons that were drawn back up the inclines. A length of rope connecting ascending and descending wagons passed around an overhead drum or sheave at the top of the incline in such a way that the weight of the loaded wagon, descending by gravity, more than counterbalanced the weight of the ascending empties.

The speed of descent was controlled by a brake mechanism acting on the sheave wheel. There must have been some doubt about the efficacy of the braking mechanism because numerous trial runs were made through the latter part of 1877 before the quarrying company accepted the system. Despite all this a terrible disaster occurred on the day of the official opening. Several blocks of stone had been successfully lowered down the main incline and Mr Beaven, the engineman, was preparing to lower a wagon loaded with a particularly large block estimated to weigh some five and a half tons. As the wagon began its descent some failure occurred in the braking system and the loaded truck hurtled down

Above: In this early 20th Century view the route of the quarry tramway can be clearly seen descending the hillside behind the Bradford Union Workhouse. In the foreground a five-ton crane is busily at work in the stone-yard at Avoncliff Sidings. The sidings signalbox is just visible amongst the trees in the centre foreground.

Below: This engraving of 1878 (involving a degree of artistic licence) gives a vivid impression of the scale of the stone industry in the late 19th Century. The horse in the left foreground seems to be galloping downhill at a prodigious rate to keep ahead of the seven-ton block of stone that appears to be chasing it. Meanwhile the other horse to the right of the picture seems blissfully unaware of the impending catastrophe.

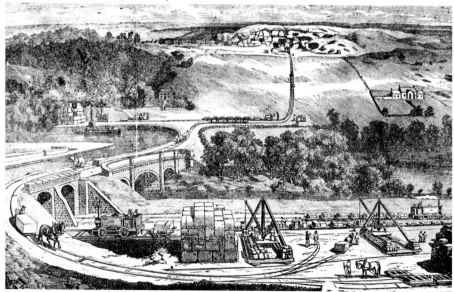

the incline completely out of control. The empty wagon was propelled up the incline at enormous speed, leaving the track at the apex where it somersaulted and struck a fatal blow to Mr Beaven as he stood struggling with the controls.

Loaded wagons were propelled across the aqueduct under gravity, using the momentum gained from their last short descent. Their speed was controlled by a brakesman riding on the back of the truck. On their return journey empty wagons were drawn back to the bottoms of the inclines by horses.

The main incline was completed by the summer of 1877 and by that time was able to serve a small wharf on the canal. Meanwhile, Randell and Saunders had been in protracted negotiation with the Great Western Railway seeking permission to lay its narrow-gauge tracks across the aqueduct on the route of the towpath. This was finally granted in July 1877 and track-laying proceeded quickly. Five months later, on 28th November 1877, the standard gauge siding and the six-lever Avoncliff Siding Signal Box that controlled it were completed and approved by the Board of Trade.

Randell and Saunders' operation at Westwood had an immediate impact upon Godwin's quarry and a fierce price-cutting war ensued. Ten years later, in 1887, several of the larger quarrying firms amalgamated to form the Bath Stone Firms Limited but Godwin was never invited to join the combination and, left out in the cold, the small company's fate was inevitable. When William Godwin died in 1900 the Bath Stone Firms was still aggressively cutting the price of its own Westwood ground stone in an effort to drive the smaller quarry operator out of business, and in 1908 William Godwin's son, Herbert, was declared bankrupt. Under the control of Herbert's younger brother the business limped on for another year or so but in 1910 he sold out to the Bradford quarry owner Issac Jones. Jones had little success at Westwood either and when he died the following year his executors abandoned the quarry.

But aggressive competition was not the only factor that led to the demise of Godwin's quarry. The early years of the twentieth century saw a severe recession in the building industry that lasted until the Great War and beyond. The downturn also had a severe effect upon the Bath Stone Firms, whose financial stability largely relied upon a buoyant building market. Despite having negotiated leases on extensive new areas of quarry ground with the view to extending there underground workings in the late 1980s, the Bath Stone Firms board decided quite abruptly, in 1930, to scale down operations at Westwood and within five years quarrying had ceased completely. Strangely, however, the stone yard beside the mainline railway remained active until 1933 despite its ramshackle accommodation and the antiquity of its machinery, which was driven by a cobweb of overhead belting and ancient gas-oil engine. Some twenty masons and labourers worked there, cutting and shaping that was shipped in by mainline wagons from the firm's other quarries in the Box and Corsham

Above: This hand-tinted view, with a pair of swans floating serenely on the canal must pre-date 1906 because there is no evidence of the steps leading down to Avoncliff Halt, which was opened in that year. To the right of the image is an unidentifiable GWR tank locomotive, its boiler surmounted by a large brass dome. Avoncliff Sidings signalbox, carrying an early-pattern nameboard, is clearly visible in the middle of the photograph. Note the sharp incline of the tramway leading off the end of the aqueduct down to the cutting yard, and the stone-loading crane on the canal wharf at the far end of the aqueduct.

Below: In this somewhat later view the steps down to the railway station are now apparent, and safety railings have been erected along the canal bank to protect railway passengers crossing the aqueduct.

Above: This photograph must pre-date 1933 because the track-side stone-cutting yard seems no longer to be at work and where the sidings' signalbox once stood there is now a platelayer's hut. The narrow-gauge quarry tramway is still in place across the aqueduct despite having fallen into disuse some twenty years earlier.

areas. The signalbox was taken out of use and the sidings removed by the Great Weston Railway in June 1937, the long-disused quarry tramway having been dismantled some years before.

Little evidence of the stone yard remains today, although the track-bed of the upper section of the quarry tramway is still well defined. The winding gear and upper terminal of the tramway was obliterated by the dumping of stone waste on the hillside when the quarry was converted for government occupation during the Second World War but the embankment that once carried the narrow-gauge tracks can be clearly identified descending the steep hillside beyond the perimeter of the waste heap. At one point the line crosses a public footpath and the simple iron girder bridge that carried the line over the pathway remains *in situ*, constructed, so it would appear, from scrap iron girders. Over the decades since the tramway fell into disuse loose material from the waste heap has gradually crept down the hillside and partially infilled the shallow cutting beneath the bridge.

Just to the rear of Avon Villa a small group of trees and an area of rough ground mark the point at which the tramway turned east towards the canal but most of its alignment from there up to the canal towpath was lost during the construction of a small electricity sub-station in the 1960s. There is no trace of the track-bed across the aqueduct towpath which has been completely reconstructed in recent years, and even in aerial photographs of Avoncliff taken in 1947 it cannot be identified. There is no remaining evidence of the location of

Avoncliff Siding signalbox, nor of the alignment of the siding itself, but much of the retaining wall that supported the loading platform survives, as does the more substantial retaining wall at the rear of the stone yard that prevented movement of the canal embankment towering above. Excavations carried out in the 1970s revealed the outline of a few buildings in the yard and also exposed a considerable quantity of cut stone. The whole area is, however, now heavily overgrown and what remains of the stone yard and of the incline from the canal towpath is concealed beneath a dense thicket of nettles, bushes and brambles. On the towpath at the end of the short aqueduct that carries the canal over the railway a substantial tubular wrought iron pillar some four feet in height that probably formed part of the capstan arrangement by which wagons were drawn up from the cutting yard survived until recently but was removed during the canal refurbishment. Only a short section remains, projecting a few inches above ground level.

MUSHROOMS

During the early years of the nineteenth century mushroom growers in France had discovered that the relatively stable ambient temperatures and high humidity found underground in the disused limestone mines in and around Paris provided ideal conditions for the cultivation of mushrooms on an industrial scale. The French system proved successful and spread across the Channel to England shortly after the First World War. The Agaric Company established itself at Bradford-on-Avon and at Corsham where large areas of the disused Hudswell Quarry were put over to mushroom cultivation. The Agaric Company's operation at Corsham was on a scale sufficient to warrant the construction of an extensive narrow-gauge railway system in the warren of underground chambers. At the same time a rudimentary ventilation system was installed consisting of a brazier of hot coals positioned at the bottom of

a ventilation shaft in order to encourage the circulation of air by convection. Unfortunately, in 1926, the mushroom beds at Hudswell became infected with 'plaster', an ineradicable virus, forcing the Agaric Company to permanently vacate the quarry. Within a year, however, the company had taken possession of the greater part of the old Godwin's workings at Westwood and was able to resume production there on a somewhat reduced scale. Aware of the risk of transferring the virus, the company abandoned the railway system and much of the other plant at Hudswell where it remained, rotting away, until 1936 when it was swept away during the major refurbishment works undertaken by the War Office during the construction of the underground Central Ammunition Depot. Initially, at least, Agaric employed the same hot-air convection system to ventilate Westwood Quarry; the curious, square stone structure capping a quarry ventilation shaft in the garden of the large semi-detached house beside the lane halfway between Westwood and Lye Green is a relic of that system.

Agaric's tenure of Westwood Quarry was fraught with difficulties and was brought to an end by the Second World War. The first crops were produced in 1928 and the business appeared destined for success but in 1934, as a result of a minor earth tremor, a series of serious roof falls occurred in the central area of the quarry, destroying many of the mushroom beds and rendering other areas unsafe to work in. Production was temporarily halted but was resumed some months later on a reduced scale after extensive remedial works had been undertaken. In some areas massive chains were clamped around the roof support pillars to prevent them bursting under the stresses imposed by the weight of the shifting ceiling strata. Elsewhere massive walls of waste stone were erected to provide additional roof support. Then, in 1936, little more than a year after business

Below: This panoramic view of part of the quarry used for mushroom growing has long been known colloquially as 'The Ballroom' on account of its extensive cleared floor area. The stout chains around the pillars were put in place to strengthen the roof supports after the minor earthquake in 1936, which caused extensive damage to the quarry structure.

Above: A long-abandoned Victorian stone crane in Godwin's section of Westwood quarry, crushed by the pressure of the roof in the partially collapsed section of the workings damaged by the 1936 earth tremor.

Above right: A hand-operated crab-winch abandoned in Godwin's workings when quarrying there ceased towards the end of the first decade of the 20th Century. This was used to haul blocks of cut stone from the working face onto horse-drawn trucks like that seen in the photograph on page 22.

Right: This view of part of Godwin's quarry adapted for mushroom growing and subsequently abandoned in 1936 shows some of the damage caused by the earth tremor. Note the severely shattered pillars seen along this main haulageway through the quarry. Westwood quarry is a maze of very similar, long underground haulage roads and to aid the mushroom cultivators with their navigation, the main roads were given local names; here we see Silver Street passing through Area No.9.

resumed after the geological disaster, it was discovered that the mushroom beds at Westwood had become infected with the same virus that had brought an end to mushroom growing in Corsham. The Agaric Company struggled on against the odds for a few more years but, by the spring of 1940, faced with the triple threats of an unsound structure, incipient viral infection and a shortage of labour due to the military call-up, things looked pretty bleak. The final blow came in November 1940 when Westwood Quarry, along with all the other quarry workings in north Wiltshire that were not already in government hands, was requisitioned by the Ministry of Works. At the same time the Ministry of Works took possession of Agaric's three other quarries in Bradford-on-Avon: Bethel Quarry, Paulton Quarry, and Jones' Hill Quarry, under the same blanket requisitioning order.

THE QUARRIES IN WARTIME

The Second World War had a profound effect on Avoncliff and Westwood and, although the passage of some sixty years has eradicated much of the superficial evidence from Avoncliff, the twin villages of Upper and Lower Westwood were changed forever. The reasons why these remote and seemingly insignificant places should have played such a pivotal role in the wartime history of Britain were determined by a single event: the fall of France in the spring of 1940.

Following the accession to power of Adolf Hitler in 1934 the intelligence services of the British government knew that another European war, if not a world war, was inevitable and, based upon their best assessments (which in the event proved to be of dubious reliability), it was thought that this conflict would probably begin in 1942. The same intelligence organization concluded that Great Britain would not be an immediate target of aggression but would be quickly drawn into conflict because of the military support she would be compelled to give to other European nations, including France and Poland, due to a series of international mutual defence agreements drawn up in the aftermath of the First World War. Germany, they said, had no wish to occupy the British Isles or snatch her lands, but would want, at the onset of the war, to neutralize her fighting capacity and her ability to intervene.

Based upon the most sketchy evidence, Britain's intelligence experts had erroneously concluded that the Luftwaffe, Germany's military air force, was much larger than it actually was in the mid-1930s, but they guessed, rather more correctly, that the range of even the best of the current German bombers would reach no further than London and the Home Counties. The intelligence consensus was that on the day war was declared the skies above London would darken with thousands of German bombers and that the city would be annihilated within minutes, wiping out the seat of government and military command centres and destroying Britain's ability to retaliate. Some comfort was gleaned from the assumption that the rest of the country to the north and west would be beyond the range of the bombers and thus invulnerable.

For nearly two decades after the armistice of 1918 the Army's entire stockpile of field ammunition was stored at Woolwich Arsenal or in lightly-built sheds at the sprawling Central Ammunition Depot at Bramley, near Basingstoke. It was assumed that both locations were well within range of the German bombers and would thus be lost in the first raid. The security of these ammunition stocks was of immense importance to the strategists at the War Office because they assumed, with an astonishing lack of foresight, that the next war would be like the last; a static battle of attrition with fixed lines of artillery pounding away at one another from opposite sides of the battlefield for months on end, expending millions upon millions of rounds of ammunition. This was the predominant War Office view, despite the fact that in the same breath the same strategists were describing an aerial war in which Britain, or at least London as her administrative heart, might be pummelled into submission by a single mass air raid.

In view of the pessimistic prediction of London's fate, a series of covert committees were convened to prepare a response to the German aerial threat. The obvious answer was evacuation on an epic scale. Evacuation of the civil population was immediately dismissed as utterly unfeasible, but during 1934 three particularly vulnerable state institutions were identified and earmarked for dispersal to the provinces. These were: the seat of government, the loss of which, it was thought, would result in the country rapidly descending into anarchy; the ammunition reserves at Bramley and Woolwich, for without these the country would be unable to defend itself; and finally the great London museums and galleries which at that time were amongst the finest in the world and which were home to much of the world's cultural heritage.

Plans for the provision of alternative accommodation for central government, for the War Cabinet and for the various Chiefs of Staff and their departments were drawn up in 1934 but need not concern us here. The schemes that were developed for ensuring the safety of the nation's ammunition reserves and cultural treasures, however, are central to our story and are explained in detail in the pages that follow.

The possibility of securing the Army war reserves of ammunition at a location less vulnerable than Bramley had been under consideration since at least 1928 and were given an added impetus by the crisis of 1934. A War and Office committee had already decided that the only truly safe storage for ammunition was deep underground, so when the first serious search for a suitable site was made early that year there were two major criteria to be met: first, that it had to be beyond the range of the current and anticipated German bomber fleet and, secondly, that it had to be underground. A third minor criterion was that on grounds of prospective cost, the underground accommodation should already exist in the form of caves or disused mines or quarries. The huge ramifications of worked-out stone quarries at Corsham were quickly identified as a likely candidate and the War Office lost no time in acquiring the first of these, Ridge Quarry near Neston, in 1934. The Bath and Portland Stone Company, which owned these quarries, was, as we have already seen, in dire financial straits at this time and its shareholders were overjoyed to see a financial return from this deal with the government. As war approached, the Army's ammunition requirements increased and three further quarries were purchased: Tunnel Quarry at Corsham in 1935, Eastlays Quarry at Gastard in the following year and Monkton Farleigh Quarry in 1937. Over a four year period well in excess of £4,000,000 was spent on the conversion of these disused stone workings into the Central Ammunition Depot, Corsham: the largest underground ammunition depot in the world.

It is important to understand that these four quarries were acquired by the government during peacetime under conventional commercial terms and, given that at the time they were a financial liability rather than a valuable asset to the Bath and Portland Company, the company was a willing vendor. Those first dealings with the War Office, however, sparked the larger idea that might have proved profitable to the stone firm under more favourable conditions. Despite the high cost of conversion the underground ammunition storage scheme at Corsham proved a success; by the time of the Munich crisis in the autumn of 1938, the directors of the Bath and Portland Stone Company realised that when war came the government might wish to acquire more of their underground quarries. It seemed obvious to the directors that if it could be shown that the quarries were profitable, working concerns rather than abandoned or worked-out relics, then they could be offered to the government on much more favourable terms. Gradually, throughout the early part of 1939 small gangs were set to work in these long forgotten quarries. At Box work began on the extraction of the lower beds of corngrit for which there had never been much demand and for which there was no demand at all in 1939 and which could not possibly have been worked profitably. Meanwhile at Westwood, where stone had not been extracted since 1908, a crane was set up and a pretence of renewed quarrying activity was acted out in a very wet area at the western end of the workings conveniently close to the entrance to be easily observed.

When war came in September 1939, however, it was something of an anticlimax. The predicted aerial onslaught did not occur and the government did not rush underground. Instead there was a long period of phoney war. It looked as if the huge expense of the Corsham Central Ammunition Depot was proving to be unjustified and, if anything, the attitude of both government and the military Chiefs of Staff was turning

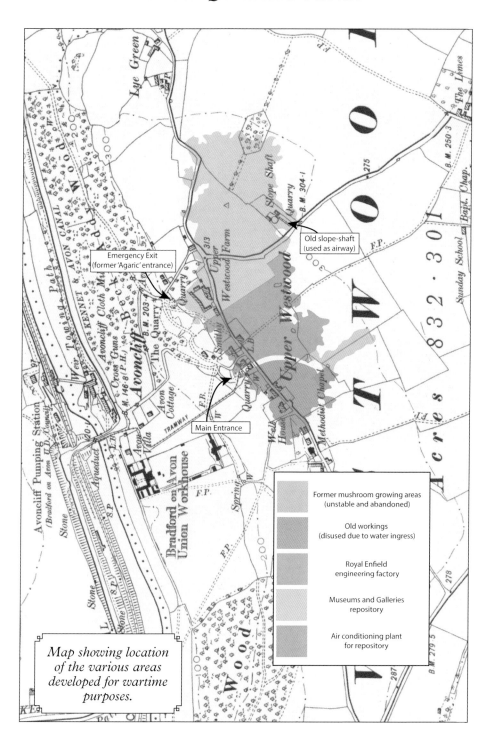

Map showing location of the various areas developed for wartime purposes.

against the concept of deep underground bunkers. The Bath and Portland Stone Company continued to quarry stone at its few remaining profitable quarries like Spring Quarry at Corsham and Hayes Wood at Limpley Stoke but quietly withdrew its dubious gangs of workmen from Westwood. It would be another year before Westwood would be called to war.

THE MUSEUMS AND GALLERIES EVACUATION PLAN

While the military men were laying plans for the evacuation of their ammunition stockpiles, consideration was being given to the safety of the priceless art treasures and irreplaceable cultural artifacts in the great London art galleries and museums. To co-ordinate these plans a special committee known as the Museums and Galleries Air Raid Precautions Committee was formed. The most prominent members of this committee were Lord Ilchester, who acted as Chairman; Sir Eric Maclagan, Chairman of the trustees of the British Museum; Sir John Forsdyke, Director of the Victoria and Albert Museum; and Sir Kenneth Clark, Director of the National Gallery. The committee was faced with a difficult task because, although it was charged with the safekeeping of the nation's cultural wealth, the Treasury was unwilling to make any significant grant from public funds to accomplish this.

The major problem that the committee had to overcome was that throughout the inter-war years the London museums and galleries were socially exclusive, the haunts of the effete and idle rich and not the place where the working man would either wish to be or would be made welcome. The British establishment, however, was aware that the greatest burdens of the war that was by now inevitable would be borne most heavily by the great mass of British working folk. The government had already made it known that it could not provide safe, deep-level air raid shelters for London's civilian population and they feared that if it became known that they were providing substantial funds for the safekeeping of the 'elitist trifles' of the idle rich while the great mass of Londoners were left to fend for themselves in the face of German bombing, then the consequences might be civil insurrection reminiscent of the October Revolution of 1917. It was acceptable to spend many millions of pounds on vast underground ammunition magazines for the Army but the two thousand pictures in the National Gallery and the contents of all the other London institutions were compelled, like the Londoners, to provide for themselves.

The scheme devised by the committee was, essentially, that it should look after its own. Discrete approaches were made to the trustees of the various museums and galleries, and through them to a wider circle of friends, family and associates from the same social and business circles – most of whom were the owners of considerable country estates – to see who would be prepared to offer their homes as secure repositories in the event of war. This approach had the full backing of the Treasury, which saw it as a means of achieving the desired ends with minimal cost to the exchequer. By the end of 1934 a list of some forty country houses, known as the *National Register*, was drawn up, detailing properties whose owners were prepared to participate in the scheme, together with a provisional allocation of individual houses to the various galleries and museums The National Gallery, for example, was allocated a number of properties in North Wales, including Penrhyn Castle; the principal repository for the British Museum was to be Boughton House in Northamptonshire, while the Victoria and Albert Museum was offered Montacute House in Somerset. Very little was destined to remain in the capital other than the Elgin Marbles, which, for the duration of the war, were buried 100 feet below central London in the disused Aldwych tube station, and a few of the British Museum's largest pieces of Assyrian statuary which were bricked-up where they stood in Bloomsbury.

With conflict imminent, it was decided that all the great London institutions should remain open until almost the very last hour before the formal declaration of war. It was felt that if the galleries and museums were to close their doors to the public and begin overtly to evacuate their contents during the days or weeks leading up to war when government propaganda was still insisting that such war could and would be avoided, then it would induce despondency, if not panic, amongst the population of London. So, on the eve of war, with the co-operation of the Great Western and the London, Midland and Scottish Railway' companies, who had been instrumental in every stage of the meticulous planning process, the great evacuation began. The evacuation was described by Sir Kenneth Clark in a memorandum to the trustees of the National Gallery shortly after the event, in which he wrote:

> 'Shortly before midnight on Saturday 2nd September 1939, to the echo of rolling thunder that marked the end of a long run of hot days and humid nights, the last of six special freight trains slipped out of Camden goods yard in North London. Hauled by the most powerful locomotive the London Midland and Scottish Railway could muster, running under the head-code of a Royal Train and with armed guards on the footplate, it sped non-stop through the night on its 240-mile journey, past Birmingham, Stafford, Crewe, Chester and Rhyl to its final destination, the North Wales coastal town of Bangor, in the shadows of the Snowdon range. All along its route lesser trains were held to wait its passing, while at every level-crossing, bridge and tunnel armed police and soldiers stood guard.
>
> Simultaneously, two mysterious road convoys departed from

the Capital, one from Kensington, bound for Somerset along the Great West Road, and the other northwards from Bloomsbury into rural Northamptonshire. Meanwhile, two heavily laden lorries with unlikely loads crept out of Bloomsbury and steered towards the London Passenger Transport Board's Lillie Bridge depot to await a late evening ballast train bound for the Aldwych tube.'

The trains carried some two thousand pictures belonging to the National Gallery, the most valuable single cargo ever carried on a British railway train, while the lorries from Bloomsbury transported the contents of the British Museum to Boughton House and the Elgin Marbles to the London Transport yard at Lillie Bridge for onwards conveyance to the Aldwych tube station. From Kensington, the other road convoy carried the treasures of the Victoria and Albert Museum westwards to Montacute.

Unrehearsed, except for a small-scale pilot run from Camden to North Wales in the autumn of 1938 at the time of the Munich Crisis, the operation ran with precision and by the morning of 3rd September every picture and artefact was secure in its new home, nothing was lost and no significant damage had occurred. For the next nine months everything went well, minor problems arose and were resolved and routines were established. There were tensions between the property owners and the museum authorities that became more prominent and threatened a crisis but, as we shall see, these difficulties were eclipsed by the events of May 1940.

THE FALL OF FRANCE

Outgunned and outmanoeuvred by the Luftwaffe and Germany's mechanized field forces, the French Army and the ill-equipped British Expeditionary Force that was supporting it collapsed. The British made their escape as best they could across the sands of Dunkirk over a nine day period from 26th May 1940 and on 22nd June the French government capitulated. With the Germans now on the Channel coast and with its air force in possession of the airfields of northern France, the British home-front evacuation and dispersal plans lay in ruins. Armament factories in the Midlands and north of England that only a few weeks before were considered invulnerable were now within striking distance of the German bombers that could range freely over the whole of Britain. Similarly, the remote country houses that temporarily housed the nation's treasures were exposed to attack from high explosive and incendiary bombs.

It was soon obvious that after the defeat of France the next German objective was the total neutralization of Great Britain, either by crushing her will to fight by massive terror attacks by air against her centres of population or, if necessary, by invasion and occupation. Before this was possible, however, it was necessary to annihilate the Royal Air Force and destroy the British aircraft industry, because until industry was rendered unable to make good the losses of fighter aircraft sustained in the air defence of Great Britain, invasion would be impossible. In July the Luftwaffe launched a series of intensive air raids against RAF fighter stations in southern England and by October these raids, which had largely failed to achieve their aim of knocking out the RAF, were turned against London and the industrial centres of the Midlands.

The targets now were obviously the aircraft factories and the aircraft component works, and in October 1940 Lord Beaverbrook, the Minister of Aircraft Production, with the full backing of Winston Churchill, ordered that drastic measures should be taken to protect these factories. Beaverbrook's plan was that all the workshops and production lines of the entire aircraft industry should be relocated to deep underground facilities built in remote, dispersed areas of the country. It was quickly apparent that such a comprehensive scheme was untenable; there was simply not enough suitable existing underground space available and to excavate in virgin rock the many millions of square feet of tunnels and chambers that would be required would represent years of labour and would be prohibitively expensive. It was recognised that the most important elements of the industry were the aircraft engine manufacturing plants because engines wore out quickly through and wear and tear and the demand for replacement units arose on top of the demand for new units to replace aircraft destroyed by enemy action. Grudgingly, Beaverbrook agreed to a series of contractions of his master plan and in November provisional consent was received from the Treasure for a limited scheme that would see the production lines of the most important engine manufacturers and those of a few key component manufacturers put underground. During the early phase of the war the Bristol Aeroplane Company, whose principal factory at Filton was severely damaged in an air raid in November, was one of the most important aircraft engine makers in Britain.

ROYAL ENFIELD

An immediate search was made for suitable underground spaces and, with the assistance of the War Office, who had been installed underground at Corsham since the mid-1930s, the remaining Bath and Portland Company's stone quarries were immediately identified as likely candidates. The Ministry of Aircraft Production then worked quickly. Writing to the company's land agent on 2nd December 1949 the chairman of the Bath and Portland Stone Company expressed his surprised that:

'On Saturday the District Valuer arrived at our office and requisitioned the whole of our Bath Stone quarries with the exception of Monk's Park, which had been requestioned a few days earlier by the Admiralty. This has come as rather a surprise to us as we did not anticipate the Ministry stepping in at all.'

The requisitioning order threw the company's plans to enhance the value of their quarries by purporting to extract stone from them into absolute disarray. They had expected to sell the freehold for a good market price, but under requisitioning their property was simply taken away from them; later they would receive a nominal sum assessed by a government inspector. Referring to the financial implications, the chairman's letter continued:

'No question of terms was discussed as he had said that would be dealt with later. I tried to find out whether we should be able to do the clearing work but could get no reply on that point. As you can imagine we are left high and dry, but I suppose we shall hear something this week.'

The most important of the quarries to be requisitioned were the 3,000,000 square-foot Spring Quarry at Corsham and the somewhat Westwood Quarry. Several other small quarries in the Corsham, Bradford-on-Avon and Limpley Stoke area were also requisitioned but they need not concern us here and, indeed, we will only look briefly at the development of Spring Quarry. Once requisition was completed the quarries were surveyed to determine their suitability, estimates of the likely costs of conversion prepared and negotiations started with potential tenants. The vast scale of the construction programme put it beyond the scope of any existing government department so one of Britain's biggest civil engineering contracting, Sir Alexander Gibb and Partners of Reading, was appointed consulting engineers under the overall direction of the Ministry of Works. Most of the building works was carried out by sub-contractors, principally Alfred McAlpine Ltd at Spring Quarry and George Wimpey at Westwood.

From the very start the entire project was a disaster and by the end of the end of the war had degenerated to farce. The problems were manifold. The scale of the project meant that numerous commercial firms and government agencies were inevitably involved, including dozens of contractors and sub-contractors, prospective tenants, the Ministry of Works, Ministry of Labour, Ministry of Supply, Ministry of Aircraft Production, Ministry of Transport, the Controller of Factories, and the Treasury, each working to its own agenda. Under these conditions unanimous agreement on even the most basic design principles was impossible; delay compounded upon delay and costs rose inexorably. The problems were exacerbated by the fact that the prime contractor, Sir Alexander Gibb and Partners, had negotiated a 'cost-plus-profit' contract with the government and thus had little incentive to speed up the work or contain the costs.

Unfortunately, costs-plus-profit contracts became common during the war and were generally viewed as licences to print money. The contractors simply presented the government with periodic accounts of money spent and the Treasury handed over the money plus an agreed profit of, say, four percent on the cost. With little or no experience of major capital projects the ministers in charge of the new departments like the Ministry of Aircraft Production were not in a strong position to question these costs.

Spring Quarry at Corsham was allocated to the engine division of the Bristol Aeroplane Company and was scheduled for conversion into an alternative underground factory for its radial engine production line at Filton. The initial cost estimate for the Spring Quarry factory was a little under £100,000 and construction was expected to be complete within twelve months. By the end of 1941, however, very little progress had been made yet already over £6,000,000 had been spent. The underground factory was finally ready for occupation, still in an incomplete state, in the summer of 1943 by which time the total cost had risen to over £30,000,000. This astonishing increase in costs prompted an unprecedented investigation by the House of Commons Public Accounts Committee which subsequently revealed just how disastrous the underground venture had been. The factory, which was designed and equipped to manufacture 260 engines per month in fact only produced 523 engines throughout its entire working life. Long before building was completed the need for the factory had evaporated after the German bombing campaign diminished to insignificance during the spring of 1942. The Treasury was highly antagonistic of the entire project, the Ministry of War Transport despised it, the Ministry of Supply were only lukewarm at best, and the Bristol Aeroplane management had never wanted to go underground. The 25,000 staff who were transferred from Bristol to Corsham, the majority of whom were relatively well-off, skilled men who were compelled to give up their comfortable homes in Bristol to live in cramped, damp, draughty huts in Corsham, detested it wholeheartedly.

On a more modest scale the same situation was developing at Westwood where conversion began a few months after the start of work at Spring Quarry. The initial survey had shown that the gross floor area of the combined Bath and Portland and Godwin's workings amounted to 719,270 square feet, but much of this was considered too dangerous to investigate in detail due to the roof falls of the previous decade. Ultimately, an area of 270,000 square feet in the most accessible areas was cleared in preparation for the conversion work. This involved the removal of some 200,000 tons of waste stone, the majority of which was tipped onto the hillside immediately in front of the quarry entrance, obliterating the upper section of the quarry tramway. Later, this area was levelled to provide a lorry park for the factory and a foundation upon which to build external offices, motor transport sheds and other facilities. Once clearance was complete little more could be done until a tenant had been found for the proposed factory in Westwood Quarry.

After prolonged negotiations during which the company continued to express serious reservations about the suitability of the quarry, Westwood was allocated to the Royal Enfield Motorcycle Company in June 1941. The company held an important contract to manufacture Type-3 Anti-Aircraft Predictors at their factory in Redditch but since the late autumn of the previous year the Director General of Instrument Production had pressed for the production line to be transferred to more secure premises. The Royal Enfield Company needed just 30,000 square feet of factory space to meet the current required output of twenty predictors per month and it was calculated that the total development cost at Westwood would be £60,000 excluding machine tools and major plant, which would add a further £50,000 to the total bill. Gauges, test equipment and hand-tools would inflate the costs by a further £10,000. Unfortunately, by the summer of 1941, much money had already been wasted at Westwood on the initial preparation of the quarry where three times the area that Royal Enfield would ultimately occupy had already been cleared. A further 12,000 square feet was added to the schedule in November after it was decided to transfer Royal Enfield's vane oil motor production facilities to Westwood, but by that time £123,500 – more than double the entire construction budget – had been spent on the rough clearance and development work alone.

There were numerous reasons for the increase in costs but the chief cause was inefficiency and incompetence on the part of the primary contractor, although inflationary price increases and rapidly rising labour costs also played their part. Conscription into the forces quickly absorbed all the available native labour and the contractors were compelled to call upon their traditional source of Irish manpower – the legendary, hard-working, hard-living and hard-drinking Mayo Men. Aware of the risks of allowing such an unruly group of men loose amongst the local population, McAlpine's, the contractors at the main Corsham site, had already made arrangements to house the tens of thousands of men working there in huge temporary labour camps, complete with bars, community centres and Catholic churches. Similar arrangements on a much more modest scale were imperative at Westwood and a small labour camp for the two hundred Irishmen employed by George Wimpey and Company was constructed in a field near the top of Avoncliff Lane. The cost of this camp had not been included in the original estimate, nor had the additional wage bill that resulted from the 'uniformity' allowance demanded by the men living there, who thought they were disadvantaged by being forced to live in so remote a location, far from the

The series of photo's on this page illustrate the development of the former Randell & Saunders entrance to Westwood quarry for wartime use as an underground factory and art treasures repository.

Above left: The entrance in early 1941 with reconstruction of the portal just under way.

Above right: A year later the wing walls are completed, temporary overhead protection is in place and narrow-gauge rails have been laid in the concrete access road to enable contractor's diesel locomotives to be used underground.

Left: By the end of 1942 the work is complete, with a brick retaining wall above the entrance.

social amenities of the main camps at Corsham.

A group of managers from the Royal Enfield plant at Redditch had been on site at Westwood through the winter of 1941-1942 acting as advisors to the building contractors. It was evident, however, that they were less than enamoured with the project and in January the company's board announced that it no longer supported the proposed move to the West Country. The Ministry of Works and Buildings, which was by that time overseeing the work for the government, was undaunted by this announcement and simply responded that they would continue with the project in its existing form as, even if Royal Enfield no longer wanted the factory, no doubt 'some other suitable end user would be found.'

By the spring the Treasury was becoming increasingly concerned about the escalating cost of the Westwood scheme and sent down Sam Brown, one of its senior officers who already had considerable experiences of the Corsham excesses, to investigate. On 3rd April Brown reported rather dispiritingly that: 'Westwood, which now stands at £227,000, as compared to an original estimate of £60,000 for the same area, is rather horrible.'

Amongst the items that had caused the cost to almost quadruple Sam Brown cited the facts that the roof was much lower and floor of the quarry sloped more markedly than the initial survey had led them to believe. This meant that the quarry floor had to be expensively terraced to provide horizontal workshop floors throughout the factory area, and the low headroom made it necessary to construct concrete-lined pits in which to position some of the larger machine tools. Despite the evidence gleaned from the earlier War Office underground adventures at Corsham, little initial thought had been given to the heating and ventilation plant that might be needed to overcome the extraordinarily high levels of humidity in the converted quarries. The provision of an adequate ventilation system including boilers, radiators, fans and an intricate system of under-floor airways and high-level extraction ducts added enormously to the costs. Finally, Sam Brown drew attention to the enormous cost of the surface married quarters, hostels and welfare facilities which were now being built at Westwood but had not been accounted for in the preliminary estimate. Astonishingly, no thought had been given to where the six hundred men and women who would work in the factory, the majority of them drafted into the area, would live.

Work at Westwood limped along through the spring and summer of 1942 and then, at the end of June as construction was nearing completion, the Royal Enfield Company performed a second volte-face and announced that it would, after all, take possession of the factory. A small group of skilled machine operators and managers were sent down from Redditch and an intensive training programme put in place under which several hundred trainees, the majority of them young women, were taught the arts and skills of precision

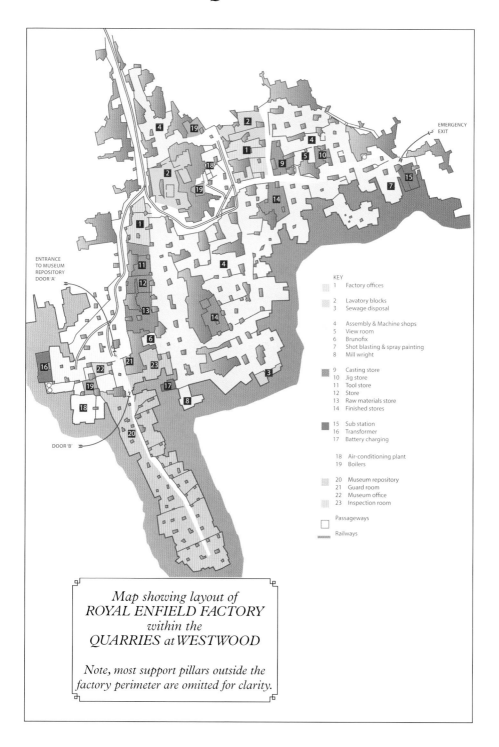

ENTRANCE
TO MUSEUM
REPOSITORY
DOOR 'A'

DOOR 'B'

EMERGENCY
EXIT

KEY
1   Factory offices

2   Lavatory blocks
3   Sewage disposal

4   Assembly & Machine shops
5   View room
6   Brunofix
7   Shot blasting & spray painting
8   Mill wright

9   Casting store
10 Jig store
11 Tool store
12 Store
13 Raw materials store
14 Finished stores

15 Sub station
16 Transformer
17 Battery charging

18 Air-conditioning plant
19 Boilers

20 Museum repository
21 Guard room
22 Museum office
23 Inspection room

Passageways

Railways

Map showing layout of
ROYAL ENFIELD FACTORY
within the
QUARRIES *at* WESTWOOD

Note, most support pillars outside the
factory perimeter are omitted for clarity.

45

engineering. Most were housed on the surface directly above the quarry on land adjoining Bobbin Lane where a sprawling estate of prefabricated bungalows for married couples and long wooden hostel blocks for single workers filled the fields between Upper and Lower Westwood. In the centre of the site a large welfare centre and entertainments hall was built, the latter reputed (no doubt with a degree of exaggeration) to have the best sprung dance floor in the west of England. Certainly, when the Peradin Rubber Company rented the near derelict building in the late 1960s for use as a temporary warehouse they discovered the disadvantages of the sprung floor. The tall, free-standing storage racks they erected in the building swayed alarmingly when anyone walked through the gangways.

Although the workers' welfare seems to have been overlooked by the Ministry of Aircraft Production and the Ministry of Works, the Royal Enfield Company was insistent from the very beginning of the project that every care was taken of its employees, many of whom would have been uprooted from their families for the duration of the war. A large, airy canteen was built adjacent to the dance hall and tea bars were established underground in order that workers could take a break without having to trek up to the surface. Special provision was made to ensure that employees working long shifts underground did not suffer unduly from the effects of living in a world of permanent darkness. During the winter months especially, they would go underground before daybreak and finish work long after sunset, never seeing daylight. To counter the effects of lack of sunlight a room was set aside underground in which each employee was compelled to sit for twenty minutes every fortnight in front of an ultraviolet lamp.

The amount of work required to transform the dripping, long abandoned Victorian stone workings into a modern factory was prodigious. The section of the quarry selected for conversion was the area immediately to the east of the existing Bath and Portland Stone Firm's entrance, the portal of which was completely reconstructed and faced with brickwork to become the main entrance to the factory. Some distance to the east, Godwin's entrance was utilized as an emergency exit. Within the quarry the main entrance tunnel was graded and concreted and a considerable amount of steelwork erected to reinforce the roof. A number of large steel doors in the left-hand wall of this passage led directly into the assembly shop while further into the quarry the main passage turned sharply to the left and became a central roadway through the quarry with numerous workshops and offices to the north and south. Throughout the greater part of the factory internal division walls were of single-skin brickwork. Towards the east end of the factory, near the section of the old mushroom workings that collapsed in the 1930s, the roof became somewhat unstable and a number of substantial brick pillars were erected to reinforce the roof support.

Four large diameter ventilation shafts were sunk together with numerous

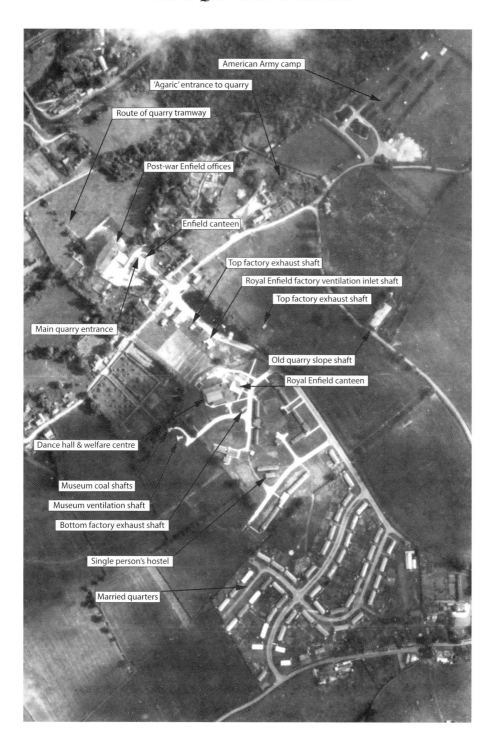

American Army camp

'Agaric' entrance to quarry

Route of quarry tramway

Post-war Enfield offices

Enfield canteen

Top factory exhaust shaft

Royal Enfield factory ventilation inlet shaft

Top factory exhaust shaft

Main quarry entrance

Old quarry slope shaft

Royal Enfield canteen

Dance hall & welfare centre

Museum coal shafts

Museum ventilation shaft

Bottom factory exhaust shaft

Single person's hostel

Married quarters

Above: The end of a shift in the underground factory. The quarry entrance is on the right, the end of the works canteen is just visible to the left of the image. The building at the end of the car park was used as an oil store.

Below: Looking in to the underground access road. At the far end the factory is to the left and the art treasure repository to the right.

smaller shafts and boreholes to carry cables, pipes and flues to the surface. At the bottoms of the inlet air shafts large fans blew incoming air through banks of steam radiators into man-sized under-floor ducts which distributed the air throughout the workshops. Stale air was extracted by subsidiary fans via steel trunking secured to the ceiling. Steam was provided by three manually fired boilers in a large, underground boiler-house, the fuel being delivered via a pair of vertical coal chutes. The prodigious amounts of boiler ash from the air-conditioning plant and swarf from the machining operations were removed from the quarry via one of the ventilation shafts by means of an old oil drum suspended from a chain hoist secured to the ceiling of the shaft top building. At the surface this vertical shaft terminated in a rectangular concrete building that was partially sunk below ground level. In the design for the surface building the engineers had incorporated a four-foot square horizontal concrete duct that ran just below ground level from the top of the shaft for a distance of approximately two hundred feet to the dance hall where it emerged behind a large cast-iron radiator within the building. By this means waste heat from the factory that would otherwise have risen up the shaft and been lost was utilized to supplement the welfare centre heating system.

Output of No.3 predictors began in July 1943 and was followed by a range of other gun control equipment including hydraulic control units for Bofors Anti-Aircraft guns. Towards the end of the war the Westwood factory was involved in the development of a radar control system for the Bofors gun codenamed 'Red Indian'. Using this system a whole battery of guns could be automatically directed onto a target which would be tracked by a single radar control unit equipped with a parabolic reflector. A tall steel-lattice pylon was erected in the yard outside the quarry entrance to support experimental parabolic reflectors that were used to track reflective balloons that were set adrift in the Avon valley to test the prototype equipment. The pylon with its rusting parabola remained as a sinister landmark on the hillside for many years after the factory closed down in 1968.

Royal Enfield remained at Westwood for more than two decades after the end the Second World War working on a number of defence contracts, although these gradually dried up as Britain's finances deteriorated and her role in world affairs contracted. Probably the most prestigious of these post-war contracts was for instrumentation for the Bristol 'Bloodhound' surface to air missile, which entered service in 1958. Thereafter government orders dwindled and the company became little more than jobbing engineers, taking whatever commercial work came their way.

The staple product of the Royal Enfield Company had always been motorcycles, and despite diversification into other engineering fields such as the design and manufacture of light-weight air-cooled diesel engines and

Above: Lathes closely placed in the upper machine shop. The sign in the background reads 'The First Component in Each Batch Must be Inspected'.

Below: A group of grinders in the upper workshop, operated mainly by young women.

Above: Stoker and his dog in the northern boilerhouse in the underground factory.

*Below: T*he Royal Enfield underground drawing office at Westwood.

precision instrumentation, this continued to be the case throughout the war years, though not at the Westwood factory. Tens of thousands of rather old-fashioned 250cc and 350cc side-valve engined bikes, together with some more modern overhead-valve types and the ubiquitous 125cc 'flying flea' were built at Redditch for the War Office. At the end of the war tens of thousands of surplus War Office machines, some unused and still in packing cases, others completely worn out after years of gruelling service in the deserts of North Africa, were returned to Royal Enfield for rebuilding and eventual resale. Most found their way to Westwood where they were temporarily stored in the disused and very damp mushroom area of the quarry while awaiting refurbishment. The bikes suffered badly in these dank conditions and to prevent further deterioration alternative accommodation was found in Greenland Mill and in the former Wilkin's Brewery in Wine Street in Bradford-on-Avon. Over a period of several years all these ex-War Office motorcycles were stripped down at Westwood, repainted and in some cases fitted with new Redditch-built engines, before being sold as new.

From the late 1950s much of Royal Enfield's motorcycle business, formerly concentrated at Redditch, migrated to Wiltshire, with component manufacture for the 250cc 'Crusader' and the Meteor and Meteor Minor moving to Greenland Mill in Bradford-on-Avon in an effort to reduce costs. The writing was, however, clearly on the wall for Royal Enfield. With an outdated range of motorcycles, a conservative, patrician management and an over-diversified structure the company was not in a competitive position and quickly went downhill after the death, in 1962, of its managing director, Major R.W. Smith. Under new owners a process of asset stripping commenced, accelerated by the formation of the Redditch Development Corporation which was eager to redevelop the main factory site.

In 1963 production at Greenland Mill and at the Wilkins Brewery site in Bradford-on-Avon ceased and production of the 700cc twin cylinder Constellation motorcycle, the company's only remaining worthwhile seller, was concentrated at Westwood. It was obvious, however, that the future was bleak for Royal Enfield and it came as little surprise to the employees in 1970 when the factory ceased production. A small part of the factory, consisting of the former assembly shops nearest the main entrance, was taken over by two ex-Royal Enfield employees who ran a very successful small engineering firm there using many of the original machine tools for a further twenty years. The firm eventually moved to more convenient surface premises at Holt in the early 1990s and the underground factory was finally abandoned after a life of fifty years.

Above: The underground tea bar in the Royal Enfield factory. Nearly all the machine operators seen in this photograph appear to be surprisingly young girls, (except for the one lad in the left background who seems to be somewhat embarrassed in so much female company).

Below: The subterranean treatment room where employees underwent compulsory twenty-minute exposures to Ultra Violet radiation every fortnight during the winter months because, working twelve-hour shifts, they never saw natural sunlight for long periods.

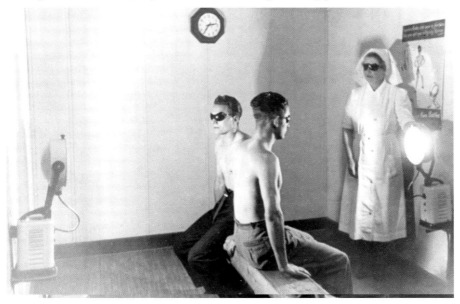

THE BRITISH MUSEUM AT WESTWOOD

The priceless treasures from the Victoria and Albert Museum arrived at Montacute House on the morning of 3rd September 1939 following their hasty evacuation from London the previous evening. For a while, in the months leading up to war, it seemed possible that the planned evacuation might be aborted and that Montacute might not, after all, be host to the V&A treasures despite the decision of the Air Raids Precautions Committee taken in 1934. The problem that threatened Montacute was created, in part at least, by an undercurrent of self interest that the committee had hoped, by keeping the scheme a closely guarded secret, to avoid. Unfortunately, however, details of the plan had leaked out and as war approached a growing number of lesser country house owners who had not been included in the original scheme approached the government and the museum authorities, offering their houses as safe repositories for the nation's treasures.

Their motive, of course, was neither altruistic nor patriotic, and it was not a motive confined exclusively to the ranks of the shabby-genteel lesser gentry. For some months, Lord Ilchester, Chairman of the Museums and Galleries Air Raids Precautions Committee, had argued strenuously against the use of Montacute House on the grounds that it was totally unsuitable. It was, he said, without mains water, sewerage or electricity, the roof leaked and, most importantly of all, it was only a few miles from the Westland Aeroplane Company's factory near Yeovil, which was a prime target for German bombers. Other members of the committee could not at first understand the vehemence of Lord Ilchester's opposition. The reason became clear, however, in January 1939 when Sir Eric Maclagan, a Director of the Victoria and Albert Museum, learned that Lord Ilchester's country home was Melbury House, just a few miles from Montacute, and that he had offered it temporarily to the nation as an alternative to Montacute. In a testy memorandum to the other committee members, Maclagan wrote, on 20th February:

> 'Ilchester has been generating concern over the Westland factory and thus proposes his own home, Melbury House, instead. We are inclined to think that his zeal is not wholly disinterested and that he hopes by sheltering the nation's treasures at Melbury to avoid having Brats from Bristol quartered on him. But this may be an unjust suspicion!'

The desperate desire of the country house owners to fill their houses with the nation's treasures in order to avoid the compulsory billeting of evacuee children, or, even worse, the risk of having their homes requisitioned for military purposes, was universal. Within a short while, however, it became apparent that the benefits were debateable for both parties. A few months after the scheme had swung into action the country house owners discovered that they, not the Treasury, were expected to foot the bill for the extra costs involved in playing host to the treasures. Fuel had to be paid for to maintain appropriate levels of heating and humidity required by the museum and gallery authorities, security had to be provided and often, too, the owners were expected to provide free accommodation and food for the museum staff that accompanied the paintings and artefacts. Misled by a rose-tinted, Edwardian image of the country house lifestyle, the civil servants who administered the scheme thought that this was a quite acceptable policy, but reality was very different. Since the end of the First World War heavy taxation, falling revenue from the land and a host of other factors had placed a heavy burden on the old estates and many, if not most, were in dire financial straits. Money was tight, the houses were in disrepair and there was a shortage of domestic staff. The situation was summed-up by Sir Patrick Duff, First Commissioner of the Office of Works, in a note to the Treasury during the first winter of the war in which he wrote:

> 'As is not surprising, we have found that these places are not entirely suited as they stand to house very valuable treasures which, in addition, are sometimes, as in the case of old pictures, highly perishable if exposed to conditions at all severe or exceptional.
>
> The owners of country houses, owing to increased taxation as well as perhaps natural conservatism, have retained standards of lighting, heating and fire protection which are by no means always sufficient to preserve the exhibits from deterioration or to reduce the fire risk to a degree which can be accepted in respect of such priceless objects.'

Museum staff also had their reservations about the country house scheme. Their concerns are encapsulated in a note from a British Museum official at Boughton House in Northamptonshire, the museum's principal repository, in which he wrote: 'The weak point of Boughton is that it is putting all our best things together in a tinderbox building where an odd oil-bomb would destroy the lot.

All this was for the future, though, and in September 1939 the scheme went ahead heedless of the difficulties to come. At Montacute the National Trust, who had owned the property since 1936, agreed with the Air Raids Precautions Committee to lease just the Long Gallery for the storage of the V&A treasures. The house was in too poor a condition to allow it to be opened to the public but the National Trust had a sitting tenant who occupied the rest of the property. The V&A were not entirely happy with this arrangement and over the next few months negotiations got under way to remove the tenant, leaving the museum in sole occupation of the whole house. There was more than just a security advantage to this move. Soon after the V&A artefacts were packed into the Long Gallery Miss Muriel Clayton, the museum's Keeper of Watercolours and now the officer in charge at Montacute, noticed that many of the tapestries and other items under her charge were developing worrying signs of mould as a result of being stacked too closely together in the poorly ventilated Long Gallery. Once the committee gained possession of the whole house Miss Clayton suggested that the museum's artefacts be spread about all the rooms in the house, allowing air to circulate amongst them more freely and allowing them to be periodically unpacked and inspected. Sir John Forsdyke, director of the V&A, immediately agreed to this arrangement.

Spurred on by her first success, Miss Clayton then suggested that as the collection at Montacute was heavily weighted with seventeenth century artefacts and they were in a house of much the same period, then why not lay them out in room-sets, rather than keep them sealed in packing cases? This plan, too, was accepted by Sir John Forsdyke. Greatly encouraged, Miss Clayton then proposed that as they had the house more-or-less set up as a quasi-museum, why not open it to the paying public at, say, sixpence a head? At this juncture Sir John felt compelled to remind her, somewhat sternly, that the museum's activity at Montacute was supposed to be a strictly guarded national secret, but Miss Clayton was not easily deterred. In response, she wrote to Sir John and the museum trustees informing them that:

> 'It is true that a great reticence of secrecy has been observed with regard the place to which the nation's treasures have been sent. But I need hardly tell you that everyone in the neighbourhood knows that our stuff is at Montacute, and I have no doubt that the same applies to the country houses that are being used by the British Museum and other national museums and galleries.'

Eventually it was agreed that the fiction of secrecy would be maintained but that serving officers of His Majesty's Forces, but not their wives, would be admitted by invitation for a token charge.

In comparison with the situation at many of the other country house repositories (particularly those occupied by the National Gallery in north Wales, such as Penrhyn Castle where the owner, Lord Penrhyn, was proving to be particularly obstructive and offensive), arrangements at Montacute quickly settled into a relatively trouble-free routine. Damp was a secondary consideration at Montacute but moths were the most persistent problem. Staff there battled for several months without success to contain a serious infestation and were compelled, in the spring of 1940, to turn to government experts for assistance. None, however, was forthcoming other than a pithy note from Mr M.G. Holmes at the Board of Education who wrote:

'I'm sorry that at Montacute, The moth's at work with teeth acute, But if your people work with zest, They'll soon eliminate the pest.'

Moths, recalcitrant owners, leaky roofs, fire risk and the host of other minor irritations in the country house repositories were, however, completely overshadowed by the Fall of France. Sir John Forsdyke had, from the start, been sceptical of the country house scheme and had long maintained that the only safe storage for his treasures was in deep underground repositories. Acting on a tip-off from W.L. Cooper, Librarian of the University of Bristol, he had begun surreptitious investigations into the possibility of utilizing one of the disused quarries at Corsham as early as February 1940. Cooper, by a stroke of good fortune, had acquired space for the University's collection of medieval manuscripts in Elm Park Quarry at Corsham some time before the war through contacts with the chairman of the Bath and Portland Stone Company, from whom the University was buying large quantities of stone for remedial work on the library building. It was this contact that Cooper passed on to Sir John Forsdyke. Initially it seemed that Sir John's approach would be successful but then, in February, the minutes of the Trustees of the V&A record that:

'Arrangements were made some time ago with the Bath Stone Firm at Corsham to inspect a quarry which they offered for storage. But we were stopped the day before our inspection by the Air Ministry who claimed all the quarries for their own use, or at least for their consideration.'

Just over a year later, with the British Expeditionary Force in France in a precarious position, with invasion imminent and with the risk of overwhelming attacks from German bombers once the Luftwaffe gained control of the French airfields (as it seemed inevitable they would), Forsdyke renewed his pleas for underground accommodation. This time he had influential support, including that of the Archbishop of Canterbury and the Prime Minister who, with reference to the National Gallery's paintings, had already given his opinion that 'if possible, they should be put in caves.' Events then moved quickly. On 11th March a meeting was arranged between Sir John Forsdyke, Sir Eric Maclagan, senior officers from the Ministry of Works and Buildings and representatives from the consulting engineers Sir Alexander Gibb and Partners at which it was agreed that the V&A and British Museum jointly should take over 20,000 square feet of Westwood Quarry previously allocated to the Royal Enfield

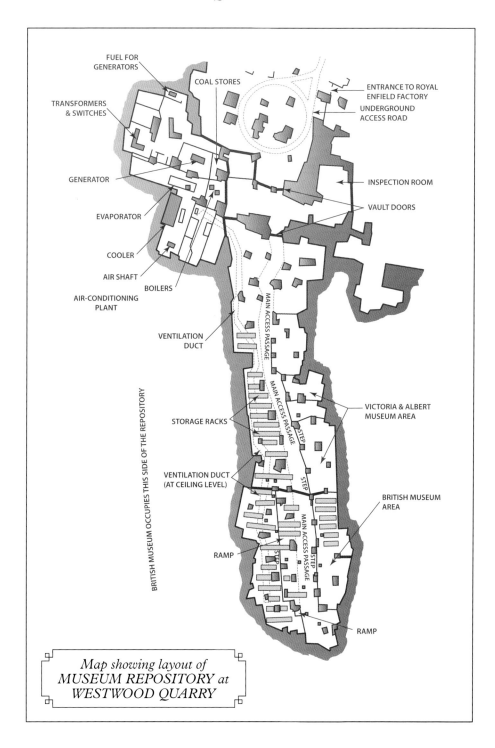

FUEL FOR GENERATORS

COAL STORES

ENTRANCE TO ROYAL ENFIELD FACTORY

TRANSFORMERS & SWITCHES

UNDERGROUND ACCESS ROAD

GENERATOR

INSPECTION ROOM

EVAPORATOR

VAULT DOORS

COOLER

AIR SHAFT

BOILERS

AIR-CONDITIONING PLANT

VENTILATION DUCT

MAIN ACCESS PASSAGE

VICTORIA & ALBERT MUSEUM AREA

STORAGE RACKS

STEP

BRITISH MUSEUM OCCUPIES THIS SIDE OF THE REPOSITORY

VENTILATION DUCT (AT CEILING LEVEL)

STEP

BRITISH MUSEUM AREA

RAMP

STEP

STEP

MAIN ACCESS PASSAGE

RAMP

Map showing layout of
MUSEUM REPOSITORY *at*
WESTWOOD QUARRY

Company. Conversion of the remote underground heading began immediately with a provisional completion date of September 1941.

It was agreed that the space at Westwood Quarry would be shared between the V&A and the British Museum to store all the V&A material currently at Montacute, together with a small number of delicate artefacts still retained in a supposedly bomb-proof vault in the basement of the Kensington museum, and all the British Museum artefacts at Boughton House, Skipton Castle and at two smaller country house repositories in Northamptonshire. Approximately one third of the gross floor area of 23,000 square feet was allocated to the V&A. This area consisted of the greater part of the section to the east of the central roadway while the remainder of the quarry was occupied by the British Museum who needed rather more space but were less demanding in their requirements. The marked slope of the quarry floor, which dropped by more than twenty feet from north to south, proved problematical. Because the majority of the British Museum artefacts were quite small they could be packed into standard cartons and stacked on racking that could be easily adapted to compensate for the sloping floor, but accommodating the many large items of furniture in the custody of the V&A was more difficult. Delicate antique furniture standing for a prolonged period on a pronounced slope, it was thought, would be prone to warp horribly. The solution was to create a series of large, horizontal terraces within the quarry by cutting away parts of the floor and building up others with concrete, a process that proved to be both time consuming and costly.

Although work on the underground repository got off to a sprightly start it soon ground to a halt, due primarily to the precedence given to other parts of the Corsham project more directly associated with the prosecution of the war. Reporting upon a site inspection on 26th June, Sir John Forsdyke wrote dispiritingly that:

> 'Arrangements have been put in hand and were going well, but latterly there has been some hold-up, possibly Treasury or possibly Service Department interference. The engineers are ready and waiting but the only activity is some architectural ornamentation of the entrance tunnel by a few stonemasons.'

Sir John was still hopeful that the work could be completed on time but his optimism was deflated following a further visit in early September, just three weeks before the scheduled completion date. The rough building work, he discovered, was three months behind schedule and the complex components of the air-conditioning plant that should by that time have been installed and running under test had not even arrived on site and, due to manufacturers delays, were now not expected until the end of October. The air-conditioning system was the key component to the entire underground storage scheme, for without it the plan would be unworkable. During the inter-war years air-conditioning was still seen as something of a black art in Europe, and even more so in the United Kingdom where our equitable climate rendered it largely unnecessary. In the United States, though, where the huge land mass created enormous and rapid fluctuations in temperature and humidity, air-conditioning had developed into a precise science. It was native mechanical expertise based upon American science that was employed to control the humidity underground at Westwood. Unfortunately this expertise was still in its infancy and consequently the installation programme suffered many setbacks.

Once the plant arrived on site it was assembled with remarkable speed and was up and running by the end of October. The plant performance fell far short of expectations, however, and it was realized that even running constantly under full power it would take at least four months to achieve a satisfactorily low level of humidity in the storage chambers. Eventually, on 17th March 1942, Mr. Bennit of the Ministry of Works and Buildings, the government department that was in overall control of the Westwood project, was able to advise the museum authorities that:

> 'I am directed by the Ministry of Works and Buildings to inform you that the quarry which has been adapted for storing museum treasures at Westwood near Bath is now complete, subject to minor points of adjustment which will be discussed with your officers locally. Arrangements may, therefore, be made to move your treasures in.'

Some months earlier, in a spirit of unwarranted optimism, Sir John Forsdyke had written to Muriel Clayton asking her to make preparations for the move from Montacute to a more secure location. At that time details of the Westwood Quarry repository were supposed to be a closely guarded secret and Sir John felt unable to reveal these details to Miss Clayton, to whom he wrote only that:

> 'I am not at liberty at present to tell you where the quarry is, but it is in the West of England and no more than forty miles from Montacute as the crow flies.'

Much to Sir John's surprise, Miss Clayton replied:

> 'I read your letter about the quarry with the greatest interest. Incidentally, I had already heard of the scheme through the medium of one of the less reputable daily papers, which had a paragraph a couple of months ago about 'art treasures in the caves' stating that several of the

great museums were proposing to take shelter in disused mine workings.'

V&A artefacts from Montacute and British Museum items from Boughton House arrived at Westwood by lorry on alternate days over the next five weeks, a special gantry having been erected in the yard near the quarry entrance to unload the heaviest packing cases. Gradually, as news of the Westwood vaults leaked out, enquiries arrived from the trustees and curators of many other institutions seeking safe refuge for their treasures. The previous November, for example, Sir John Forsdyke received a letter from Mr. Mackintosh, keeper of the Science Museum, asking:

> 'Could you possibly be very kind and give me a small corner of your stone quarry, if you could spare it? It is to house the Wright Aeroplane [Kittyhawk] in absolute security. By special request of the individual who is our liaison with Orville Wright, it has not been sent to a country house and is still in our basement which I consider far from safe.'

After some debate about whether the packing cases containing the dismantled aircraft would fit through the vault doors at Westwood, Kittyhawk finally arrived in May 1942 and was later followed by vast quantities of other items from the Science Museum. A little later most of the pictures from the National Portrait Gallery were transferred from their temporary home at Mentmore House followed by a flood of priceless artefacts from the Bodleian Library, the Wallace Collection, the Kenwood Collection and a host of other national museums and galleries. As the war progressed thousands more irreplaceable artefacts accumulated at Westwood including a mass of ecclesiastical treasures, amongst them the thirteenth century stained glass from the windows of Salisbury Cathedral, oak carvings from many of Wren's London churches and tapestries from Durham Cathedral. By the end of 1942 Westwood probably housed the greatest and most valuable collection of cultural and artistic artefacts assembled in one location anywhere in the world.

Throughout the war the Westwood project was plagued by Treasury parsimony. Whereas money was thrown at the underground factory scheme with such abandon that the resultant scandal gave rise to an unprecedented wartime inquiry by the House of Commons Public Accounts Committee, the museums authorities had to fight for every penny. The Treasury, for example, refused to sanction the purchase of new safe doors to secure the underground repository. Instead, old, nineteenth century iron doors from the vaults in the basement of the British Museum in Bloomsbury had to be ripped out and transferred to Westwood, where it was discovered that, because they were of odd sizes, they would not fit properly without expensive additional engineering work.

Above: Watercolours and other delicate artefacts arriving at Westwood from their previous refuge at Montacute House in the summer of 1942. The packing cases are being lowered onto electric trucks (probably borrowed for the purpose from Royal Enfield in the adjacent factory), for transfer into the underground repository.

Above: A view along the main access road through the art treasures repository at Westwood. Some of the French furniture from the Salt bequest, belonging to the V&A, can be seen on the terraced areas to the left of the passageway, with boxed British Museum artefacts on racks to the right.

Left: Packing cases on the left of this image contain items from the British Museum's Greek & Roman department, while those on the right, marked 'ETH' are from the Ethnographic collection.

Above: Contained within one of these canvas bags which hold part of the V&A's collection of carpets and tapestries, is the Ardabil carpet of 1530, the world's oldest dated carpet and one of the largest, most beautiful and historically important in the world.

Below: Packing cases in the foreground contain sculptures from the British Museum's Greek & Roman Department; in the background are pictures from the National Portrait Gallery.

Above: Terracotta panels from the Victoria & Albert Museum stacked against the bare stone wall in Westwood Quarry.

Below: After the discovery of a moth infestation, textiles from the British Museum's Ethnographic Collection were sprayed with DDT in a chamber set aside for the purpose.

Similarly, funds were not forthcoming for the purchase of a reliable standby generator, upon which the uninterrupted working of the air-conditioning plant depended. Sir John was compelled to employ the services of a dealer to scour the country for a suitable second-hand machine which was eventually found in September 1941 in the possession of the Exe Valley Electricity Company at Dulverton in Devon.

The electricity company demanded the outrageously inflated price of £860 for the machine (equivalent to approximately £35,000 at the time of writing), but when it was delivered to Westwood it was found to be little better than scrap. The diesel engine was over twenty years old, vital components were missing and after a thorough inspection it was discovered that all the moving parts including the pistons, main bearings, big and small end bearings, rockers and cams were so badly worn as to be useless. Lister-Petter, the manufacturers, was unable to provide spare parts off-the-shelf because engines of that type had not been made for over a decade. The company offered to manufacture new parts to order but warned that the price might prove prohibitive. With no alternative source of supply available, the Ministry of Works, on behalf of the museums committee, was compelled to take up Lister-Petter's offer.

A year later the new parts had still not arrived and as a temporary measure a portable generator was borrowed from the Bristol Aeroplane Company at Corsham. Eventually, on 12th December 1942 the parts had arrived, rebuilding was complete and a test run was scheduled under the guidance of Ministry of Works engineer, Mr. Pallot. Starting the archaic semi-diesel engine necessitated the tedious process of removing a series of blanking-plates and inserting a kerosene lamp into each cylinder to heat them up. Once the required temperature was reached the lamps were removed, the plates bolted back into position and the engine turned over by compressed air. Much to the engineer's relief this process went without a hitch and the engine fired-up and appeared to run quite smoothly for several seconds, but then there was an enormous explosion which dislodged the cylinder heads and completely demolished a large brick exhaust expansion chamber that connected the engine exhaust pipes to a vertical ventilation shaft. The engine was completely destroyed and, subsequently, an inquiry was set up to discover the cause.

It soon became obvious that the accident had its roots in the acrimonious relationship that had existed between the Treasury and Sir Alexander Gibb and Partners throughout the history of the Corsham project. The Treasury placed the blame for the huge increase in the cost of the project squarely upon the consulting engineers accusing them in only the most thinly veiled words of profiteering. By the late summer of 1942 Treasury officials despaired of the construction work, and hence the cost, ever coming to an end and determined that all outstanding contracts, either with Alexander Gibb and Partners or with

Above: Long abandoned, much of the historically important air-conditioning equipment in the museum plant room at Westwood still survives today.

Below: Disused coal-fired boilers in the museum repository plant room in Westwood quarry.

their sub-contractors, would be classified as completed even if there were still tasks outstanding. Little work remained to be done at the Westwood site other than completion of the boiler-house and air-conditioning plant in the museum repository and George Wimpey's men were urged to complete this as quickly as possible. There were heaps of empty cement sacks and a great deal of builders' debris in the vicinity of the generator room and in order to get this cleared away quickly the workmen simply shovelled it all into the still incomplete exhaust expansion chamber where it was bricked-up out of sight. Unfortunately the rubbish and debris completely choked the gas outlet into the vertical shaft and, when the engine was run-up on test, pressure built up in the expansion chamber resulting, inevitably, in a catastrophic explosion. Disheartened, the engineers abandoned the now completely wrecked Lister-Petter engine and instead made an arrangement with the War Office to borrow an old mobile searchlight generator which was stationed at the top of the exhaust shaft and connected to the underground switch-room by trailing cables.

Although the destruction of the standby generator plant was the most serious accident to occur at Westwood there was another less dramatic but potentially more catastrophic disaster that was only narrowly avoided. When the Westwood scheme was first proposed the Treasury reluctantly agreed to finance the underground air-conditioning plant because it was impressed upon them that without air-conditioning most of the items it was proposed to store there would suffer rapid and irreparable damage. Treasury officials were concerned, however, at the prospective running costs of the plant and refused to pay for full-time plant attendants, insisting instead that automatic monitoring equipment should be installed and that day-to-day maintenance should be undertaken when necessary by Ministry of Works men engaged on general duties in the quarry. The only dedicated member of staff was to be the boilerman who stoked the two coal-fired boilers that provided steam to heat the repository. A technically advanced infra-red smoke detection system was installed that would shut down the circulating fans if a fire was detected and a ten-point remote temperature and humidity sensing system automatically controlled the running of the plant to ensure that atmospheric conditions within the museum store were maintained within strict limits. Chart recorders kept a record of daily fluctuations in temperature and humidity and an alarm system connected to the recorders would sound if the limits were exceeded. Within the vaults strategically placed thermo-hygrographs maintained an independent record of conditions.

The system appeared at first to be working well until, on 18 April 1943 warders working in the repository noticed that the humidity was increasing very rapidly and that heavy condensation was forming on the walls and on the ventilation ducting and packing cases. No alarms had sounded and a quick check of the chart recorders indicated that the plant seemed to be operating normally. Then it was realized that the recording instruments were not revolving as they should. Ministry of Works engineers were called in to investigate and it was very quickly discovered that the main air-conditioning plant and the warning and monitoring equipment all ran off the same electricity supply so that, when a power failure stopped the plant, the alarms and recorders also stopped. Thus the system was incapable of ever sounding an alarm. To prevent such a situation arising again changes were made to the electrical circuits and arrangements to ensure that the plant room was permanently manned by properly trained attendants.

From the outset it had been decided that despite the evacuation from their London headquarters all the museums and galleries would continue to perform their normal functions of cataloguing, conservation and acquisition. The evacuation of artefacts was, therefore, paralleled by an exodus of staff, together with their library and research resources and workshop equipment, all of which had to be found suitable accommodation. At Westwood the British Museum Identified the former workhouse, by then functioning as the Old Court Hotel in the valley at Avoncliff as an ideal location for its temporary headquarters. Sir Eric Maclagan had become aware of this rather isolated and run-down establishment when he stayed there as a guest during an earlier foray into Wiltshire. The building, one of the few such establishments in the immediate area not already taken over for war purposes, was quickly requisitioned and handed over to the museum authorities. Senior staff of the V&A and the British Museum were found quarters in the hotel along with their offices while lesser staff were billeted in the temporary huts built in Westwood village for Royal Enfield employees. Throughout the latter war years all the British Museum's activities were conducted from the hotel and the Public Records at Kew are full of correspondence issued from Avoncliff on old British Museum headed notepaper, the address 'Bloomsbury' either over-stamped 'Old Court Hotel, Avoncliff' or with the temporary address simply scribbled in by hand.

Although, by the end of the war, the underground repository contained artefacts from dozens of different institutions, the bulk of the material was the property, in more-or-less equal proportions, of the V&A and the British Museum. The safekeeping of all these treasures was vested in a departmental head from one or other of these two museums and responsibility was rotated every six months. The first keeper, and the man who established the rules and systems of operation that would remain unchanged for the rest of the war, was Mr. C.J. Gadd, the Keeper of Egyptian and Assyrian Antiquities at the British Museum. In an idle moment in 1942 Gadd doodled graffiti on the wall of his office deep underground at Westwood but, being a world-renowned Egyptologist he chose to write not in English but in cuneiform characters. The ten lines of Gadd's inscription, in translation, read:

'In the year of our Lord 1942
The sixth year of George, King of all lands,
In that year everything precious,
The works of all the craftsmen
Which from palaces and temples
Were sent out, in order that by fire
Or attack by an evil enemy they might not be lost,
Into this cave under the earth
A place of security, an abode of peace,
We brought them down and set them.'

POST-WAR AND COLD WAR

As soon as victory in Europe was judged inevitable in the summer of 1944 the government decided that all the pictures and other artefacts belonging to the London museums and galleries should be returned to the capital as soon as possible after peace was declared and the museums re-opened to the public. This was thought to be an important step in bolstering public morale and creating a sense of returning normality after six years of war. Most of the V&A material stored at Westwood was returned to London by the end of December 1945. The majority of the British Museum artefacts were also returned during November and December 1945 but, because parts of the museum had been badly damaged during the war, some items remained at Westwood until repairs were completed in 1950.

Although all the museum artefacts had left Westwood by the beginning of 1950 the quarry was retained by the government as a safe refuge for the nation's treasures in the event of an atomic war with the Soviet Union, which, given the deteriorating political situation in Berlin at that time, seemed to some to be inevitable. A permanent Ministry of Works and Building maintenance staff kept the air-conditioning plant in running order and, towards the end of the decade, a new Crossley four-cylinder diesel generator set was installed to replace the dilapidated wartime unit. Staff at Westwood kept the air-conditioning plant ticking-over for nearly thirty years, maintaining it in a state of immediate readiness for the Third World War, when *'Operation Methodical'*, the meticulously planned Cold War evacuation scheme, would swing into action. This unworkable plan was abandoned and the plant finally shut down in July 1973 but the government continued to keep the quarry on Care and Maintenance for a further twelve years until 1985 when it was transferred to the private sector.

Westwood Quarry saw a flurry of sinister activity between 1950 and 1952 when it was temporarily occupied by scientists from the government's chemical

Above: This photograph, taken in 1945, shows the first batch of artefacts being prepared for return to the V&A at the end of the war, while on the right can be seen the first of some 20,000 ex-army Royal Enfield motorcycles that were returned to Westwood for refurbishment.

Below: Royal Enfield technicians operating an experimental *Red Indian* Bofors gun radar control unit at Westwood which tracked small balloons launched down the Avon valley.

and biological weapons research establishment at Porton Down. At that time the British government was deeply involved in the development of biological weapons as a less expensive alternative to the atomic bomb. Numerous trials were conducted using non-toxic simulants to test the dispersion patterns of various biological agents. Many of these tests involved the exposure of large areas of southern England to simulated pathogens sprayed from aircraft flying an arc of forty miles radius north of Salisbury, while in others passenger trains entering tunnels were sprayed by hidden lineside equipment. The Westwood experiments involved the contamination of the museum repository with the bacterium *Serratia marcesens* in the form of an aerosol during which staff on site wore full protective suits and respirators, despite the fact that the bacterium was supposedly classified as non-pathogenic. Archives from the Porton Down Microbiological Research Department record that in 1952 something went wrong and:

> 'The aerosol was disseminated into ducting serving the chamber and within the chamber, both in continuous ventilated state and recirculated state. Air from the system found its way back to the surface through the entrance tunnel, thus some emission to the outside air occurred.'

At first this caused little concern but some years later an independent review conducted on behalf of the Ministry of Defence by Professor Brian Spratt concluded that:

> '*Serratia marcesens* was used as a biological warfare simulant up to the 1950s. At that time this bacterium was believed to be harmless, but it is now known to be an opportunistic pathogen that is a significant cause of disease in seriously ill patients in hospitals, particularly those who are imuno-deficient. A well publicised release of live *Serratia marcesens* from a ship off San Francisco in 1950 has been associated with a number of cases of *Serratia marcesens* disease and one death, and live *Serratia marcesens* is no longer considered to be a safe biological warfare simulant.

In the United States in 1981 the Federal Government was charged with responsibility for the death of a San Francisco citizen resulting from tests conducted in 1950 when the San Francisco bay area was sprayed with *Serratia marcesens* by the US army.

WESTWOOD QUARRY TODAY

The quarry experienced something of a renaissance in the 1980s when Wansdyke Security Ltd took possession of the old museum repository and the Bath and Portland Stone Company resumed quarrying to the south-east of the mushroom area.

Wansdyke Security was established in 1953 to provide high security underground storage for essential commercial documents and company records where, as their publicity material explains, there are 'ideal conditions to guard against the combined risks of fire, flood, theft, industrial espionage and environmental deterioration, which are difficult to achieve at an economic cost.'

The business, which began as a subsidiary of the Bath and Portland Stone Company but is now independent, was established in the abandoned underground Royal Navy ammunition depot at Brockleaze Quarry near Neston and expanded into the museum repository at Westwood when it became available in 1985. Ten years later the company acquired the much larger underground ammunition depot at Monkton Farleigh which offers some 1,250,000 square feet of storage space.

Much of the wartime underground infrastructure still remains at Westwood. The entrance to the Wansdyke Security site is still secured by the nineteenth century iron doors transferred from Bloomsbury in 1942 but now supplemented by a modern, massively secure, Chubb vault door. The company has installed independent air-conditioning units but the wartime plant remains in situ, though disused and abandoned. Although untouched and undamaged there has been no effort made to preserve it and the equipment is gradually deteriorating. The generator installed in the 1960s remains but is disused although the original wartime electrical switchgear and sub-station is in its original state and continues to provide power to Wansdyke Security. Switches and fuse-boxes in the powerhouse bear the labels 'Museum Power & Lights', 'Enfield Power', etc. Within the vault C.J. Gadd's office is still in existence and is used by Wansdyke Security staff. Gadd's cuneiform text is in remarkably good condition, protected now by a glazed frame.

The Royal Enfield factory remained in good condition for a decade or more after its closure in 1970. Part was occupied by Messrs. Willet and Wilkins and used as a small engineering workshop for many years, but the bulk of the factory was simply abandoned. All the machine tools were removed but the fixed plant – boilers, ventilation fans, sewerage and water supply apparatus, paint-spraying booths and electrical substations – remain in place. All the offices and workshops are identifiable with many of the doors lettered-up with their function. Here and there odd items of plant can still be seen while the fluorescent light fittings – very much a novel innovation in Britain in 1942 – hang precariously from

Above: The new Crossley diesel generator installed in the museum plant room at Westwood in preparation for the repository's re-use in the event of a nuclear war with the Soviet Union.

Below: Since the mid-1980s the former Westwood art treasures repository has found a new use as a high-security document storage facility.

the ceilings on rusty chains. Unfortunately, in the late 1980s, the Bath and Portland Stone Company resumed quarrying at Westwood from an area on the far side of the Enfield works and used the main road through the factory as a highway for their plant and a route via which to remove the huge blocks of cut stone. This, inevitably, has resulted in a certain amount of disruption, but much worse damage has been done where the stone company has used the old workshops as a dumping ground for waste stone. Most of the large chambers to the south of the roadway are now choked with debris and are inaccessible. In the more accessible offices and workshops to the north there is much evidence of renewed roof movement similar to that which caused the catastrophic collapse in 1934. Massive brick reinforcing piers are being crushed by the weight of the overburden and cracks have appeared in many of the stone pillars.

There is still plenty to be seen on the surface. The quarry entrance is much as it was during the war, except for the addition of a steel roller-shutter security door. The large Royal Enfield office block is now a motor bodywork repair shop while the tall vehicle garages and a range of single storey offices on the opposite side of the access road are occupied by a small business. Hanson Minerals, the successor to the Bath and Portland Stone Company, uses both the former employees' car park to the left of the quarry entrance and the yard where the museum's unloading gantry and Royal Enfield's radar testing tower once stood as a stone stacking yard. In recent years a few smaller buildings in the vicinity of the quarry entrance have been demolished and parts of the area are now overgrown.

The village of Westwood was changed completely by the war. The influx of over one thousand new residents and the erection of a large estate of temporary dwellings and ancillary buildings to accommodate and service them changed the landscape of the village irreversibly. Wartime housing development filled the fields between Upper and Lower Westwood, effectively joining them into a single community. During the early 1960s the temporary housing was acquired by the District Council which replaced them with modern council houses. More recently the area around Bobbin Lane, which was previously the site of the community hall and numerous industrial buildings associated with the underground factory, has been redeveloped as a private housing estate. It was Intended that the Bobbin Park estate should be much larger, extending northwards to Upper Westwood Lane, but concerns about the instability of the quarry workings below prevented this.

The area is now a public park but is littered with relics of wartime occupation. Large red-brick bomb-proof buildings mark the tops of two of the ventilation shifts from the factory, the eighty-foot-deep shafts protected by strong iron bins clearly visible through the buildings' grilled entrances. Unfortunately both structures were given a white cement rendering a few years ago which destroyed

Above: A Samson arc shearing machine and a low profile mine loading shovel in the re-opened section of Westwood quarry in 1990.

Right: Preparing a Samson machine for a top-cut. Note the cutting chain on its universal rotating head.

Below: Cut stone blocks awaiting transfer to the surface.

Above: The decaying remains of the northern boilerhouse in the Royal Enfield factory as it is today. The photograph on page shows this plant in pristine condition in 1945.

Below: The northern machine shop in the underground factory as it is today. This image shows the same area of the factory as the lower photograph of the grinding machines on page 50.

Above: This panorama of the crossroads in the middle of the factory gives some impression of the scale of the works.

Left: The rusting remains of the 440 volt switchgear in the factory substation. The 11,000 volt transformer and switchgear can just be seen in the background.

Below: A brick roof-support pillar in the upper machine shop, crushed by the weight of the overburden.

Right: One of the factory ventilation induction fans, built by Keith, Blackman & Co, installed in 1942.

Left: Hand-wash sinks in the women's ablutions in the southern factory area. Seventy years after this part of the underground factory was abandoned, the deco style swivelling soap dispensers remain intact.

Above: The switchroom in the underground substation serving the British Museum section of Westwood quarry, still in use when this photograph was taken in 2005, and still bearing its wartime labelling.

Below: The wartime Royal Enfield Canteen at Westwood, until recently used as a car repair shop.

their wartime character and has made them rather vulnerable to the modern graffiti artist. Smaller structures nearby mark the tops of the chimney from the underground boiler-house and the top of the coal chute down which fuel for the boilers was heaved. The single storey building beside the village road, currently used by a playgroup, was formerly the site engineer's office. There is another ventilation shaft from the underground factory in a field some way to the east of the main group and a fourth shaft just across the road from the northernmost house in Bobbin Park. It is a low, enclosed concrete building partially hidden in bushes and quite difficult to identify. This is the shaft that one contained the rudimentary hoist mechanism for bringing swarf and boiler ash to the surface and is now used by Wansdyke Security for ventilation.

The assortment of shaft-head buildings for the British Museum plant room was In a separate compound to the west of the welfare centre behind Chestnut Grove. The principal buildings consisted of a T-shaped bomb-proof shaft head building and a concrete-roofed, open-fronted brick structure, similar to a bicycle shed, which protected the tops of the two coal chutes. The latter building still stands in the garden of one of the small group of executive homes built on the site at the end of the twentieth century. The developers had intended to demolish the unsightly shaft-top building and level the ground but then, to their misfortune, discovered that the shaft was still used by Wansdyke Security and that there were certain legal rights associated with it. So the shaft still survives, within just a few feet of one of the new houses, its top protected by an ornate, open-sided structure rather like a gazebo which more-or-less blends in with the architecture of the house.

Below: The bomb-proof surface structure above the powerhouse air shaft in its original condition.   *Below:* The shaft top building reconstructed to blend in with a newly constructed house.

3

THE KENNET AND AVON CANAL

There is no doubt that the construction of the Kennet and Avon Canal at the very end of the eighteenth century had the most profound effect upon the hamlet of Avoncliff and, indeed, from casual observation it would be easy to assume that the little group of industrial and residential buildings that seem to cling to its embankment have grown around it as a consequence of its very existence. The immediate commercial effects of the canal's completion were, however, minimal. Godwin's stone quarry seems to have benefited only marginally from the reduction in transport costs offered by the canal but that may have been due to the conservatism of the quarry-master. The canal did not tempt any of the larger quarrying firms in the Corsham district to exploit the Westwood reserves and it was not until nearly two decades after the opening of the Great Western Railway line through Avoncliff in 1857 that the Bath and Portland Stone Company took an interest. Old engravings of the aqueduct show stone from Westwood Quarry being loaded onto barges in the 1880s, but such traffic, by then, must have been marginal.

Although the economic impact was minimal, the visual impact of the great stone aqueduct striding across the valley was immediate and enormous, bisecting the hamlet, disrupting the age-old pattern of lanes and tracks and effectively forming a topographical full-stop, blocking the valley at its narrowest point. The picture would have been very different, however, had the Kennet and Avon Canal Company not been dogged by financial difficulties just as construction was due to commence. Extravagantly planned at the height of the Canal Mania, when investors fought in the streets to purchase shares in canals that went from nowhere to nowhere, their virtues puffed by the most ludicrously optimistic prospectuses, the Kennet and Avon received its Royal Assent and started to make financial calls on its promoters just as the Napoleonic wars panicked the financial markets and caused price inflation to soar.

Before studying in detail the building of the canal through Avoncliff we should take a brief look at the more general history of the canal and of the Avon Navigation which was later taken over by the canal company.

Various proposals were made in the 1780s to build a canal westwards towards Newbury in order to form a link with the River Thames and London via the River Kennet. It was soon realised that this scheme would only be viable if it was extended much further to the west towards Bristol to form a navigable waterway between the Thames and the River Avon at Bristol. Thus, in April 1788, a committee of the proposed Western Canal, under the chairmanship of Lord Dundas, agreed that:

> 'It appears to this meeting that a Canal from Newbury to Hungerford only would not be likely to meet with the general approbation and that nothing short of a junction of the Kennet and Avon Rivers would answer, and be of material benefit to the Country at large.'

The scheme had immediate appeal and, with the first tranche of money subscribed by the investors a survey was commissioned from Messrs. Barns, Simcock and Weston and presented to the shareholders in the summer of 1789. The plans were scrutinized by a number of eminent engineers including Robert Whitworth, who questioned the adequacy of the water supplies to the higher pounds. The committee then called in the engineer John Rennie who, although he was later to achieve great eminence as a civil engineer, had as yet little experience of canal building and was perhaps at that time an odd choice.

Rennie completed his own survey in July 1793 which advocated a more southerly route than that proposed four years earlier but which required less heavy engineering and could be completed in two years rather than the three- -and-a-half years that had been estimated for the earlier scheme. Rennie's new route was approved by the Western Canal Committee on 27th August 1793 when, in recognition of the significance of the waterway as a strategic east-west transport link, the name of the undertaking was changed from the Western Canal to the Kennet and Avon Canal. The Kennet and Avon Canal Act received Royal Assent on 27th August 1793 and one month later John Rennie was officially appointed engineer. With the same caution that had led the committee to call in both Rennie and Robert Whitworth to examine the plans of Barns, Simcock and Weston, the committee called upon another rising canal engineer, William Jessop, – an immensely skilled but unassuming man whose reticence to some extent robbed him of the recognition he deserved – to prepare independent costings for both a wide and a narrow canal on Rennie's route.

Both engineers favoured a wide canal. Jessop suggested a deviation that would avoid the two-and-a-half mile long tunnel that featured in Rennie's plan, but which would require more locks and a pumping station to maintain water levels in the summit pound at Crofton. A short tunnel would still be required, but construction costs would be cut by £47,000 and further savings would be made by routing the canal north of Trowbridge, obviating the need for a substantial aqueduct in the town. The committee also looked at Rennie's more controversial proposal to take the canal through Sydney Gardens and the Bathwick Estate to join the Avon at Bath rather than via a flight of five locks at Bathampton as initially planned. This latter scheme was not finally agreed until 1798 at which time the canal company was compelled to pay the considerable sum of 2,000 guineas in compensation to the owners of Sydney Gardens.

THE AVON NAVIGATION

Seventy years earlier, in 1724, work had begun on a scheme to make the River Avon navigable from Bristol to Bath. Through navigation had been impossible for centuries due to the weirs at Hanham, Keynsham, Swinford, Saltford, Keynsham and Weston and the intention of the promoters of the Avon Navigation was to build six sets of locks to bypass these obstacles. Although the scheme had first been discussed by Bath City Council as early as 1712 it was not until 1724 when the interests of private commerce came to the fore under the leadership of Ralph Allen, John Hobbs and others that any substantive progress was made. Excavations for the first lock pits started in April that year and all six were completed and the navigation opened for traffic by 15th December 1727.

Throughout the rest of the eighteenth century the Avon Navigation returned a satisfactory although not spectacular profit to its shareholders. There is evidence that the undertaking was held back to some extent by conservatism on the part of the proprietors who showed little interest in a number of independent schemes, put forward at regular intervals, to extend the navigation to the east, first to Lacock and then to Chippenham. Aware of the importance of the Avon in the vision of the proprietors of the Kennet and Avon Canal, however, the Avon Navigation offered itself to the canal company in 1793 but the offer was refused, presumably because the price asked was too high. But this did not mean that the canal company was uninterested, for over the following two years they furtively bought up Avon Navigation shares as they became available. By 1795 the canal company had fully realized just how pivotal the river was to the overall success of their undertaking and made a formal offer to the Avon Navigation to purchase the river outright. In a fit of pique, the river proprietors refused to sell and the canal company was forced to buy shares by a number of devious means including the use of nominee shareholders in order to hide the fact that they were gradually accumulating a majority holding in the Avon Navigation. This was achieved in 1796, though at exorbitant cost. Minority shareholders continued to cause local difficulties and it was not until December 1803 that the Kennet and Avon Canal Company achieved complete control.

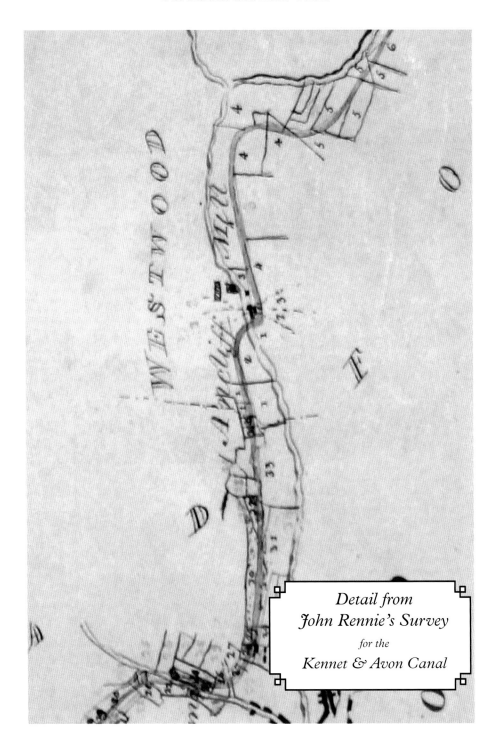

Detail from
John Rennie's Survey
for the
Kennet & Avon Canal

CONSTRUCTION OF THE CANAL, 1794-1810

The construction of the network of artificial inland waterways in the British Isles which began in the latter part of the eighteenth century was the first large-scale civil engineering task undertaken in modern times and, at that date, there was not a correspondingly large civil engineering industry to support it. The huge contracting firms we see today – the likes of McAlpine and others – are essentially a product of the railway age and, for the most part, simply did not exist in the eighteenth century. Although, as L.T.C. Rolt makes clear in his biography of Thomas Telford, men did emerge towards the end of the century who were prepared to take on substantial canal contracts employing many hundreds of labourers, the great majority of all such excavation and building work being undertaken by small local contractors; typically they would tender for no more than one or two miles of excavation or the building of a couple of lock chambers or a single bridge or an aqueduct. Work started simultaneously at the eastern and western ends of the Kennet and Avon Canal in 1795. The specification for the first contract, which was advertised in the Gloucester Journal in May 1795, was for works near Bradford-on-Avon and is typical of the small scale of such contracts:

> '... for the purpose of letting a length of about 1,500 yards of deep cutting on the line between Bradford and Widebrook, the depth at the summit thirty-one feet including the bed of the canal.'

Work proceeded steadily from Bradford-on-Avon towards Bath with contracts let for all the building and excavation of the fifteen-mile length by the beginning of 1796, except for the underwater foundations for the aqueducts at Avoncliff and Limpley Stoke. No suitably competent contractor could be found so the canal company was forced to undertake these difficult tasks using directly employed labour.

Rennie's original plan shows the aqueduct at Avoncliff located approximately 200 yards east of its final position, upstream of the weir and approached from the Westwood bank of the river by a long, sweeping embankment. Building the aqueduct in that position, while avoiding the disruption of the hamlet that resulted from its subsequent repositioning, would have necessitated a long, expensive embankment on the south bank of the river and difficult earthworks, mainly through oolitic limestone, in the meadows below Turleigh. Acting upon the advice of William Jessop, Rennie decided, principally upon grounds of economy, to reposition the aqueduct downstream of the weir to the point at which it now stands. Although this decision must have met with much opposition from the inhabitants of Avoncliff, whose day-to-day lives were

86

greatly inconvenienced for several years while building was in progress, their concerns were overridden by the financial plight of the canal company. Building the aqueduct in its final position, where the valley is at its narrowest and its sides most steep, involved much less heavy engineering and allowed the construction of a simpler, cheaper and more elegant masonry structure. Crucially, too, was the fact that the final position was much closer to the main source of stone used in the aqueduct's construction as the cost of transporting stone to the building site was proving to be a major element in the overall cost.

Shortly after construction work began on the canal the availability of suitable building materials became critical. Rennie had intended to build most of the bridges, aqueducts, lock and stop-gate chambers of brick, manufacturing them from the deposits of clay that it had been anticipated would be found along the route of the canal. Partly as a consequence of the limited understanding of geology that existed in the latter part of the eighteenth century, Rennie's predictions regarding the abundance of clay proved wildly optimistic and, apart from a small amount discovered near Devizes, virtually none was available along the western section of the canal. No clay meant no bricks, and without bricks the canal builders were compelled to fall back upon limestone, a material that was in abundance in Wiltshire and Somerset but in the use of which they had little or no experience. But the contemporary shortcomings in the science of geology upset Rennie's use of stone as well. Although the use of oolitic limestone was growing quickly towards the end of the eighteenth century, particularly as a result of the building boom that saw the transformation of Bath, there seemed to be a marked inability amongst many masons to tell good stone from bad in the short term. The situation was improving however and, in the light of experience, quarry masters were developing an instinctive feel for those beds of Bath stone that appeared to combine the advantages of workability and durability, though little of this was based on science.

In December 1794 Rennie requested George Fletcher, who had been recently appointed Inspector of Buildings and Works by the Western Area Sub-Committee, to enquire the price of stone at the various quarries in the vicinity of Avoncliff and Limpley Stoke. Fletcher discovered that prices were as high as eight shillings (40p) per ton at Bradford-on-Avon, while Godwin's of Westwood could offer good building stone at five shillings (25p) per ton at the quarry plus three shillings (15p) per ton for haulage to the building site. He was also quoted 16 shillings (80p) per day for the hire of a wagon and four horses. Such a wagon, he was told, could carry 36 cwt of stone in summer and 30 cwt in winter, which perhaps says something of the condition of the roads at that time. These prices very much alarmed George Fletcher ('his prices are extraordinary,' wrote Fletcher to Rennie regarding a quote received from one quarry master), and in desperation he sought out other more economical sources of stone. Fletcher proposed to purchase virgin quarry ground on behalf of the canal company, who would then work it themselves, and on 20th December 1794 he informed Rennie that:

> 'I have the pleasure to inform you that I have found excellent stone for the purpose within 150 yards of Avoncliff Aqueduct on one side, and one mile on the other, and within 750 yards of Monkton Combe Aqueduct, which may be got down to each place for 1 shilling and 6d [2.5p] per Ton by a small Machine and Railway.'

In a temporary mood of optimistic elation following the discovery of a stratum of oolitic limestone along the line of the canal between Avoncliff and Limpley Stoke, Fletcher was also able to report that:

> 'We shall get a large quantity of stone in the line of the Canal in lots 6 and 5 which will serve for the stop gates and bridges in those lengths.'

Unfortunately George Fletcher's optimism was ill-founded. Without exception, all the stone he had discovered was from beds much lower than those already worked by the established quarrymen at Westwood and elsewhere and was of a very inferior quality. Unaware of this, the company went ahead on Fletcher's recommendation and opened their own quarries at Avoncliff and Murhill to supply building stone for the aqueduct. The cliff-like face of the huge, open quarry from which stone for the aqueduct was extracted can be seen towering above the lane from Westwood, on the left hand side of the lane as one descends towards Avoncliff. The earliest quarries at Murhill are probably those that are lower down the hillside and would also have provided some of the stone for the aqueduct. The more extensive of the Murhill quarries are near the top of the hillside and were worked from the early nineteenth century, initially to provide stone for the reconstruction of Avoncliff aqueduct in 1803. Scars caused by the random extraction of stone for the bridges and stop-gate chambers along the section of canal west of Avoncliff are clearly visible on the precipitous hillside north of the waterway towards Limpley Stoke.

Using coffer dams, the canal company's small workforce of directly employed labour began work on the underwater foundations for the piers of Avoncliff and Limpley Stoke aqueducts early in 1795. The works at Avoncliff were above flood level by March 1796 and during that month the contractor, James McIlquham, began construction of the main span of the above-water masonry arch. McIlquham was also responsible for the construction of the Dundas aqueduct at Limpley Stoke, starting work there in August 1796. The company's cash crisis of 1796 led to numerous stoppages of work when bills and wages could not be paid, and further serious delays were encountered due to frosts and inclement weather during the harsh winter of 1796/7. Avoncliff aqueduct was finally completed towards the end of 1798, nearly a year behind schedule, but several more months were to pass before the Dundas aqueduct was finished.

Rennie's proposed location for the Dundas aqueduct at Limpley Stoke was also altered following Jessop's recommendation. Rennie's survey of 1794 shows the canal crossing the Avon upstream of Limpley Stoke weir and then passing through the grounds of the Manor House to follow the line of the present day railway before sweeping northwards in a three-quarter mile horseshoe loop up the valley of the Midford Brook almost as far as Monkton Combe before returning to its current alignment below Basset House. This line would have avoided a certain amount of excavation through solid rock on the escarpment below Conkwell but otherwise involved a long embankment before crossing the Avon, the purchase of expensive estate lands in the parish of Limpley Stoke and prodigious earthworks near Monkton Combe. Stone for Dundas was obtained from a company-owned quarry, evidence of which is still just discernible, cut into the hillside below Conkwell at the eastern end of the aqueduct and was brought down to the works via a short tramway which was apparently the earliest example of a true railway constructed in southern England. This line must not be confused with the much longer tramway that was constructed in 1801 to bring down stone of marginally better quality from a quarry nearer the top of the hill when it became necessary to make urgent repairs to the original work.

Although the two major aqueducts in the Avon valley might have been finished by the end of 1798 no work at all had been done on the line of the canal from Claverton to Bath, tenders for this work being advertised in the Bath newspapers on 29th November of that year. For most of the section that was completed between Bradford-on-Avon and Limpley Stoke, the canal clung precariously to steep hillsides consisting of badly fractured oolitic limestone interspersed with thin seams of clay. This treacherous combination was what Rennie had been keen to avoid and, to some extent, explains the somewhat devious route of his original survey. Almost immediately after the completed sections were filled with water there were serious collapses as the embankments gave way. Near Bradford-on-Avon over seven acres of land slipped down the hillside completely destroying a substantial length of the canal. These underlying geological difficulties on the nine-mile pound between Bradford and Bath plagued the canal for two hundred years, causing frequent landslips and stoppages of traffic on the waterway, and were not properly overcome until the very end of the twentieth century.

Terribly serious problems developed at Avoncliff within a year of the completion of the aqueduct. Shortly after the trough was first filled with water it was noticed that the central arch of the aqueduct had sagged, causing a major distortion of the whole structure. It is impossible now to determine whether the design was at fault or whether poor workmanship or the poor quality of the stone was the main factor in the aqueduct's partial failure. Certainly the winter frosts of 1798-99 took their toll on the masonry work which disintegrated dreadfully. The stone, which was of extraordinarily poor quality in the first instance, had not been allowed to 'weather' after it was quarried and was thus still full of moisture when the aqueduct was built. In the frosts this moisture froze, splitting and spalling the blocks and this, in combination with the stone's insufficient compressive strength, led to widespread structural failure.

Emergency repairs were made during the following year using stone that was probably obtained from a new quarry at Avoncliff north of the river. This quarry, which is now the site of the former waterworks pumping station opposite Mill House, together with a strip of land upon which an access road was laid linking it to the end of the aqueduct, was acquired by the canal company in 1799. These repairs, and similar repairs made to the aqueduct at Limpley Stoke, were not successful; in September 1800 the company opened another quarry higher up the hillside at Conkwell in the hope of obtaining stone of adequate durability. Stone from the quarry was brought down to a wharf close to Dundas aqueduct by means of a double-track, self-acting inclined tramway consisting of short cast-iron rails with interlocking ends, spiked to wooden sleepers. The route of this tramway is still clearly evident where it descends the hillside.

The performance of the Conkwell stone was disappointing and the aqueducts and other masonry work continued to deteriorate at an alarming rate. In 1803 the company acquired further quarrying rights at Murhill to extract stone from the upper beds of oolitic limestone which they hoped might finally meet their requirements. Some means was required to lower the stone down the steep hillside to the canal in the valley some 500 feet below, and on 1 April 1803 a contract was let for: '...a wooden railroad for the new stone quarry at Murhill to be laid from thence to the canal.'

The tramway was probably finished by the summer of 1804 but in the meantime Rennie wrote despairing of the terrible quality of all the masonry work in the Western Sub-District, telling the management committee that:

> 'Seeing the great loss that the company have sustained and the great detention which the works have experienced from the badness of the stone, I feel it my duty to repeat again to the committee, what I have frequently done before, the propriety of again considering whether it would not be better to use brick generally, instead of stone in the works which are yet to do.'

Murhill Quarry was no longer operated by the Kennet and Avon Canal by 1812 when it was in the hands of Ambrose and John Heal. In 1825 it was leased to Messrs Dunkin and Baber who, in the following year and after some acrimonious correspondence with the canal company, replaced the old wooden tramway with a more modern system using iron edge-rails. Dunkin and Baber were also probably responsible for the erection of steam-driven stone-cutting machinery near the quarry in 1835. During the mid-1800s the quarry was worked by a succession of moderately successful tenants until 1863, after which trade deteriorated; by the early 1890s it had become derelict.

The route of the 48-inch gauge Murhill tramway is still remarkably intact. A double-track incline descends from the hilltop quarry to the cutting yard adjacent to Murhill Lane from which point a second incline descends at a slightly obtuse angle to the wharf, becoming a single track approximately half-way down the hillside. At the wharf the line turns sharply to the east, splitting into two short sidings running parallel to the canal. In recent years the lower section has been covered with tarmac to form a lane giving access to Wharf Cottage and a few other houses that cling to the hillside, but beneath the tarmac the stone sleeper blocks that supported the rails are still *in situ*. Remarkably, most of the trackwork at the wharf remains intact despite having fallen into disuse well over a century ago. The rails, which were excavated and recorded by English Heritage in the 1970s and subsequently scheduled as an Ancient Monument, have been reburied for their own protection although a few exposed sections are easily visible to the casual observer.

The upper section of the tramway passes diagonally through the woodland north of Murhill Lane and is still a prominent feature of the landscape. Although the rails were removed over 100 years ago all the stone sleeper blocks remained in place until very recently when, unforgivably, this superb example of Wiltshire's industrial archaeology was bulldozed up to make way for a sewer pipe that was laid along the route of the incline. The blocks still survive, piled up amongst the undergrowth, many of them still retaining the threaded bolts grouted in place by lead plugs that once secured the cast iron rail chairs. At the bottom of the incline and adjacent to Murhill Lane it is just possible to make out the location of the celebrated steam sawmill and the reservoir that once held water for its steam engine. Two short parallel tunnels burrowing into the hillside at the north end of the masonry-walled reservoir tapped springs of water.

It is not until one has walked the upper incline, and also the new road to the east of Murhill, laid by Colonel John Richard Magrath in 1880, that one realizes the true extent of the quarries there. Towering cliff faces of quarried stone hang over the woodland fringing the lanes in both directions while half way up the incline short, abortive underground mine workings burrow into the faces of the open quarries, hopelessly chasing poor quality stone. The most

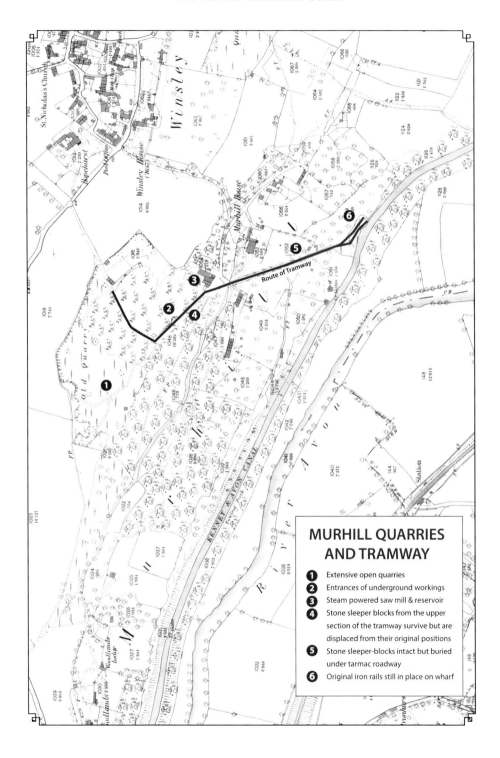

Route of Tramway

MURHILL QUARRIES AND TRAMWAY

1. Extensive open quarries
2. Entrances of underground workings
3. Steam powered saw mill & reservoir
4. Stone sleeper blocks from the upper section of the tramway survive but are displaced from their original positions
5. Stone sleeper-blocks intact but buried under tarmac roadway
6. Original iron rails still in place on wharf

Above: A short section of the original early nineteenth century tramway track exposed where it crosses a public footpath near Murhill wharf.
Below: A point assembly in the trackwork at Murhill wharf exposed during excavation in the early 1970s. A good example of fish-bellied rail is evident in the mid-foreground.

Above: The twin tunnels visible in this photograph tapped springs supplying water to the boiler house reservoir for the steam-powered sawmill at Murhill. The reservoir was directly in front of the tunnels, while the undergrowth to the left conceals the remains of the demolished buildings.

Below: The 1930s architect's drawing for proposed new wards at Winsley Chest Hospital. The buildings were ultimately completed to a much simpler design.

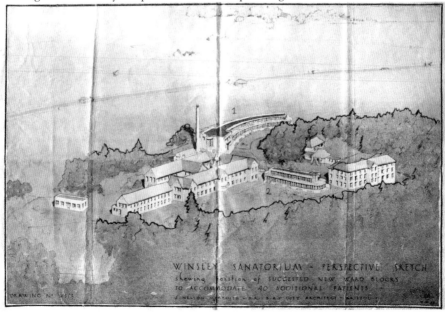

extensive workings, though, are near the top of the hill where a broad plateau, now softened by undergrowth and partially obscured by new development, marks the area where the whole south-facing hillside has been taken away. In 1904 this large tract of derelict wasteland, high above the stagnant valley bottom, caressed by gentle breezes, exposed to the warm southern sun for most of the day in summer and protected by the high quarry face from the worst of winter's northerly winds, was identified by the medical authorities as the ideal site for a tuberculosis recuperation sanatorium. Within a short time a complex range of wards and chalets were built, each with its wooden, empire-style veranda upon which beds were placed for recovering or dying patients to take the air. When visited one October evening in the early 1990s, the long disused and semi-derelict sanatorium, known in more recent years as the Winsley Chest Hospital, still exhaled an air of Edwardian grace as the breeze shifted the autumn leaves that had fallen on the ancient wicker bath-chairs standing abandoned on the verandas.

It is probable that the rails on the upper section of the incline were removed when the land was purchased by the hospital authorities in 1904 because just a few years earlier, in 1893, a visitor to the area remarked upon the 'very old-fashioned rails on an inclined plane running from the quarries down the hill.' In recent years the old sanatorium has been sensitively redeveloped and is now known as the Avon Park Care Centre.

During the summer of 1803, some five years after its supposed completion, the aqueduct at Avoncliff was still causing despair and in June it was reported to the committee that: 'We still keep sets of masons repairing the work which have been torn to pieces by the frost on the Western district.'

Despite being opened for through trade between Bath and Foxhanger (near Devizes) in 1803 there were still constant stoppages and upsets to trade on the canal due to problems with collapsing masonry at Avoncliff and elsewhere. The problem was not that Bath stone was, *de facto*, a bad building material, it was simply that in seeking economy George Fletcher had used the worst and cheapest stone available and in his haste to complete the works had failed to allow the freshly quarried stone to weather, thus compounding the error. Eventually, in 1808, the canal company finally grasped the financial nettle when it decided to utilize stone of the best quality from the Hampton Down quarries to complete the repair work. Details of this arrangement are somewhat vague but it would appear that the canal company did not own quarries on Hampton Down but merely purchased large quantities of stone from Messrs. Bowsher and Company. Tenders were invited in June 1808 for the construction of a tramway from the quarry to join the Kennet and Avon at a wharf on the canal near Claverton. A record of disputes between the quarry owners and the canal company over the exact location of the wharf indicates that neither the quarry nor the tramway was canal property.

The Hampton Down incline is the longest and most impressive of the early quarry tramways along the Avon valley, any one of which will provide the opportunity for a rewarding afternoon's walk to anyone with even the most cursory interest in industrial archaeology. Arranged as a double-track, self-acting incline with a gauge of 3' 4", the 2,658-foot-long Hampton Down tramway was in fact two linked tramways. The upper line, terminating just above the present A36 trunk road was 1,658 feet long while the lower section that descended through the meadows to the canal wharf was 1,000 feet in length. Rather primitive, 'L'-section cast iron plate rails were used on the incline, secured to the stone sleeper blocks by nails driven into wooden plugs which were themselves fixed in sockets bored in the blocks. The rails, each approximately three feet in length, were not up to the job, a contemporary description of the tramway noting that:

> 'These rails are too weak for the load which is lowered upon them, which amounts to 80 cwt [four tons] including the wagon. This is proved by the large heaps of broken rails that lie beside the line.'

This account, published in 1827, has been verified in recent years by the discovery of a number of discarded rails buried in debris and undergrowth along the line of the incline, all of which were broken. Throughout the upper section the line is substantially intact with the majority of the sleeper blocks still in place. Below the main road, however, tipping in the 1970s, changes in property boundaries and the re-routing of a footpath have pretty well obscured all evidence of the lower tramway although the general alignment can still be made out.

Just below the bottom terminus of the upper tramway a low arched masonry bridge was built in 1809 to carry the line over an ancient trackway that threaded its way to Bath from Claverton via Hengrove Wood and Bathampton Wood. With the opening of the Black Dog Turnpike extension (the current A36 Warminster Road) in 1830 the old lane fell into disuse. Between Claverton and Bathampton the new turnpike ran parallel to the lane but was more gently graded, taking a lower contour as it turned west around the promontory of Bathampton Down before making its final approach into Bath. At this point a new bridge was required to carry the tramway across the turnpike. During most of the twentieth century this bridge – the infamous 'Bathampton Dry Arch' – presented a notorious hazard to traffic on the increasingly busy A36 trunk road until it was finally demolished in 1966. The original bridge of 1809 still stands, hidden by undergrowth and spanning a little-used footpath.

THE CANAL 1810 to1850: THREE DECADES OF PROSPERITY

Following the completion of the Widcombe locks at Bath in November and of the troublesome flight of locks at Devizes on 28th December, the canal was finally opened for through traffic at the end of 1810. Trade increased steadily for the next forty years, bolstered by heavy freight traffic from the Somerset Coal Canal which joined the Kennet and Avon at Limpley Stoke.

The opening of the Great Western Railway main line in 1841 marked the beginning of the end of the canal's prosperity. Traffic on the canal declined slowly at first as traders gradually became aware of the advantages of speed and lower transport costs offered by the railways, but by the late 1840s little remained other than the Somerset coal trade (the railways did not really penetrate the Somerset coalfields until the 1870s) and the canal company paid its last dividend to its shareholders in 1850. The following year, in March 1851, the canal company, now facing the prospect of bankruptcy, took the only realistic option that was open and offered itself to the Great Western Railway. Transfer of ownership took place on 30th June 1852. Following acquisition by the Great Western Railway tolls on the canal rose steadily and traffic declined. During the early 1860s ice-breaking in winter was suspended, pleasure craft were discouraged and attempts were made to close the canal during darkness and during periods of low water in summer. Economies were made across the board and in 1864 the Cleveland House headquarters in Bath was closed and management of the canal transferred to Paddington. By 1905 annual traffic had fallen from a peak of 360,000 tons in 1848 to just 60,000 tons and continued to decline thereafter.

IN DECLINE

The section of canal between Avoncliff and Limpley Stoke continued to cause problems for the new owners with frequent blow-outs and collapses of the embankment. A spectacular and potentially fatal landslide occurred near the occupation bridge at Murhill on 3rd September 1902 when a thirty-foot section of the embankment burst just as a canal maintenance barge was mooring nearby. Seconds after the workmen stepped out of the boat the towpath beneath them was washed away and their boat, swept away by the torrent of water escaping from the great rent in the side of the canal, was dashed down the precipitous hillside into the River Avon below.

In an attempt to contain the damage from possible blow-outs on the nine-mile pound, the canal company had from an early date installed a number of 'stop-gates' on the section between Bradford-on-Avon and the top lock at Bathwick. These gates, which looked superficially like conventional locks, were constructed in pairs along with masonry channels on each side of the canal into which heavy boards or stop-planks could be inserted. By using the stop gates and planks, sections of the canal could be isolated to minimize water loss in event of a breach or to allow short sections to be drained for maintenance. Within each section drainage adits or 'syphons' were let into the bed of the canal and sealed with two-foot-square hinged wooden plugs. Stout chains attached to the syphon plugs connected them to hand-operated windlasses beside the towpath. Most of the runways that conducted water from the syphons into the River Avon are still evident today. One, for example, in the form of an open, stone-lined gulley for most of its length, runs through a tunnel beneath the roadway at the beginning of the Barton Farm Country Park. At Avoncliff another, situated some fifty yards east of the southern end of the aqueduct, takes the form of an enclosed tunnel that runs below the Cross Guns public house.

'Restoration' of the Kennet and Avon in recent years has led to the disappearance of much of the canal's historic infrastructure, including the stop-gates and syphons. The position of many of the stop-gates are, however, still evident and at a few modern stop-planks have been fitted. Every mile or so on the nine-mile pound the canal mysteriously narrows between masonry walls, and it is there that the gates were fitted. The locations of the syphons are given away by the few surviving remnants of the windlass mountings beside

Below: One of the many syphon windlasses that could once be found on the Bradford-Limpley Stoke pound of the canal. This example was above the Cross Guns Inn at Avoncliff.

the towpath. Twenty years ago they were all still intact; substantial, iron-bound wooden rollers mounted between massive upright stone or iron-rail supports and fitted with forged ratchet and pawl mechanisms to stop the weighty plugs crashing back into the water if the operator temporarily lost his grip or footing.

Despite their stringent policy of cost cutting and their apparent eagerness to close the waterway for long periods on the weakest of pretexts, the Great Western Railway initiated a considerable programme of work during the early years of the twentieth century to stabilize the canal in the Avon valley. The main motive for this work was not, however, the improvement of the canal's commercial viability but simply to minimise the danger to the railway embankment in the valley below, which was at risk of being washed away by a serious breach. This work, which was completed with remarkable economy, would probably never have been done had it not been for an unexpected local windfall that fell, in the timeliest manner, into the lap of the Great Western Railway. This windfall fluttered from the financial failure of a dismal early nineteenth century railway venture which, though not at first sight remotely relevant to Avoncliff, is briefly told below, after which its tenuous relevance will hopefully be clear.

THE AVON AND GLOUCESTERSHIRE RAILWAY

Very early in the nineteenth century there was much interest in expanding the coalfields north of Bristol but development there was held up by the lack of adequate transport. Aware of the potential commercial benefits to its waterway, the Kennet and Avon Committee gave its backing to a number of proposals to build tramways from collieries in the Pucklechurch and Coalpit Heath areas between 1803 and 1814, but none came to fruition. Eventual success came in 1828 in the form of a rather complicated arrangement consisting of two linked tramways – the Bristol and Gloucester Railway, which ran from Coalpit Heath to Bristol, and a separately owned branch from this line, the Avon and Gloucestershire Railway, which left the Bristol and Gloucester at Rodway Hill Junction in Mangotsfield and trundled off through Warmley and Oldland Common to feed wharfs on the Avon Navigation near Keynsham. The Avon and Gloucestershire opened in 1832 and from its inception, as a result of its interest in the Avon Navigation, was almost wholly owned by the Kennet and Avon Canal Company.

Trade on both lines was good in the first few years but soon, due to its strategic location and the fact that it had a terminus within the city of Bristol, the Bristol and Gloucester attracted the attention of the larger railway companies. Eventually, following a number of extensions and alliances, the Bristol and Gloucester was purchased by the powerful Midland Railway Company in 1846 and became part of that company's main line to Gloucester, and Bristol's principal route to

Above: The Avon & Gloucestershire Railway near Willsbridge Tunnel, around 1906.
Below: A length of handrail at the end of the parapet of Avoncliff aqueduct showing the distinctive fish-bellied shape of the Avon & Gloucestershire rails, re-used as support posts.

the north. Meanwhile the fortunes of the Avon and Gloucestershire ebbed away as it became a difficult and embarrassing adjunct to the main line. The problem lay in the fact that while both undertakings had always been standard-gauge lines, the Bristol and Gloucester had been upgraded by the Midland Railway to carry express steam-hauled trains while the Avon and Gloucestershire remained resolutely a horse-drawn freight tramway. Worse still, the Avon and Gloucester retained statutory running powers over the original section of the Bristol and Gloucestershire as far as Coalpit Heath. By 1846 this was intolerable as horses and steam locomotives did not mix.

By 1852, when the Great Western Railway acquired the line as part and parcel of the Kennet and Avon Canal it was pretty well moribund, the victim of unassailable competition from the Midland Railway, constant litigation over running powers, and the terminal decline of Bull Hall, Siston Hill and Crown Collieries, the line's main sources of traffic. The Great Western applied for an Act of Parliament to wind up the railway in 1865 which, for reasons never explained, was not followed through. At a Kennet and Avon Committee meeting in 1871 it was admitted that there had been no traffic on the line for the past twenty years but it was resolved to leave the rails in place just in case any new commerce developed in the area. A tiny dribble of traffic came from California Colliery after a new deep shaft was sunk there in 1874 but was of little value to the proprietors. When California pit ceased winding in 1904 the line was closed permanently and the rails lifted in July 1906.

Due to the relatively steep incline of the line as it headed towards the river (198 feet over its five-and-a-half mile length), earthworks on its route were necessarily heavy, including a number of bridges, embankments, and three tunnels at Warmley, Oldland Common and Willsbridge. The line was laid using iron fish-bellied rails, each fifteen feet long, laid on rough stone sleeper blocks by means of iron shoes. Many of these blocks, along with most of the major engineering works and vestiges of Londonderry and Avon Wharfs, are still visible today.

Because the tramway had never been truly viable very little upgrading had been done throughout its seventy-two year life, so when the Great Western lifted the track in 1906 it found itself in possession of some eleven linear miles of apparently useless, seventy year-old, fish-bellied iron rails that by now looked distinctly antique. Coincidentally, this stockpile of scrap iron came to hand just as the Great Western Railway was planning both the improvements to the nine-mile pound and the construction of its new passenger facilities at Avoncliff, and large numbers of the scrap rails were artfully employed in those works.

New stop gates were constructed in 1906, one every mile between Bradford-on-Avon and Limpley Stoke, and to ensure that they offered the least obstruction to the waterway they were designed so that when open the wooden gates were concealed within rebates below the edge of the towpath. Whole lengths of fish-bellied rail were used as girders to support the towpath above these openings and many more were bent, shaped and riveted to form the large racks upon which the stop-planks were stored when not in use. Following the opening of Avoncliff Halt on the Great Western line in 1906 the short aqueduct over the railway became the only means by which passengers could cross the line. To avoid the risk of late night revellers from Avoncliff, Westwood or Winsley (for the tiny station had a large catchment area) on their return from the fleshpots of Bath or Bradford-on-Avon, stumbling into the canal to meet an ignominious end by drowning in its turgid waters, the railway company erected iron railings, fabricated from lengths of fish-bellied rail, on the towpath edge. Unfortunately, because for most of its length the towpath had to be kept clear for the ropes that hauled the barges, it was not possible to protect the whole length of the pathway over the aqueduct in this way, so natives of Avoncliff and Westwood were compelled to fend for themselves for the latter half of their journey. Short lengths of railing were erected at the Avoncliff end of the aqueduct to save pedestrians, feeling their way on a foggy night by holding on to the stonework of the parapet, from tumbling off the edge when the masonry ran out.

When the station was opened the Great Western thoughtfully provided paraffin lamps on ornate cast-iron standards on the steps from the station platforms and at each end of the aqueduct and beside the lane below the

Below: A stop-plank rack at Murhill, constructed from Avon & Gloucestershire fish-bellied rails.

102

aqueduct. All these lamps were attended to by a porter from Bradford-on-Avon who trimmed the wicks of the lamps and kept his stockpile of paraffin in a corrugated tin shed beside the line in the shadow of the aqueduct which he shared with the signal linesmen who maintained the signal lamps. The beautiful Edwardian lamps were taken away in the early 1950s but the area remained lit by paraffin for another fifteen years or so by utilitarian storm-lanterns hung from the old posts. All the cast-iron lamp standards were removed some forty years ago except for the one by the lane below the aqueduct which disappeared under suspicious circumstances during the recent restoration.

Lengths of old Avon and Gloucestershire fish-bellied track also served as posts for the ubiquitous and sorely missed warning signs erected along the towpath warning the riders of bicycles against their nefarious activity on pain of a fine of forty shillings. There must be many poor walkers today who use the towpath for their Sunday afternoon jaunt who bitterly regret the passing of the signs and of the legislation that gave them teeth, wishing perhaps that the rules were still in force and that the penalty was not just forty shillings but included the confiscation and destruction of the miscreants' machine along with the incarceration of the rider and his extended family for long periods of penal servitude.

Nearly all the period features fabricated from Avon and Gloucestershire rails were destroyed during the restoration of the canal in recent decades; the stop-gate casements are gone, the sign-posts are gone, all but one or two of the marvellous stop-board racks are gone (the exceptions being a fine example at Murhill and another above the locks at Widcombe, now partially dismantled) and almost all the railings at Avoncliff have been removed and replaced by horribly bland mild-steel fencing which does nothing for the aesthetic appeal of the aqueduct. Some fish-bellied railings have survived at Widcombe and at other odd locations as far east as Devizes, but overall the unnecessary and wholesale removal of these historically significant artefacts has made the canal a poorer thing by their absence.

DECAY AND RESTORATION

By 1950 the canal was in all practical senses moribund although legally still open. It was just possible to navigate its whole length but the journey was likely to take a month or more and would require the assistance of a team of up to a dozen Railway Executive maintenance men, which the Executive was legally required to provide if requested. Thus they found themselves in the ludicrous and unsupportable position of having to pay wages in excess of £80 to collect a £5 toll. In 1951 the locks from Devizes to Bath had fallen into such a poor state that they were all padlocked against traffic and in the following year orders were issued that maintenance work on the western end of the canal should be limited to ensuring the safety of bridges and culverts over and under the waterway and that no effort should be wasted on trying to keep the canal navigable.

My first truly lucid childhood memory (I was far from a precocious boy) is of standing beside the canal at the end of a long walk with my Aunt Molly to Avoncliff in October 1954 where we watched a barge and tender pass over the aqueduct making its way towards Limpley Stoke. I vividly recall standing beside the cold, white-painted railings and seeing the thin wisp of smoke curling from the crooked chimney on the roof of the barge cabin and the black tarpaulin that covered the tender that it towed. Four decades later I was to learn that what I had seen that day was the last vessel to navigate the nine-mile pound for thirty years, for just days after my chilly autumn walk the clay puddle collapsed between the aqueduct and Winsley Bridge at Murhill, draining that section of the canal and marooning the two vessels on the dry bed. Fearful that the weakened embankment, which towered high above the railway line on a tight curve, might collapse upon the railway line below with potentially fatal consequences, the British Transport Commission closed-off the stop-gates east of Avoncliff aqueduct and at Limpley Stoke bridge and permanently drained the intervening section.

In 1965, under increasing pressure from the Kennet and Avon Canal Association, the British Waterways Board which by that time controlled the canal agreed to a tentative restoration programme. During 1965 and 1966 the accumulating undergrowth was cleared from the dry bed of the canal west of Avoncliff aqueduct and the rotting hulks of the two stranded maintenance boats removed. Efforts were made to repair the clay puddle that sealed the canal bed using material from the canal's own clay-pit in Bradford-on-Avon, which lay beside the towpath a hundred yards or so east of the Frome Road lock. By the early 1960s the clay-pit was a sorry sight, some thirty feet deep with its precipitous walls subsiding and its flooded bottom choked with reeds. A wartime pillbox, part of the Ironside anti-invasion defences of 1940, was perched on the very edge of the pit and during the winter of 1967, as a result of erosion of the subsoil by heavy rain, the pillbox and its massive concrete foundations tilted alarmingly. Standing inside the tilted pillbox, devoid of any reference point to the outside world except for the tiny gun-slits, one experienced the bizarre misconception that instead of standing upright in a canted universe one was leaning at an unfeasible angle in a horizontal world. A little later this rather surreal spectacle slid gracelessly into the bottom of the quarry where it was eventually broken up.

With the aid of some two-foot gauge decauville track and a small fleet of tatty skip trucks kindly provided by Farr's, the Westbury civil engineering firm, a group of volunteers began the laborious task of digging clay and transporting it to the Frome Road bridge where it was transferred to lorries for onward delivery to Limpley Stoke from where it was carried to a point near Murhill by means of more narrow gauge track laid on the towpath. It soon became apparent that the task was beyond the capabilities and resources of the available workforce and soon petered out. During 1966 the experimental use of polythene sheeting as an alternative waterproof membrane was also abandoned on account of its cost. Thereafter restoration more-or-less halted for a decade and shrubs and dense undergrowth again took control of the canal bed.

Negotiations were going on in the background, however, that would lead eventually to a comprehensive solution to the problems that had dogged the nine-mile pound for the best part of two hundred years. In June 1974 Wiltshire County Council, the Manpower Services Commission and the Kennet and Avon Canal Trust agreed upon a plan prepared under the auspices of the British Waterways Board for a jointly funded scheme to concrete the dry section of canal between Avoncliff aqueduct and Limpley Stoke bridge. The Trust would supply the materials, initially estimated at £75,000, while the Manpower Services Commission would provide labour to a notional value of £100,000. The work, which involved the laying of a continuous concrete lining over heavy-duty polythene sheet on the bed of the canal, the construction of concrete and masonry side-walls and the strengthening and grading of the towpath, was expected to be completed within a year. Inexperienced (and in some cases unwilling) labour, atrocious winter weather and a severe bout of vandalism delayed progress and inevitably increased costs. As a direct result of these manifold difficulties costs were increased by at least £20,000 and a new completion date of April 1978 announced.

The condition of the two aqueducts at Dundas and Avoncliff continued to cause concern. Dundas aqueduct at Limpley Stoke appeared structurally sound but suffered from severe leakage which it was hoped could be stemmed by the use of clay puddle over polythene sheet. The problems at Avoncliff, however, were of a much greater magnitude and necessitated enormously expensive engineering works that were, eventually, fully funded by the British Waterways Board. It was feared that the weakness of the underlying structure of the aqueduct caused by the settlement that occurred during its construction and further exacerbated by nearly a century of neglect might have rendered it incapable of carrying the anticipated levels of leisure traffic once the waterway was fully re-opened. The plan adopted, implementation of which began in 1980, involved the construction of a reinforced concrete trough within the original masonry structure which was supported only by the abutments at each end so that no additional load was thrown upon the arch.

Following the failure of the polythene-lining at the Dundas aqueduct the same concrete trough technique was employed there too, the task being completed in July 1984. By that time restoration of Bradford lock was complete, allowing

Above: This view of Avoncliff aqueduct must date from the early 1950s. The canal is clearly disused, GWR lamp standards are still in evidence, and at the top of the station steps the wartime pillbox is still camouflaged as a pitched-roof toll booth.

Below: By 1955 the canal west of Avoncliff was dry and weeds were taking hold of the bed.

Above: By the time this photograph was taken, some time before 1966, footpaths have become well established across the dry bed from the Westwood side of the canal. At the top of the steps from the railway platform the square outline of a large wartime pillbox can be clearly seen.

Above: Another 1960s view of the aqueduct with the pillbox at the top of the steps and another in the bushes at the north end of the aqueduct. Note the handrail made of Avon & Gloucestershire rails on the right hand side of the dry canal bed.
Below: Work under way on reconstructing Avoncliff aqueduct in 1981.

Above: Construction of the new concrete trough within the structure of the original aqueduct has been completed' stop-planks are in place on the Westwood side and water is being slowly let in.

Below: Repair work under way on the external facing of the aqueduct in 1981.

Above: Reconstructing the canal bed in reinforced concrete near Murhill.

Below: With the new concrete canal bed near Limpley Stoke bridge finished loads of random Bath stone have been delivered in preparation for building the side walls and towpath.

Above: Reconstruction of the towpath retaining wall well advanced near Limpley Stoke.
Below: At Winsley bridge, (very close to Murhill wharf) the canal bed has been cleared and levelled with a layer of hardcore over polythene sheet prior to the new concrete bed being laid.

Above: With reconstruction complete, here we see the canal being slowly re-watered.
Below: With the canal refilled all that remains to be done is to level and resurface the towpath.

through navigation between Devizes and Widcombe. Success was short-lived, however, for the following summer there was a failure between Bradford and Avoncliff necessitating the drainage of that section for re-puddling, which took almost a year to complete. The final stage of restoration at Avoncliff involved the re-facing of the badly deteriorated masonry of the aqueduct, particularly on the eastern elevation. Included in this work was the replacement of the ugly engineering brick patchwork that was the legacy of over one hundred years of Great Western bodged repairs, undertaken on an *ad-hoc* basis at the cheapest possible cost and with no eye at all for aesthetics. The recent programme of repairs, using Bath stone of the highest quality, was begun at the turn of the millennium and has only recently been completed.

So, the canal at Avoncliff is now fully restored and in terms of the number of vessels passing across the aqueduct on a summer afternoon it is probably busier today than it has ever been. However, in the opinion of many observers what has been accomplished is not 'restoration' in the true sense of the word; the canal is not restored as a piece of antique furniture or a vintage car might be restored, but has instead been reincarnated with minimal reference to the past. What we see now is not an early nineteenth century commercial waterway restored, as the hackneyed phrase has it, 'to its former glory', with all its period features lovingly refurbished and its grace and character retained. It is instead an immensely successful but utterly characterless twentieth century tourist and leisure amenity superimposed upon the route of the old canal which has brought enormous commercial benefit to businesses new and old along its route. This latter fact alone is probably sufficient to justify the way the job has been done, but there are many amongst us who would have seen it otherwise.

Surviving features that still show evidence that the Kennet and Avon was once a proper, working canal upon which heavy horses lumbering along the towpath pulling heavily-laden commercial barges are now few and far between. At the southern end of the downstream side of Avoncliff aqueduct the stonework of the parapet shows the deep wear marks created by the haulage ropes from countless barges as the horses that pulled them turned off to go under the aqueduct to join the towpath on the opposite bank. Once, a steep cobbled track led down to the lane but this has now been replaced by concrete steps. Similar but shallower marks can be seen on the opposite parapet where the track drops down to the Cross Guns public house. At the point where the canal turns sharply to the east towards Bradford-on-Avon a tall stone was erected in the garden of a cottage on the corner to guide the haulage ropes around the corner. This stone is deeply scored and grooved; had it not been there the haulage ropes would have cut into the corner of the cottage. A few yards further to the east a similar but small fender-stone was erected, close to one of the few surviving Kennet and Avon boundary markers, to protect a second

Above: A view from the south end of the aqueduct looking towards Bradford-on-Avon along the dry bed of the canal in 1973. This is how the canal at Avoncliff looked throughout most of my childhood and is how I remember it at its timeless best.

cottage but did not do its job so well. Careful inspection will show a series of shallow grooves cut into the cornerstones of this cottage, caused by the ropes slipping over the top of the stone. Originally replaceable baulks of timber had been bolted to the parapet of the aqueduct to protect the stonework but in latter years they fell into disrepair and were not replaced. The bolts holes that once secured them are, however, still clearly visible.

For me, Avoncliff and the canal that ran through it were at their most magical in the late 1950s and very early sixties when no-one went there, when the few who knew would drink through the night at the Cross Guns (for the writ of the licensing magistrates seemed not to run in so remote a spot); when the little station was still lit by paraffin lamps, the stagnant canal, blocked off just east of the aqueduct was alive with iridescent dragonflies and the dry canal bed and its towpath near the railway bridge was smothered with rampant hops that clambered wildly over the parapets and railings. It seemed always to be Saturday afternoon and sunny; school was two long days away and the canal bank and the lane from Turleigh were dotted with pillboxes, relics of the 1940 invasion-that-never-was, to play in. Until recently one such pillbox stood at the very edge of the aqueduct near the top of the railway steps, but this was pointlessly and inexplicably destroyed along with many others during the restoration. Towards Murhill the remains of the two maintenance barges still rested in the dry canal, rusting, diamond-shaped cast-iron signs on Murhill bridge warned darkly about attempting to cross with 'Vehicles Above The Normal Traffic Of The District', the towpath was overgrown and rutted and cycling was strictly prohibited. Nothing worked in Avoncliff, which was glorious for us children. Hardly any trains stopped at the little station, and the big pump-house with its thirty-foot well was disused and abandoned, presenting a dusty, cobwebbed mystery ripe for exploration. Neither mill was at work and the one on the north bank of the river was filled, as it was until just a few years ago, with sinister machinery, giant wheel-driven cogs and overhead belting providing a perilous playground that – had he been aware of my adventures there – would have horrified my father who a decade earlier had been marginally involved in the management of the mill. In high summer, provided one was brave enough to take the first few shaky steps across the narrow, perilous plank that spanned the waterwheel and the rushing leat on the north bank, it was possible to walk across the weir from one mill to the other without getting your feet wet.

4

THE RAILWAY

The railway which, as we have seen, slowly strangled the life from the Kennet and Avon Canal, came unwillingly through Avoncliff during the mid-nineteenth century but didn't bother to stop until 1906.

The main line of the Great Western Railway between Bristol and London was opened in 1841 and had an immediate impact upon the economy of all the towns along its route. Within a year or two the financial benefits of the coming of the railways to Britain were manifest, not just to the shareholders of the companies, who enjoyed extravagant dividends, but also to the landowners, businessmen and communities that were prepared to take advantage of the opportunities that the railways offered. A rash of new lines were proposed; some well thought out, logical extensions to existing lines, others no more than hopeless local ventures going nowhere and with no prospect of ever attracting commercial traffic. Amongst the former class was the Wilts, Somerset and Weymouth Railway, a line proposed with the backing of the Great Western Railway, which would link with the main line at Thingley Junction near Chippenham and follow a route through Trowbridge, Westbury and Yeovil to the south coast port of Weymouth. A number of subsidiary branches were proposed, including lines to Devizes, Bradford-on-Avon and Salisbury.

The Wilts, Somerset and Weymouth Railway Company applied to Parliament In 1846 for an Act enabling it to compulsorily purchase land for the new railway which was eventually granted upon the strict condition that the short branch from Staverton to Bradford-on-Avon should be extended through Freshford and Limpley Stoke to a junction with the main line at Bathampton in order, in the words of the Act, 'to effect a better line of communication with Bath and Bristol.' The Great Western Railway, which was supporting the nominally Independent Wilts, Somerset and Weymouth, vehemently opposed this condition but was compelled to accept it in order to get the Bill passed. The company's motive for its objection was blatantly commercial. The Great Western Railway anticipated heavy traffic on the Wilts, Somerset and Weymouth from the ports of Southampton and Portsmouth destined for Bristol and, as their revenue was based upon mileage, they could expect substantially higher tolls from cargoes carried to Bristol via the roundabout Trowbridge – Chippenham – Bath route than from the shorter Trowbridge – Bradford-on-Avon – Bathampton route which Parliament and the Board of

Trade insisted upon. The Wilts, Somerset and Weymouth Railway Company began the purchase of land along their route late in 1846 and started the major engineering works on the northern part of their main line between Chippenham and Westbury the following year. Unfortunately for the company, the rampant railway speculation of the early years of the decade led to financial collapse in 1847. Money was suddenly hard to find and shareholders were unwilling to meet outstanding calls on their shares. Although work limped along on the main line through the following eighteen months, allowing the railway to open as far as Westbury in September 1848, elsewhere it ground to a halt. The short branch to Bradford-on-Avon was almost complete by the summer of 1848; the embankments and cuttings were finished, the bridges over the River Avon near Bradford Great Wood and across the weir at Greenland Mill were built, Bradford Tunnel and the two road bridges immediately east of the station were ready, Bradford station was built and ready to receive passengers and some but not all of the rails to Bradford were laid. Then, despite the expenditure of some £1,500,000 that had already been sunk into the line, work suddenly stopped and was not resumed for nearly nine years.

In an effort to extract the Wilts, Somerset and Weymouth from its financial quagmire the Great Western Railway purchased the entire share capital, absorbing the complete undertaking in March 1850. Work resumed on the main line to Weymouth via Yeovil but the Great Western immediately announced its intention to abandon the Bradford branch, a move that was strenuously opposed by a whole host of local interests. Action was taken against the company in the Court of Queen's Bench at Somerset Assizes in 1853, which found in favour of the complainants. In November the Great Western Railway lodged an appeal against the earlier decision which was promptly thrown out by the Exchequer Chamber.

Compelled to complete the line, the Great Western Railway resumed negotiations with the property owners upon whom compulsory purchase orders had been served seven years earlier. Due to the precarious future of the old Wilts, Somerset and Weymouth Railway many of these orders had not been acted upon, much of the land was yet to be acquired and much that had been taken had been leased back to the original owners when it seemed unlikely that the line would be built. In some cases the original owners had been allowed to continue in occupation of their properties by default without legal title. It seems likely that the brickwork for one or two occupation bridges in the Freshford and Limpley Stoke area had been at least started in the 1840s, but for the most part the route of the line had not even been marked out.

Although the almost complete section of the branch to Bradford-on-Avon was laid as a double-track, broad-gauge (seven-foot) line, it was decided that from Bradford-on-Avon to Bathampton Junction it would be laid only as a

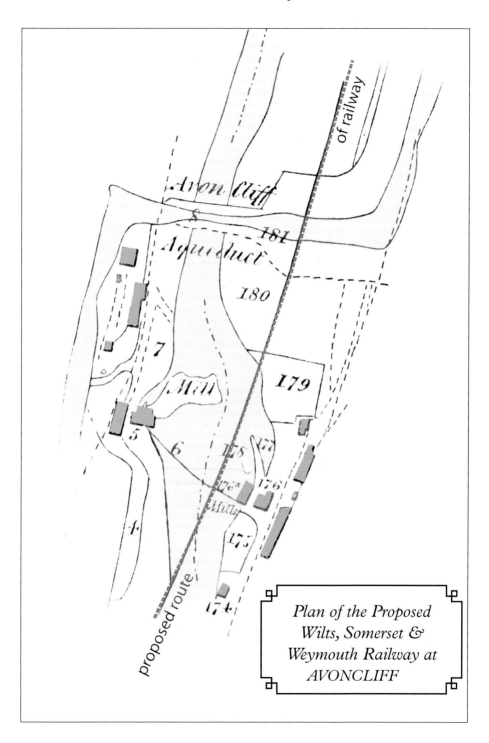

Plan of the Proposed
Wilts, Somerset &
Weymouth Railway at
AVONCLIFF

single track. Rather bizarrely, despite this decision, all the engineering works on the entire branch, including the substantial viaduct at Freshford and the two aqueducts that carried the Kennet and Avon Canal over the line at Avoncliff and Limpley Stoke, were built to accommodate a broad-gauge double-track railway. When first completed even the ballast was laid wide enough for a double track. Even odder was the decision to construct a double-track timber viaduct over the River Avon immediately west of Bradford-on-Avon station which extended the two platform tracks over the river where they joined to become a single track at the point where the footpath from Barton Orchard now crosses the line.

The original parliamentary plans show an alignment from Bradford-on-Avon to Claverton that differs markedly from the final route. The proposed route shows the railway crossing the Avon just west of Bradford-on-Avon station as it does today, but then re-crossing to the south bank of the river opposite Belcombe Court to continue its approach to Avoncliff through the water meadow, where a massive retaining wall was required to support the canal embankment. Just upstream of the mill on the Westwood bank the railway crosses the river again by means of a spectacular viaduct that spans the centre of the weir at an acute angle to make landfall on the north bank adjacent to the aqueduct where it tunnels under the embankment close to the site of the present day bridge. Had the railway been built to this plan then the Cross Guns public house and all the buildings adjacent would have been condemned to a life of stygian gloom, hemmed in and overshadowed by the high canal bank on one side and the bridge girders on the other. A similar scheme was proposed at the Dundas aqueduct at Limpley Stoke where the line was to have crossed the river one hundred yards upstream of the aqueduct, traversed the meadows on the Warleigh bank for approximately a quarter of a mile before crossing back to the Claverton side of the river by a bridge close to Warleigh Manor. The reason for this seemingly expensive diversion is unknown but it is possible that Brunel had hoped to use the existing arch of the aqueduct on the east bank of the river, despite the necessity of building two bridges over the river. The alternative option which was later implemented, of tunnelling obliquely beneath the canal on the west bank, was seen as a hazardous enterprise best avoided. Once work got underway on the alternative west bank scheme Brunel's apprehension proved to be well founded, for in his own account of the building of the railway he describes the negotiation of the canal at that point as 'a tedious and difficult operation.'

Work got under way again on the completion of the line early in 1854. Property along the route had been blighted by the company's unwillingness to proceed for eight years or more and much had become unsaleable. The granting of an Act of Parliament authorized the railway company to compulsorily purchase land along the route of their line, but this right was often not confined

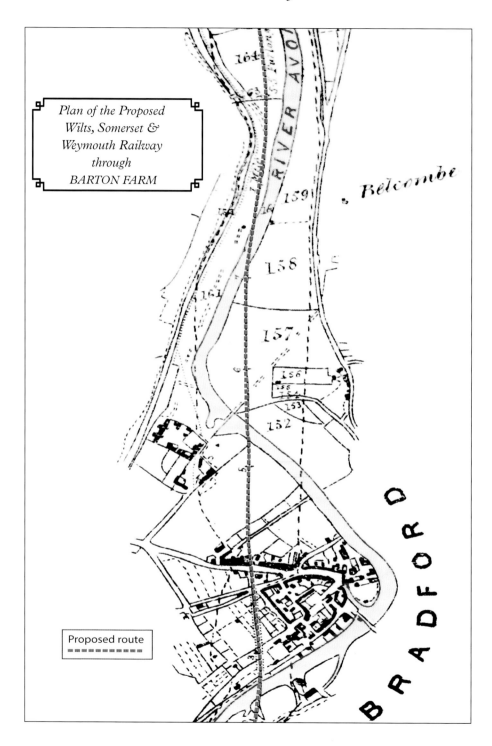

Plan of the Proposed
Wilts, Somerset &
Weymouth Railway
through
BARTON FARM

Proposed route

within tight limits. Parliamentary plans invariably show the centre line of the proposed railway together with a tract of land sometimes up to 100 feet wide on each side of the centre line that represents the company's 'limit of deviation'. This allows the company to make slight local alterations to its route without having to apply for separate Acts in each case. The difficulty with this arrangement was that until the railway was actually built landlords with property on the edge of the limit of deviation did not know for sure whether or not their property would be snatched from them. While this was of marginal importance in the case of rough, common or agricultural land where compensation was simple to determine, in the case of inhabited or commercial premises the consequences could be disastrous. Through Avoncliff the southern limit of deviation followed the canal towpath from Barton Farm, dropping down to include the mill complex south of the weir, but excluding the Cross Guns and the nearby cottages, before running along the frontage of the workhouse and thence onwards to Freshford. To the north the limit ran close to the grounds of Belcombe Court then along the fields below Turleigh and on to the canal, encompassing within its grasp all the mills and other buildings north of the river.

The company's decision to route the railway north of the river, thus avoiding the costs of a long embankment through Barton Farm, substantial retaining walls for the Kennet and Avon Canal (which was already perilously unstable at that point) and the construction of an exceptionally difficult bridge across the weir at Avoncliff, perhaps reflects its parlous financial position at that time. Other than plunge most of the buildings into a perpetual semi-darkness, the southern route would have had no material effect on properties in Avoncliff but instead, compensation payments being obviously lower than engineering costs, a number of properties on the north bank were sacrificed to the railway company's economic imperative.

There had long been two independent mills on the north bank of the river at Avoncliff, a fulling mill of ancient origin (but substantially rebuilt at least twice in the nineteenth century), which still stands today with its cast-iron waterwheel beside the weir, and a grist mill built probably in the early eighteenth century that once stood between the fulling mill and Mill House, right on the line of the railway. The fulling mill belonged to the Yerbury family but during the first half of the nineteenth century was leased to a number of tenants, most of them well known Bradford clothiers, including Saunders and Company (1813-1824), Yerbury, Tugwell and Edmunds (1835-1841) and J.E. Davis (1841-1845). The grist mill had belonged to the Shepherd family since at least 1750. Thomas and John Shepherd also owned a row of four dwellings nearby known as Ford Cottages.

By the end of 1845 the coming of the railway must have been common knowledge because both mills, by now under the black cloud of potential compulsory purchase, were empty and disused. The following year Francis Yerbury was advertising without success for tenants for the fulling mill and Shepherd's Mill. The latter was leased to Charles Lewis and was also vacant and to let, notices in the local newspapers advertising:

AVON CLIFT MILL, Near Bradford

> To be let and entered upon immediately, the corn and flour mill on the River Avon two miles from the town of Bradford and six from Bath. The premises are in an excellent state of repair and are well adapted for carrying on an extensive and lucrative business. The mill is furnished with three pairs of stones, flour-dressing machine and every suitable requisite. For full particulars apply by letter, pre-paid, to Mr C. Lewis, Avon Clift Mill near Bradford.

In 1854 Shepherd's Mill and Ford Cottages were demolished to make way for the railway but the fulling mill and its associated Mill House were saved by a hair's breadth. Although not obvious when viewed from the public road, the railway through Avoncliff runs on a substantial embankment, the height of which can only really be appreciated from the small yard in front of the mill. At the Bradford end of the mill the embankment is supported by a ten-foot-high blue brick retaining wall that presumably continues for the length of the mill, as it is unlikely that the subsoil of the embankment would be piled directly against the wall of the building. At the west end the retaining wall is of unfaced masonry that appears to be bonded into the end wall of the mill.

West of the mill, after crossing the age-old approach to Avoncliff ford by means of a small bridge, the railway was faced with the obstacle of the canal embankment that stood in its path. Here, rather than tunnel under it as at Limpley Stoke, Brunel's solution was to completely remove a short section of the existing canal and towpath and replace it with a relatively lightweight wooden trough and decking supported on brick abutments. Elsewhere on the Bathampton branch similar wooden trestle bridges and viaducts had been constructed with great success and at a fraction of the cost of comparable masonry arched structures. It is perhaps indicative of the power still held by local landowners that while Francis Yerbury could not stop the railway from passing uncomfortably close to Belcombe Court, a mile or so east of Avoncliff, he could insist that the under-bridge that gave access to his riverside land opposite the house was built with a most elaborate, highly decorative cast-iron balustrade, despite the railway's stringent economy in the construction of bridges elsewhere on the line. The timber aqueduct was probably replaced by the current brick and

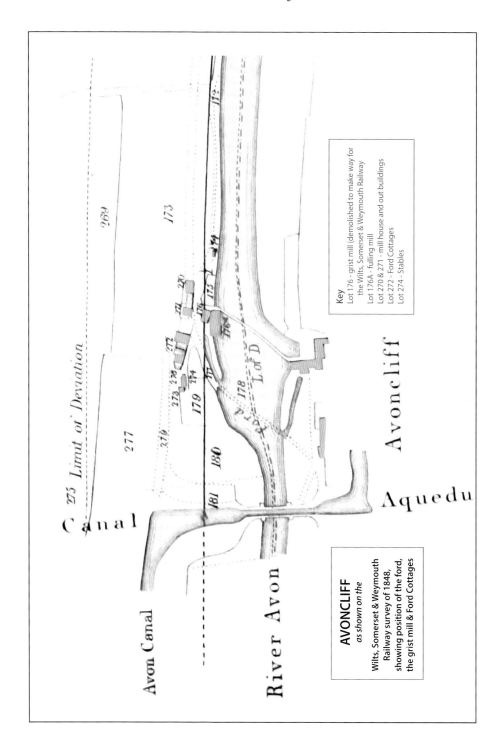

Key
Lot 176 - grist mill (demolished to make way for the Wilts, Somerset & Weymouth Railway
Lot 176A - fulling mill
Lot 270 & 271 - mill house and out buildings
Lot 272 - Ford Cottages
Lot 274 - Stables

AVONCLIFF
as shown on the
Wilts, Somerset & Weymouth Railway survey of 1848, showing position of the ford, the grist mill & Ford Cottages

masonry structure in 1878 when the timber viaducts east of Bradford-on-Avon and Bath stations were also rebuilt.

The broad-gauge single track line was completed and scheduled for opening on 20th January 1857 but on the previous day Colonel Yolland, the Board of Trade inspector, travelled the line and declared the running too rough. The problem was rectified during the following week and the line finally opened, after a delay of nearly nine years, on 2nd February 1857. There was no station at Avoncliff and the Great Western Railway seemed to have no intention of providing one, even after the stone yard sidings were laid in 1877.

The Great Western Railway had stuck stubbornly to Brunel's broad gauge for nearly forty years despite the fact that every other railway company in Britain had adopted the standard gauge of 4' 8", but by the early 1870s the inconvenience was becoming intolerable. In 1874 the company decided to accept defeat and abandon the broad gauge and in just five days, between 18th and 22nd June 1874, the entire length of the Bradford Junction to Bathampton branch was changed to standard gauge by simply slewing one rail on the existing cross sleepers and refitting the shoes. Nine years later, in May 1885, the line was doubled throughout and new platforms built at Freshford and Limpley Stoke stations. Finally, in 1906, when the Great Western inaugurated rail-motor services on the Bathampton branch, passenger facilities were provided at Avoncliff. Traffic was not considered adequate for a proper station so a minimal, unstaffed halt was built with just a simple shelter on one platform and a couple of benches. Early in the Second World War, as part of the anti-invasion plan, the small bridge that carried the rails over the approach to Avoncliff ford was removed and the cutting filled with rubble.

Trespassing upon the railway or, more importantly, neglecting to close the gates at occupation crossings (level crossings that were not necessarily public rights of way but just allowed farmers, for example, to access fields cut off when the railways were built) appears to have been regarded as a heinous offence and the Great Western Railway seems to have spent a considerable part of its revenue on the erection of notices to warn the public of that fact. Avoncliff Halt and the nearby railway property soon bristled with a profusion of such signage. Every railway company erected similar warning notices but many of those on the Great Western were most peculiar in character, tending towards unintelligible, lugubrious verbosity or, alternatively, towards a notoriously ambiguous terseness.

The large cast iron signs attached to every crossing gate not only asked the user to close it behind him, but also quoted, chapter and verse, the provisions of the Act of Parliament that required the gate to be kept closed. The exact wording of these notices read: 'Great Western Railway. By 8 Vic. Cap. 25. S. 75. Any Person Not Fastening This Gate After Having Passed Through Is Liable

To A Penalty Of Forty Shillings.'

Remembering that much of the Great Western line ran through rural countryside inhabited by agricultural labourers who, even if not completely illiterate, would certainly be absolutely baffled by the '8 Vic Cap 25 S 75' that threatened to rob them of the best part of three months wages, it is difficult to understand the logic that led to the erection of such signs. It was, incidentally, proved on more than one occasion that, in strict compliance with the phrasing of the Act, if a person with a malicious turn of mind was to open the gate and leave it unfastened without actually going through it, then he was immune from punishment. By contrast the North Eastern Railway Company in Yorkshire put up signs on their gates that simply read 'Shut This Gate', but set in a menacing type face that implied dark consequences for anyone that did not take heed. On the backs of the Yorkshire gates was a second sign for the benefit of the absent minded that read 'Penalty For Neglect £2'.

At the ends of the platforms at Avoncliff there were signs, as there were

on every station on the Great Western Railway, whose notorious ambiguity is legendary. These read, quite starkly, 'Passengers Cross The Line By The Bridge'. What did they mean? Were they instructions, requests or merely observations about the behaviour of railway passengers in general? Did passengers cross the line by the bridge but other itinerant pedestrians throw caution to the wind and rush headlong across the tracks regardless of the consequences? It was not until a number of passengers had met untimely ends after misconstruing the signs by walking the length of the platforms at various Great Western stations in order to cross the line close by (but not actually by means of) the footbridges that the company realised that the signs could be interpreted in a number of ways. The result was a new notice stating that 'Passengers Must Not Cross The Line', which, of course, had the potential to abandon most of the railway's passengers on the wrong side of the tracks in perpetuity.

The occupation bridges, like the example at Murhill which crossed the

Above: Avoncliff Halt. The telegraph poles on the left hand side of the line indicate that the signalboxes at Freshford and Bradford-on-Avon were still in use, connected by the block telegraph system, so this photo dates from before 1966 when colour light signalling was introduced. Note the level crossing which replaced the under-bridge leading to the ford in the post-war years

Below: Notice in this view of Avoncliff Halt the tall poles taking the telegraph wires up over the aqueduct. The tin shed at the bottom of the steps is a lamp hut, used to store fuel for the oil lamps used to light the platforms, steps and path over the aqueduct at night.

Kennet and Avon Canal and which became Great Western property when the railway company bought the canal in 1852, offered great scope for confounding notices. Most of these bridges had been built around 1800 and were constructed at a time when the heaviest traffic they were likely to carry was a herd of cattle or a hay wagon. Elsewhere in the country many other canal undertakings were being absorbed by the railways and similar conditions applied there too. Towards the end of the century mechanised transport was becoming more widespread and the prospective loads on these bridges were increasing dramatically. In the hope of averting unseemly accidents the railway companies put up signs warning that 'This Bridge Is Insufficient To Carry Weights Above The Normal Traffic Of The District'. The problem was that an assessment of what was the normal traffic of the district was somewhat subjective, and it was not until the drivers of a few twenty-ton Fowler steam ploughing engines found themselves at the bottom of the canal, surrounded by the shattered masonry of the bridges they had tried with a spectacular lack of success to negotiate, that the railway companies realised that something a bit more definitive was required. Luckily they were helped by the provisions of the Motor Car Acts of 1893 and 1903 that were just coming into force and which created mandatory weight limits on many bridges. This resulted in a rash of new, perplexing and, to the average farm labourer utterly incomprehensible diamond-shaped cast iron signs which read:

Notice. This Bridge Is Insufficient To Carry A Heavy Motor Vehicle the Registered Axle Weight of which Exceeds Three Tons, or the Registered Axle Weights of the Several Axles of which Exceeds in the Aggregate Five Tons, or a Heavy Motor Vehicle Drawing a Trailer if the Registered Axle Weights of the Several Axles of the Heavy Motor Vehicle and the Axle Weights of the Several Axles of the Trailer Exceed in the Aggregate Five Tons.

Perhaps the most enigmatic of all the signs on the railway stations on the Bathampton branch of the Great Western Railway were to be found in the gentlemen's toilets. There was, of course, not one to be found at Avoncliff because it was never provided with the luxury of toilets, but examples survived at Trowbridge, Bradford-on-Avon and Limpley Stoke until relatively recently. These wonderful notices, which were placed prominently by the exit from the gent's urinals, read 'Gentlemen Adjust Their Dress Before Leaving', which rather implied that gentlemen might very well do so, but the lower orders, as a rule, didn't bother.

Unfortunately, during the late 1970s, all these notices became desirable antiques in their own right and their values soared, with the inevitable result that they all disappeared in the night, prey to the nocturnal depredations of hordes of railwayana collectors descending on the railway line under cover of darkness, armed to the teeth with hacksaws and bolt-cutters.

Below: Until its mysterious nocturnal disappearance by the hands of an unscrupulous collector of railwayana in the mid-1970s, this Great Western Railway cast iron notice gave warning of the dire financial consequences of trespassing upon the railway at Avoncliff.

5

THE MILLS

Wool has been a staple industry of England since medieval times. Just as rhododendrons grow like weeds on acid soil and rosebay willow herb thrives on bombsites, sheep bred like rabbits on the chalk and limestone uplands of Wiltshire and South Gloucestershire. Indeed, sheep bred so successfully on the luscious coarse grasses of the Wiltshire Downs that, with the incidental help of the occasional epidemic of myxomatosis, they soon pushed the rabbits (who were their only real competitors for the grass upon which they grew fat and indolent) most determinedly into second place in nature's hierarchy. In their turn, the sheep provided the English weaver with wool to clothe the world and, as a by-product, a surplus of mutton for shepherd's pie.

From the very start the many and diverse processes required to convert raw fleece into fine woollen cloth has been an industrial enterprise requiring considerable capital and the labour of large numbers of men and women. Long before the classical English 'Industrial Revolution' enterprising capitalists had risen from the lowly ranks of spinners, weavers and shearmen to organize the industry into a vast commerce upon which Britain's position in the world would depend for over two centuries. These merchant middlemen, whom we know as 'The Clothiers', supplied the capital to purchase wool from the farmers, carried it to the carders for cleaning and the separation of the matted fibres, delivered the carded hanks to the spinners who produced an even continuous thread and thence to the weavers who wove the cloth. The cloth was then fulled (a process by which residual oils in the wool were washed out and the material matted and shrunk). After fulling, the cloth would be air-dried or 'tentered' and stretched to a predetermined size. The final finishing processes, and those requiring the most skill, were raising and shearing, by which the loose short fibres were raised from the surface of the cloth using hooked teasels and cut flush with shears. The final product was a dense, heavy broadcloth with a lustrous doeskin surface with no sign of weave. The clothier would then collect the finished cloth and arrange its marketing.

The important point to note is that, with one exception, all of these processes were undertaken under the domestic system; that is by 'putting-out'. Everything was done by individual workers, expert in their own limited field, paid by the piece by the clothier and worked in the labourers' own cottages using their own tools and equipment. In effect, the clothier's job was to synchronize the work of hundreds of individual, self-employed craftsmen. For convenience these workers tended at first to be concentrated in the towns and gradually, from the Tudor period onwards, a complex system of statutes developed that protected the interests of the clothiers and the labourers and the financial security of the nation at large. At the same time the various branches of the industry formed Guild organizations that imposed further regulation upon their members.

Inevitably as technology and the economics of production advanced, the Tudor statutes and the conservative Guild regulations remained entrenched in the past with the result that what had been initiated as protective measures became instead stultifying, restrictive practices. There then followed a gradual move from the towns and cities out into the country villages where the restrictive writ of the Guild system did not run. This was the state of affairs in the middle of the eighteenth century, just a few decades before the widespread introduction of the first generation of textile machinery (though still used in the worker's cottage) and the eventual concentration of these machines in the factories from about 1790. The rapid growth of the factory system seems to have been typical of the wider social and economic developments of the time and it is difficult to overestimate the profound change that swept through Britain in the latter part of the eighteenth century. Despite the upset of the Civil War and the later restoration of the Monarchy, the culture and ethics that ruled every aspect of life in 1750 was still essentially Elizabethan in character. Within fifty years, though, this had changed completely and the social and economic values of that period, as reflected, for example, in the novels of Jane Austen, are much more identifiable with those that prevail today than with those of the seventeenth century. The complex causes of this broad-brush change in national character are far outside the scope of this little book, but suffice it to say that the same profound developments that so revolutionized and democratized wider English society also heralded the introduction of the factory system, of joint stock finance and the ethic of protestant capitalism.

In the textile trade, the first spinning machines made their appearance in the 1770s; first Richard Arkwright's Spinning Jenny, then Hargreaves' Water Frame followed by Crompton's celebrated Mule which combined the advantages of both the Arkwright and Hargreaves machines and was able to produce yarn that was good for warp and weft. Gig mills and carding machines were introduced into Wiltshire some ten years earlier and by the turn of the century workable shearing frames were being introduced. At first the Jenny simply replaced the spinning wheel and was still essentially a domestic machine; often, for example, two Spinning Jennies might be found in the cottage of a more prosperous handloom weaver. Towards the end of the eighteenth century the advantages to the clothier of concentrating all the different stages of production on a large scale and under one roof, in terms of economy, efficiency and quality control, were becoming manifest.

The advantages of concentration were not so great while the machinery, like the scribbling engine and the Jenny, was still operated by hand. It was the successful application of power to the machinery that made the factory feasible and the first machines to be adapted were those used in the primary preparation of the wool, followed soon after by the water frames and mules that spun the yarn. Up until the turn of the century only scribbling and carding were performed in the mill, the resultant slubbings being sent out to the cottages for spinning. These machines were revolutionary inventions but there was no such rapid revolution in weaving. Improvements in the loom enabled the hand weaver to work faster, but the loom itself remained fundamentally unchanged and stubbornly refused to adapt itself to power operation. For the clothier there was little incentive to bring the hand loom into the factory if it could not be made to work faster and more efficiently there, so weaving remained very much a cottage industry, certainly into the 1830s and beyond. A power loom of sorts was invented by Cartwright in 1787 but a quarter of a century passed before this was developed into an even remotely practical device. Successful power-operated cotton looms were in use by the mid-1820s but were unsuited to the weaker woollen thread and, somewhat surprisingly, although John Jones installed the first Wiltshire power looms in Staverton Mill in 1839, power weaving of woollen cloth did not become common until the 1870s.

The introduction of machinery and its later concentration in factories was a development that met with vehement opposition from the hand-workers, not so much because they feared a loss of income by going into the factories but because of the loss of the traditional independence that they had for so long enjoyed. One class of worker that did suffer real hardship, however, were the scribblers and pickers. These were often less able men, often physically handicapped and sometimes blind, who were unable to adapt to the machinery and had little hope of other employment. Unfortunately it was their processes that were first to be mechanized, resulting in the first violent confrontation between master and man. At first, the disgruntled labourers tried with some success to invoke the ancient statutes that could be construed as making the introduction of textile machinery illegal. In 1787 some 1,500 Trowbridge and Bradford handloom weavers were successful in a suit to prevent John Yerbury from introducing machinery into his workshops and, in high spirits, marched *en-mass* to Bradford-on-Avon in order to celebrate their success at their master's discomfiture. At Belcombe Court, however, faced with the menacing prospect of two small artillery pieces mounted in the windows of the mansion, their ardour quickly evaporated so they mumbled their excuses and left.

The action at Belcombe Court is often quoted as the first of the wool riots but this can hardly be justified. Firstly, it was not a riot but more an arrogant show of strength as the protestors had already achieved their aim by legitimate legal action and, secondly, there had been a series of much more serious riots during the preceding twenty years. In 1766 a machine was destroyed by the mob at Horningsham Mill and there were further riots following the introduction of spinning machinery at Shepton Mallet in the same year, and at Frome in 1781, Chippenham in 1786, Keynsham in 1790 and Westbury in 1791. On 14th May 1791 a 500-strong mob gathered menacingly outside Westbury House in Bradford-on-Avon, the home of the clothier Phelps, demanding the destruction of the scribbling machine he had recently converted from an older carding engine and installed in his workshop. Shots were fired into the house and missiles thrown. Fearful for is own safety Phelps and his supporters returned fire, killing a man, a woman and a child in the crowd. But far from quelling the crowd the deaths only inflamed the situation, so, in order to prevent further bloodshed and the probable destruction of his home, Phelps handed over his machinery to the rioters who promptly burned it on Bradford Bridge.

By the 1790s the first wave of opposition had more-or-less blown itself out, although prudent clothiers chose, where possible, to erect their new factories in areas remote from the town mobs. The difficulty for the workers who felt themselves under threat was that they were predominantly women and children who even collectively could muster little real power and who could not rely upon the support of the relatively few male textile workers whose interests were often contrary to theirs. It was not until the employers tried to introduce power-operated gig mills and shearing frames into the factories from around 1801/2 that the real troubles began. The final finishing processes of raising and shearing the cloth were the exclusive domain of male workers and were highly skilled occupations. The hand shearmen were the absolute elite of the woollen industry. They were jealous of their craft, requiring a seven year apprenticeship for new entrants and they were very well paid. The wages of the Wiltshire shearmen, unlike those of any other manual worker, were sufficient to allow them to save, a fact deplored by the employers when disputes arose because they found themselves unable to starve the shearmen into submission because they had reserves to fall back on. Inevitably, over time, the power of the shearmen led to abuse and by the early years of the nineteenth century this abuse of power was helping to sustain anachronistic, conservative working methods and a reactionary attitude amongst the workforce. The introduction of power gig mills and shearing frames was seen by the clothiers as a way to break the restrictive powers of the shearmen and was pursued with some vigour. Quite correctly, the shearmen saw that the introduction of such machinery would quickly bring about the end of a comfortable lifestyle. A startling modern parallel to the situation that existed in 1802 was the dispute in Fleet Street a quarter of a century ago between the newspaper proprietors and the printing unions over the alterations demanded in working practices associated with the introduction of new technology in the printing industry. Such a conflict of interests could only end in violence and tragedy and that is what occurred during a brief period between April 1802 and March 1803.

Unable to stop the machines by legal means, the combination of shearmen decided in early April 1802 upon direct action and resolved to destroy the Warminster Mill of Mr Warren who had recently installed the hated gig mill. Foiled in their fumbled attempts at arson the protesters withdrew, their tails between their legs, only to return a little later to burn down a dog kennel and a hayrick, which was at least a gesture of defiance though it did little to forward their cause. Over the following few months a few more half-hearted gestures were made against clothiers in Bradford-on-Avon and Warminster before the mob returned again to Mr Warren's premises in June and this time burned down his stables. Then, on 4th July, they turned their attention to John Jones' mill at Staverton which was the largest and most completely mechanized textile factory in Wiltshire. About a hundred armed shearmen attacked the building shooting out some of the windows, but were repelled by Jones' private army who returned fire with startling effect. Realizing that the large factories of Bradford-on-Avon and Trowbridge were too well defended the protesters turned against a softer target and on 6th July attacked Clifford Mill in Beckington which was completely destroyed.

Next to be engulfed in flames was Littleton Mill, the property of Mr Naish of Trowbridge which was burned on the night of 21st July. There the attackers made the fatal mistake of holding the defending occupants hostage until they had completed their work and one of the men detailed to guard them, a young shearman's apprentice called Thomas Helliker, was recognized by his captives and subsequently arrested. Meanwhile the shearmen had withdrawn their labour and the mills ground to a halt. Early in August another unsuccessful attack was launched against Staverton Mill, but a few nights later, on 3rd August, the mob were more successful in Trowbridge when Conigre Mill, another factory owned by the reviled Mr Naish, was burned to the ground. With this attack and the consequences for Thomas Helliker of the earlier arson at Clifford Mill, the shearmens' resolve seemed to die away and there were no more mill burnings in Wiltshire. Later that year, while Helliker languished in Salisbury jail, Parliament took the first steps to wipe away the anachronistic statutes that the shearmen had hoped to use to bolster their case against the machines and by the end of 1803 the shearmen's combination was a broken reed.

The case against Thomas Helliker was heard at Salisbury County Assize Court before Justices Sir Alexander Thompson and Sir Simon le Blanc on 14th March 1803. Helliker was found guilty of arson and hanged at Fisherton jail in Salisbury on the chill morning of Tuesday 28th March 1803.

THE FACTORIES

So, as we have seen, the development of more efficient textile machinery led to the concentration of the industry, first into workshops (where much of the machinery was still manually operated) and then, by the 1790s, into much larger factories – the archetypal 'dark satanic mills' of northern legend – with the machinery worked by water power or steam or a combination of both. For the first fifteen years or so the development of the factories was dogged by violent labour disputes but, in Wiltshire at least, this had subsided by about 1805. The factories saw the decline of the oldest of the Wiltshire clothier families like the Hortons of Bradford-on-Avon. These families, whose wealth had been based upon 'rotating capital', that is capital that was tied up in raw materials and finished cloths awaiting sale, were replaced by newer and more transitory dynasties whose businesses depended upon fixed capital – the money tied up in the cost of their factories and machinery – often provided in the form of commercial credit. Some older families, like the Yerburys, maintained their interest for a while but only as partners in the new-style firms until they too, with their memories of older and more genteel business practices, faded away to be replaced by the Edmonds, Tugwells, Phipps, and a host of others.

From about the mid-1790s the banks of the Avon through Bradford-on-Avon became increasingly crowded with splendid new woollen mills, some newly constructed and others developed on the sites of fulling and grist mills of ancient origin. The following table is a simplified chronology of the principal nineteenth century mills in Bradford-on-Avon and in the villages of the lower Avon valley.

GREENLAND UPPER MILL

1804	Factory built by John Hinton.
1810-1825	Occupied by Thomas Tugwell.
1832-1836	Occupied by Yerbury, Edmonds & Co.
1836-1851	Probably disused.
1851-1905	Occupied by J.W. Applegate of Trowbridge. When Applegate ceased trading in 1905 wool production in Bradford-on-Avon came to an end.

GREENLAND MIDDLE MILL

1807-1808	Existing fulling mill converted to factory.
1808-1825	Leased to Stoddart, Gale Howell & Co.
1825-1855	Occupied sporadically by the Spackman family.
1855	Occupied by J.G. Jones who was bankrupt the same year.
1862	Occupied by H.M. Dunn of Trowbridge who used it as a

flock mill. The building was destroyed by fire in 1862.

1866-1884	Occupied by a succession of rag millers.
1884-1889	Occupied by George Harman (who also owned Avoncliff Mill) as a flock mill.
1889-1905	Occupied by J.W. Applegate and operated as part of the Upper Mill

GREENLAND LOWER MILL

1797	Existing fulling mill purchased from Duke of Kingston and converted into a factory by John Rennison and William Shrapnel.
1806	Rennison's share of the business transferred to Phillip Shrapnel.
1811-1824	Leased to Yerbury, Tugwell & Edmonds.
1824-1841	Leased to Saunders, Fanner & Co. until the company was declared bankrupt in 1841,
1841-1850	Empty.
1850	Incorporated into Moulton's rubber works.

KINGSTON MILL

1805-1820	A much earlier corn mill, acquired from the Duke of Kingston in 1805 and converted into a factory by Divett, Price, Jackson & Co.
1820-1826	Occupied by Hopkins & Howard.
1836-1842	Occupied by Samuel Pitman of Trowbridge until his bankruptcy in 1842.
1848	Converted into a rubber factory by John Moulton.

BRIDGE FOOT MILL

1796-1800	Earlier woollen workshop converted to a factory.
1804-1818	Enlarged by Bush, Newton & Bush.
1818-1825	Empty.
1825-1836	Occupied by S. & J. Mundy until their bankruptcy in 1836.
1839-1842	Occupied by Samuel Pitman of Trowbridge until his bankruptcy in 1842.
1842-1867	Sold to Charles Spackman and used intermittently as a dye house. Purchased by Harpur, Taylor & Little.
1867-1882	Occupied by Ward & Taylor.
1882-1898	Purchased by Spencer, Moulton & Co. and operated as a 1898 rubber factory.

BULLPIT FACTORY

1794-1807	Purchased by John Moggridge and worked with his partner Thomas Joyce as a wool workshop. Moggridge and Joyce also owned Avoncliff Mill at this time.
1807-1813	Occupied by Yerbury, Tugwell & Edmonds.
1813-1832	Occupied by Benjamin Glass, later Baker & Glass.
1832-1841	Leased by William Holwey.
1848-1850	Empty factory purchased by Thomas Butterworth.
1850-1858	Leased to Edmonds and King who were bankrupt in 1858.
1865	Purchased by Henry Edmonds and James Harpur.
After 1865	Purchased by Daniel Jones.
1882	The factory was destroyed by fire around 1882.

ABBEY MILL

1807-1824	New mill built by Saunders, Fanner & Co. Bradford's largest factory employing over 300 hands.
1824-1866	Sold to Yerbury, Tugwell & Edmonds who also acquired Church Street Mill adjoining in 1833 and ran both mills as one business.

CHURCH STREET MILL (and ABBEY MILL after 1833)

1798-1833	New mill constructed for Jones and Tugwell.
1833-1865	Sold to Edmonds & Co. who, alone amongst the major Bradford wool companies, survived the depression of 1841-42 but were bankrupted in 1862.
1865-1869	Empty and disused.
1869-1899	Purchased by Harper & Taylor a firm that, due to partnership changes over its two decades of existence, traded under a variety of names including Harper Taylor & Willis, Ward, Taylor & Willis and later H.H. Wills & Co. In 1874 the firm commissioned the architect Richard Gane to design the new factory which still survives as a residential complex.
1902	Purchased by a speculator named Clay who published great plans for the factory but achieved nothing.
1915	Purchased by George Spencer, Moulton & Co. for use in the rubber industry.

FRESHFORD MILL

1795	Existing fulling mill sold by Paul Methuen to Samuel Perkins.

1796-1807	Occupied by Bush, Newton & Bush (of Limpley Stoke Mill) and converted to a woollen factory.
1807-1816	Occupied by Moggridge & Joyce.
1816-1818	Occupied by H.J. & J. Joyce.
1818-1829	Occupied by Stoddart & Gale.
1829-1840	Empty.
Circa 1840	Occupied by William Gee.
C1850-1855	Occupied by Henry Edmonds until his bankruptcy in 1855
1860s	Reverted to fulling mill during 1860s, viva.
1875-1939	Used by C. Freeman as a flock mill.
1939-1992	Purchased by Peradin Bonded Polymers for use in the rubber industry.

DUNKIRK MILL - FRESHFORD

1792-1795	Factory built by Thomas Joyce.
1792-1810	Occupied by Moggridge & Joyce.
1810-1813	Occupied by Joyce, Cooper & Co.
1813-1816	Empty.
1816-1820	Occupied by W.H. Jones.
1820-1828	Various short-term tenants.
1828-1853	Purchased and occupied by Thomas Spackman.
1853-1856	Empty.
1856-1902	Occupied by C. Freeman, used as a flock mill.
1902-1912	Occupied by Harman, used as a flock mill.

LIMPLEY STOKE MILL

1796-1822	Former fulling mill purchased by Bush, Newton and Bush who rebuilt it as a factory employing 200 hands.
1822-1826	Occupied by James Baker.
1826-1835	Empty.
1835-1842	Occupied by Saunders, Fanner & Co. of Bradford-on-Avon until their bankruptcy in 1842.
1842-1852	Empty.
1852-1853	Occupied by Kemp and Edmonds. Destroyed by fire in 1853.
1875-1890	Rebuilt and occupied by precursors of the Avon Rubber Company. Destroyed by fire in 1890.
1890	Rebuilt and used as a timber mill. Gutted by fire for the third time in 1939. Subsequently rebuilt and again used in the timber trade. Currently occupied by an IT company.

What this table clearly indicates is the slow decline of the woollen industry in Bradford-on-Avon after 1825, accelerated by the collapse of the banking firm of Hobhouse, Phillot and Lowder in 1841, and its inability to adapt to changing markets in the latter half of the century. Through the Napoleonic War demand was buoyant despite the slump elsewhere and remained so during the post-war boom, but by the 1820s costs were rising and demand was falling away. Crucially, too, taste was changing amongst both home and export consumers, away from the heavy broadcloths which were the staple of the Wiltshire trade towards lighter and more stylish cassimere and, later, worsteds. The Wiltshire mills were not technically disadvantaged against the Yorkshire factories to take up the challenge of the new markets – the machinery employed in the west was equal to anything used in Yorkshire, steam power had become commonplace immediately after 1805 when the opening of the Somerset Coal Canal gave access to cheap fuel, and cassimere, after all, had been invented in Bradford-on-Avon. The problem was one of conservatism, an unwillingness to change production from the expensively finished, traditional broadcloths (which no-one wanted to buy) to either lighter, high quality cloths or to the cheap low woollens that Yorkshire later thrived upon. Trowbridge was one exception to this general trend, for some businesses there, more willing to bend to the demands of the market, survived into the second half of the twentieth century.

In Bradford-on-Avon the collapse of Hobhouse, Phillot and Lowder's bank in 1841 marks the turning point in the town's fortunes. It has been suggested that the bank failed through its own ineptitude and brought the woollen industry down with it, the speculation being that Henry Hobhouse, who became a director of the bank following the death of his father in 1831, had other outside interests, both business and pleasure, that distracted his attention away from the interests of the bank. It is much more likely, however, that the catastrophe was caused by the failure of Saunders, Fanner and Company, who were deeply indebted to the Hobhouse bank and who had greatly over-extended themselves. Saunders, Fanner and Company fell first, taking the bank with it; a host of smaller firms already in precarious circumstances then fell like dominos. The only major firm to survive the failure was Edmonds and Company at Abbey Mill, but they too succumbed in 1862.

MILL BUILDINGS

Earlier in this chapter it was noted that under the domestic system all except one of the processes involved in the transformation of fleece to broadcloth were undertaken in the cottage. The one exception is fulling, which had been a universally mechanized process since at least the thirteenth century. Fulling is

BRADFORD-ON-AVON
1837
Showing Woollen Factories &
Mill Leats along the bank
of the River

a two-stage process by which the finished cloth is first thoroughly washed to remove its natural lanolin content and also any oil that may have been added to the thread to make weaving easier; this then beaten in water by heavy hammers for a prolonged period to felt the cloth. A typical water-powered fulling mill would contain perhaps two or more pairs of enormously heavy, pivoted wooden mallets or 'stocks' which were alternately raised and dropped by means of cams mounted on the mill wheel shaft. The hammers would beat the cloth which was submersed in a large tank full of a rather disgusting liquid consisting, for the most part, of human urine, the ammonia content of which made an admirable detergent. Nightly rounds by the 'sig' cart (rather like a milk float in reverse) would collect the contents of chamber pots left outside the door each night to supply the fulling mills. Workhouses, apparently, made a small but regular supplement to their income by selling their inmates' urine which, because of their restricted diets was of a purity perfectly suited to the fuller's purpose. The final process of beating-up the cloth would take many hours and it was for this reason that it had long been done mechanically.

In almost every case the fulling mill had been manorial, that is, it was the property of the lord of the manor and every weaver within the manor was obliged to take his cloth there for fulling. Often the milling rights would be leased to an enterprising individual and eventually, by the middle of the sixteenth century, many fulling mills were privately owned business ventures. Frequently, too, depending upon the state of trade, fulling mills would be converted to grist mills and vice-versa. The mill at Stowford, near Wingfield on the River Frome, is a fine example of this evolution. In his book *Wiltshire and Somerset Woollen Mills* Kenneth Rogers comments that:

'The environment of the sixteenth century clothier is vividly recalled at Stowford. The large house, now a farm, is of that period. Nearby is another stone house of similar date which appears to have been built as a mill. The present mill dates from the later eighteenth century.'

Kenneth Ponting, in his excellent but now sadly scarce little book *Wool and Water*, eulogises in a similar way about Stowford Mill, writing that:

'Stowford, a short distance along the river [from Farleigh Hungerford] is the perfect example of a clothing hamlet, cloth having been made there up until the middle of the nineteenth century. Here is the typical group, with the clothier's house next to the mill. That was how it usually began, and one suspects that the business often declined when the two were separated.'

I have fond memories of Stowford from the late 1960s and I recall that even then it had lost little of its sixteenth century charm. Since 1166 Stowford had been the property of the Abbey of Keynsham but was held under copyhold by William Sewey until 1458 when he was granted a 96-year absolute lease. Sewey's successor, Thomas Baily, purchased the freehold from the Crown when the abbey was dissolved in 1539. Thus we see a fine example of the evolution from monastic or manorial ownership into private hands. By the mid-seventeenth century the property was in the hands of the Ashe family and there was a grist mill on the site adjacent to the fulling mill. Towards the end of the century Stowford had developed into a small scale workshop involved in almost every stage of woollen manufacture. There was a dye house and shearing shop established there as well as the fulling mill but, although it was still producing its own cloth after 1800, it never made the transformation to a factory and some time between 1842 and 1851 Stowford had become a grist mill, its connection with the textile trade severed after seven hundred years. The surviving records are inconclusive but it is possible that there had been a grist mill in continuous operation there since 1658 when such a mill was first mentioned. In 1842, the year in which so many local woollen mills failed, the workshop at Stowford failed too, leaving just the grist mill in operation.

When looking at West Country mill buildings it is important to differentiate between the two types: fulling mills – which are generally small one or two story buildings, usually with small windows and often, too, of ancient origin, and the woollen mills proper, better described as factories, almost all of which were built between 1795 and 1810. These later factories usually have four or six floors, are long, narrow buildings with many windows on both sides. The large windows and narrow design ensured that the maximum natural daylight fell upon the machinery before the advent of artificial illumination. Examples of both types survive at Avoncliff, a fine fulling mill on the north bank of the river and an early factory on the south bank. These are described in detail below.

AVONCLIFF WOOLLEN FACTORY

The weir at Avoncliff was undoubtedly built for a grist mill on the north bank which certainly existed in the mid-sixteenth century and may well have been three hundred years older. The first evidence of a building on the south bank, in the parish of Westwood, is a deed of 1700 indicating that a corn mill of unknown age was purchased by William Chandler. By 1742 ownership had passed to the Goldney family of Chippenham who sold it to Richard Stratton in 1763 when it was converted to a fulling mill. Over the next few years the mill changed hands frequently, being sold in 1767 to Joseph Saunders who occupied it until 1772. He was then declared bankrupt after which it fell into the hands of the Bradford Clothier Stephen Beavan. In 1781 Beavan sold out to John

Yerbury at which time the building was still operated solely as a fulling mill with four pairs of stocks.

In 1790 or shortly before, John Yerbury leased the mill and some adjoining land to the partnership of John Moggridge and Thomas Joyce, who completely rebuilt the old fulling mill as a substantial water-powered woollen factory of four floors, 67 feet in length and 21 feet wide. Two years later Moggridge and Joyce erected another mill at Dunkirk, near Freshford, and in 1794 took premises at the Bullpit in Bradford-on-Avon, creating something of a little woollen empire in the Avon valley. A few years later, in 1807, they rationalised their premises, concentrating manufacture at Freshford Mill where they remained until they apparently ceased trading in 1816.

The period through which Moggridge and Joyce were proprietors of Avoncliff Mill is of fundamental importance to the history of the woollen industry in Wiltshire. In December 1791, shortly after Moggridge and Joyce started trading at Avoncliff, an inquest was held into the death of twelve-year-old William Gibbence, a parish apprentice employed at the factory. The record of this inquest is regarded as the first evidence of power-driven machinery in use in a Wiltshire mill. It was reported that Gibbence:

> 'who with many others younger as well as older was employed at Ancliffe Mill in Westwood in managing and working the late improved machines and engines for cloth making, and having inadvertently in his playtime put and buckled one part or end of a long strap of leather round his waist, the other end was taken hold of by a large upright piece of timber called the mainshaft, constantly going round, turning, and working the engines, whereby he was whirled round with great force, his body bruised, his limbs shattered and beaten off, so that he was instantly dead.'

Too much must not be read into this, however, as it is simply the first written reference to power machinery and is not proof that Avoncliff Mill was the first in the county to employ such plant. However, given the early date and remote location, such could well be the case. In Gloucestershire and elsewhere power machinery had been first installed in obscure country locations remote from the attentions of the mob and a similar policy may have been adopted by Moggridge and Joyce. In 1791 communication with Avoncliff would have been poor; it would be almost sixty years before the railway reached Avoncliff and even the canal was ten years in the future. Its only links to the outside world were the tortuous trackways down from Westwood and Winsley and the obscure paths through Becky Addy woods to Bradford-on-Avon.

Above: In this 1971 view, the derelict remains of the mill on the Westwood side of the weir at Avoncliff are almost completely submerged within the undergrowth. The riverbank in front of the Cross Guns, which is now laid out as a terraced beer garden, was just overgrown wasteland.

Below: This view, taken forty years later, looking across the weir and waterwheel in the North Mill, shows the buildings of the South Mill restored as residential properties.

Above: This view of the South Mill leat shows the surviving two floors of the spinning mill (note the numerous blocked windows), and the vertical shaft of the turbine.

Below: The main mill building (reduced from four stories to two) is on the right, with the subsidiary two-storey workshops to the left.

Moggridge and Joyce also leased the land upon which stands the intriguing range of buildings, now known as Ancliff Square, which, between 1836 and 1917 served as the Bradford Union Workhouse. The building was erected by Moggridge and Joyce at some time between 1793 and 1795, but its original purpose is unclear and has given rise to much speculation. It has been suggested that the building, which currently forms three sides of a square but was once enclosed by an entrance block and flanking walls, was built to employ weavers who would work yarn spun in the mill. For the years up until 1807 when Moggridge and Joyce dominated the Avoncliff wool industry this is probably unlikely for a number of reasons. In its original form the main range consisted of a larger central bay that comprised a single, fairly substantial residence flanked by fourteen small three storey apartments. The design is quite unlike any other surviving purpose-built weavers' housing in that the majority of the original windows are quite small and would not allow in sufficient light. Also, the 'U' shape formed by the central bay and the two wings would virtually ensure that many of those windows would be in shadow for most of the day. The use of the building for this purpose would not explain the existence of the larger central residence; the idea that it was occupied by a manager of sorts would be very much at odds with the traditional independence of the hand-loom weaver. It seems, too, that such a sophisticated building would be something of an extravagance for just fourteen or sixteen families when we consider that when it was purchased by the Bradford Poor Law Guardians it was anticipated that it would house a minimum of 250 inmates.

It is also argued that the building was intended to house families that worked in the mill, which, whilst a possible explanation, still leaves questions unanswered. Certainly, while in the more industrialized north where competition for workers was higher, employers sometimes (though rarely) offered inducements including subsidized housing to attract workers, this was not usual in the West Country. In 1787, for example, Evans' Cotton mill in Darley advertised that they wanted:

> 'families, particularly women and children to work at the said mill. They may be provided with comfortable houses and every necessary convenience either at Darley or Allestry; particularly a milking cow to each family. It is a very good neighbourhood for the men getting work who are not employed in the manufactory.'

John Jones of Staverton Mill built a couple of terraces in Staverton for his workers but this was most unusual. The situation in rural areas was very different to that in the big industrial conurbations. For their mills, the country factory proprietors wanted predominantly women and children, not adult men. The few men that were required were normally specialist in the new technologies millwrights, engineers, carpenters, smiths, etc. There was little point in importing whole families into a rural area if there was no work for the men to do. The architecture of the building once again argues against this sort of use: it is too large and complex for the small number of families that would be housed there and also the previous argument still stands regarding the larger central apartment which would have no function.

Bearing in mind the large number of children that Moggridge and Joyce employed in their mills the most likely explanation is that the building was constructed to house pauper apprentices. Both boys and girls were employed in the mills from the ages of seven to fourteen although the majority were between the ages of eight and ten years. Such children were apprenticed for periods of between one and eight years and it was common for the Bradford Commissioners, amongst others, to pay a premium of £5 to get such pauper children off their books. If this was the function of the peculiar building at Avoncliff then the larger central house in the middle range may have been the home of the Overseer responsible for the welfare and discipline of the children. This arrangement is supported by contemporary evidence from the north midlands where a visitor to a mill in Cuckney in August 1793 noted that:

> 'Children employed at the respective mills are kept in excellent order. They live in cottages built for the purpose, under the care of superintendents; boys under one roof and girls under another; an apothecary attends them at stated times to preserve health. They are trained to the duties of religion and are fed plentifully.'

An apprentice house situated at Avoncliff would have been ideally suited to house children working not only at Avoncliff Mill but also at the other factories owned by Moggridge and Joyce in Freshford and Dunkirk, both of which were within easy walking distance.

Anthony Dunsdon, who has owned the property for over thirty years and has had the opportunity to study its structure in detail, has found evidence on the upper floor of fittings for looms which correspond with some windows on that floor which have been enlarged (and subsequently filled-in). The late Moggridge and Joyce period seems an unlikely one in which to enlarge windows as it corresponds with the highest rate of window-tax which occurred in 1808. It is possible that two windows for adjacent upper floor rooms were joined together to make a single double-light window (which would have counted as only one opening for tax purposes), but without drawings of the original arrangement this is hypothetical. Unfortunately, the oldest surviving plans of the building date from 1797 and show only the ground and first floors. Even on these plans the arrangements of staircases and chimney breasts (which may have been altered when the building was converted to a workhouse) leave too many questions unanswered. The most solid evidence that the building was at some time used for manufacture is the presence of a most impressive cloth-drying stove within its precinct. This architecturally striking building has a vaulted stone roof and double-skin walls with two fireplaces and a roof chimney or vent. The building may date from some time after the tenure of Moggridge and Joyce as most known examples in Wiltshire seem to be early nineteenth century rather than late eighteenth. Later patterns of drying houses were built on land adjoining the mill by subsequent tenants. It is most likely (though based upon scanty evidence) that the main building was first constructed solely as an apprentice house and that at some time, probably between 1810 and 1825, at least a part of it was used a workshop.

With the decline in trade after about 1825 there may have been little use for the building but in 1836, when unemployment in the clothing industry was escalating and the Bradford Poor Law Commissioners were contemplating the construction of a new Workhouse under the terms of the 1834 Poor Law Amendment Act, this purpose-built structure, previously in quasi-institutional

Below: The early nineteenth century drying stove behind the former workhouse at Avoncliff.

use at Avoncliff and now, fortuitously, up for sale for £3,000, must have seemed ideal.

Shortly before they gave up at Avoncliff in 1798 Moggridge and Joyce built the new, three-storey South Mill, which is close to the main mill but at a right angle to it, tucked up against the canal embankment. Moggridge and Joyce were succeeded by members of the Yerbury family who were involved in the mill as partners in a number of different firms including Yerbury, Oriel and Company, and Yerbury, Tugwell and Company. The latter firm pulled out in 1811 and thereafter a number of small clothiers tried to operate the factory but with only limited success:

1811-1814	Samuel Davies. Bankrupt in 1814.
1814-1819	John William Yerbury
1819	Francis England
1820-1823	Richard Pool
1824-1825	Thomas Spackman
1826-1828	James Porch and Samuel Jennings
1831-1841	Mundy and Jones

After the collapse of 1841, to which Avoncliff was not immune, the mill never again participated in the fine woollen trade.

RAGS AND FLOCK

The mill probably lay derelict for nearly twenty years until 1860 when the freehold was purchased by J.A. Wheeler of West Wharf, Cardiff. One of the many entrepreneurs who realized that the traditional woollen industry in the west was in its death throes, Wheeler, who took up residence for some years in Avon Villa near the workhouse, adapted the factory for use as a flock mill, breaking up the fibres of old textiles for use as fillers for upholstery and for a variety of other uses. During Wheeler's tenure, which lasted until 1878, several new buildings were erected including a two-storey tearing and willeying shop. The sixty-foot high red-brick and Bath stone chimney that is still a prominent feature of the site may have been erected during this period to replace an earlier stack, although it is also possible that it is more recent, dating from the period when a well sunk on the site was briefly used as a municipal water source. It is possible that steam power was used before 1860 but the very short periods of the previous tenancies makes this unlikely. When Yerbury, Tugwell and Company vacated the mill in 1811 its power was derived from two conventional water-wheels and there was no mention of a steam engine on the premises, but in the sales particulars produced in 1878 when Wheeler advertised the factory for sale it was described as having a 37-horsepower water turbine and a 25-horsepower high-pressure steam engine. The particulars suggest that the power plant, which included 'a capital multi-tube boiler' was in excellent condition but in his report prepared for a potential purchaser in October 1879 an inspecting engineer noted that:

> 'The existing boiler is nearly worn out. I have provided for a new boiler in my estimates as well as for overhauling and re-erecting the engine with the shafting and gearing in the mill. There is a considerable amount of shoddy-making machinery and appliances which will not be of any use and may be disposed of.'

The asking price for the freehold of the factory, all the plant and machinery contained within it and four acres of land adjoining was £2,028/2s/6d.

The mill was eventually purchased in 1883 or 1884 by George Harman who also acquired Greenland Middle Mill in Bradford-on-Avon at the same time. Both factories were used for the manufacture of flock and shoddy. Harman vacated Greenland Mill in 1889 but appears to have continued at Avoncliff until 1901 when the factory was almost completely destroyed by fire. The company then transferred its business to Dunkirk Mill near Freshford where it continued for a further ten years. Meanwhile the ruins of Avoncliff Mill were purchased by W. Selwyn of Toadsmoor Mill near Stroud and partially rebuilt. Both principal buildings were reduced in height, the Main Mill and the South Mill each lost their upper storeys. Shortly afterwards Selwyn also purchased the mill on the north side of the weir and operated both sites as flock mills until 1939.

The Second World War saw the end of the flock business in the Avon valley and during the early post-war years the mill was disused and rapidly fell into decay. For a while the grounds were used as a tea garden where one could also hire boats on the river but this did not last for long. Both the main and south mills have now been converted into houses and the whole site quite tastefully renovated. In its new incarnation the main mill is known as 'Weavers Mill' although weaving was never undertaken there. It is possible that the name is a corruption of 'Wheeler's Mill', the common name that became attached to the site during Mr Wheeler's tenure, (1860-1878). Wheeler's was the longest continuous occupation and the name appears to have stuck during subsequent nineteenth century ownership.

THE NORTH BANK MILL

We have already seen that there were originally two mills on the north bank of the river, and that Shepherd's grist mill was demolished when the railway was built in the 1850s. The mills had become the property of the Hungerfords of

Farleigh Castle at the Dissolution and in 1606 were leased to John Yerbury. By 1712 the freehold was held by Robert Hillman and then by Edward Davis. In 1740 ownership of the two mills was divided, the grist mill being purchased by the Shepherd family and the fulling mill by Francis Yerbury. The previous occupier, Edward Heylyn, had used the mill to grind timber for the production of dyestuffs for the woollen trade from 1718 until his bankruptcy in 1740. The building then appears to have reverted to a fulling mill and remained with the Yerbury family until 1811 when it was offered for sale.

Saunders, Fanner and Company, who for a decade were the biggest employers in the woollen industry in Bradford-on-Avon, purchased the mill at Avoncliff in 1813 in order to secure adequate, dedicated fulling capacity for the cloths produced in its factories in the town. As the fortunes of Saunders, Fanner and Company declined in the 1820s their interests in Abbey Mill, Church Street Mill and Avoncliff were bought out by Messrs Yerbury, Tugwell and Edmunds who acquired the freehold of Avoncliff Mill in 1824. Ten years later the mill was disused, probably following the rebuilding of Church Street Mill and the installation there of Dyer's rotary fulling machines which had been developed with great success in Trowbridge the previous year and which, certainly for the more prosperous manufacturers, rendered the traditional fulling mill redundant. A few years later the mill was purchased by Davies of Holt to full cloths produced at the factory there but by 1846 it was disused and to let, seemingly without much success.

With little demand remaining in the area for fulling capacity the mill was reconstructed in 1860 as a corn mill and fitted with a new cast-iron waterwheel and five sets of grinding stones. There are no records to indicate how successful this venture was but by 1875 Avoncliff Mill, along with Dunkirk, Tellisford, Freshford and Monkton Combe mills, had been purchased by members of the Freeman family and was converted for use in the flock trade. Freeman's activity at Avoncliff could not have appeared promising because in January 1880 the Bradford-on-Avon Town Improvement Commissioners approached Mr Freeman's agent with an offer to buy the mill in connection with a new waterworks project that was currently being considered. It was thought, briefly, that the wheel at the mill might be suitable for pumping water from a well in Avoncliff to a reservoir in Winsley but, as we shall see in a subsequent chapter, this plan was later abandoned. Initially, Mr Mitchell, Mr Freeman's agent, replied that the mill was not for sale because: 'Mr Freeman purchased the property from one of his sons who is not disposed to have it sold.' The Commissioners made a second offer in July with little success, reporting to their committee that:

'We offered Mr Mitchell on behalf of Mr Freeman £800 for his mill at Avoncliff but the offer has been declined. Mr Mitchell in his reply to the offer stated that Mr Freeman considered the mill to be very valuable and that he had no idea of parting with it unless at a price which would command a mill equally good.'

Freeman was not prepared to sell for less than £1,200. He did, however, offer the Commissioners the opportunity to install their own turbine in part of the mill and guaranteed a constant supply of water to drive it for the sum of £1,000 but this was declined. A few months later, in October 1880, a similar offer was made but the asking price was reduced to £500. This, too, was rejected.

Then in 1881, the mill was completely gutted by fire and partially collapsed. Freeman seemed unwilling to repair the structure and in May 1882 offered the freehold of the entire site to the Town Commissioners for £800. The offer was considered and costings made for the repairs that would be necessary to meet the needs of the waterworks project. Ultimately a completely different scheme was adopted, but the costings prepared by Mr Robinson, the Commissioner's consulting engineer, give some indication of the condition into which the mill had fallen after the fire:

Purchase of Mill, lands and cottages	£800
Rebuild as much of the mill as would be wanted	£150
Repairing water wheel, foundations and works	£50

It is interesting to note that Dunkirk Mill and Tellisford Mill also fell into very poor condition during the Freeman tenure.

The derelict remains were eventually purchased and rebuilt, almost from the ground up, in 1883 by William Selwyn who by that time also owned the factory on the south bank of the river. Between the wars Selwyn replaced a large timber storage shed in the yard in front of the factory (standing on stilts to raise it above the flood line) with a two-storey stone office block. Sympathetically designed, this building looks much older than it actually is. Its relatively recent provenance is given away by the internal steel framing of the roof and by the concrete-filled iron lattice panels used to construct the upper floor. Selwyn operated both mills in tandem for the processing of flock until the start of the Second World War when the business seems to have been wound up.

CHLOROPHYLL AND DERIVATIVES

During the early 1950s the United States and the United Kingdom were swept by a mania for all things chlorophyll.

Chlorophyll, the green pigment in the leaves of plants, is a complex organic chemical – or more accurately, a group of complex organic chemicals – strikingly

Above: Avoncliff fulling mill shortly after the devastating fire of 1881.

Below: The fulling mill shortly before the First World War whilst in use as a flock mill. Note the large wooden storage shed on the site of the later laboratory building, supported on wooden stilts to raise it above flood level.

similar in chemical structure to the red pigment haemin in blood. Whereas blood contains the element iron, chlorophyll contains magnesium. This similarity between the two substances and their obvious importance to the maintenance of plant and animal life prompted scientists since the earliest days of organic chemistry to probe deeply into their structures and mechanisms. Unfortunately, in non-scientific circles these investigations, coupled to the common, junior--school-science-lesson awareness that the chlorophyll in green leaves absorbs atmospheric carbon dioxide and releases oxygen, has imbued chlorophyll with a chemical prowess rather beyond that which it actually possesses. Carbon dioxide was seen as a bad thing and the fact that chlorophyll could convert it into oxygen, which was seen as a good thing, endowed the green stuff with powers little short of mystical. A mythology developed in the hygiene-obsessed United States of the early 1950s that anything even mildly unpleasant or malodorous that threatened to contaminate the atmosphere would be absorbed by properly prepared chlorophyll and be transformed into sweet, life-giving oxygen. The American advertising machine, never slow to seize an opportunity, was soon loudly trumpeting the wonders of chlorophyll and by 1952 the public were barraged with advertisements for chlorophyll toothpaste, chlorophyll mouthwash, chlorophyll breath-fresheners, chlorophyll toilet paper and even chlorophyll dog-biscuits.

Chlorophyll had been used quite legitimately in the soap and cosmetic industry for many years as a simple, stable pigment but the sudden escalation in demand created by the chimerical deodorant craze left the traditional users in short supply. Previously, much of the United Kingdom's supply was provided by Allen Chlorophyll Ltd, an East Anglian company that also specialized in the production of essential oils derived from organic sources for use in the perfumery trade. The eminent organic chemist Henry Jefferies, who lived in Bradford-on-Avon, was a world-renowned expert in the field of essential oils and artificial perfumes; through a chance connection with the Allen company he became aware of the impending chlorophyll shortage. As well as being an expert in his own field of chemistry Henry Jefferies was, amongst many other things, an accomplished development engineer; in fact he was something of a renaissance man, quite remarkably able and talented in almost every field of life. Pulling together his various strings of competence Mr Jefferies took steps to make up some of the deficiency in chlorophyll supply by purchasing the disused mill at Avoncliff and converting it to a chlorophyll extraction plant. He was aided in this by my father who was at that time a young engineer, a near neighbour and something of a disciple of Henry Jefferies. Despite the age gap of a generation between them they got on well although, I rather suspected at the time, and am quite certain now, that my father was always more than a little in awe of Henry Jefferies.

At Avoncliff chlorophyll was extracted from dried stinging nettle leaves, which were bought-in, by the use of acetone and a range of other organic solvents. Natural chlorophyll is actually a mixture of four separate substances: alpha-chlorophyll, which is blue-green in colour, beta-chlorophyll, which is yellow-green, reddish-yellow carotin (the main colorant, *quel surprise*, in carrots), and brownish-yellow xanthophyll, bound together with a protein to form chloroplastin. Extraction was a multi-stage process which first required that the nettle leaves were ground to a fine dust in a mechanical mill before being agitated in a mixture of water and ether which dissolved out the chloroplastin. The murky liquid produced by primary extraction was then centrifuged in a machine that operated rather like a monstrous spin-dryer which concentrated it to a thick sludge that was then pumped into a pair of large steel solvent extraction vessels. In these tanks the solvent acetone was used to break down the chloroplastin and dissolve out the various forms of chlorophyll. These were then further separated by a process that took advantage of their differential solvency in a range of organic solvents. Once the required purity had been obtained the bulk of the solvent was evaporated for recovery in steam-heated vessels and the highly concentrated solution passed to a high-speed Sharples centrifuge to produce a finished product in the form of a dense, waxy substance. Some was further dried and reduced to powder form.

Most of the chemical plant, which was rather archaic, cast-iron and extremely heavy, was set up in the concrete-floored, corrugated-steel clad extension over the waterwheel that most visitors to Avoncliff now consider to be a terrible eyesore. A small amount of packaging machinery was installed on the ground floor of the main mill building while the attic floor was used to store bulk nettle leaves. From there they could be shovelled directly into the crusher from a platform high above the machine room which was accessed via an opening knocked through the upper wall of the mill. The basement floor flooded regularly and was prone to silting-up with mud so it was used only to house a pair of collection tanks where used solvent was stored prior to purification. The basement also contained the enormous reduction gearing from the waterwheel and the main drive pulley that transmitted power to the upper floors. The largest cog wheels turned in pits cut in the floor which often became clogged with mud after a flood and had to be dug out. All of the plant, including the grinding mill, mixers, extraction agitators, centrifuges and even the crane which lifted bags of nettle leaves to the attic floor, were worked by power from the waterwheel, transmitted by a network of shafts and pulleys and overhead belting. A small British Thompson Houston electric motor, connected via belting to the overhead shafting, drove the plant at times when high or low water rendered the waterwheel inoperative.

A large proportion of the plant in the factory was associated with the

Above: The north mill in the early 1960s, shortly after both chlorophyll extraction and 'Flights' firelighter packing had ceased and the building lay abandoned with all its plant intact.

Below: The main frontage of the mill in 1968. During its last days as a factory, the main building was used for packing firelighters, the tin shed to the left, over the waterwheel, contained chlorophyll extraction plant, while the building in the foreground was Henry Jeffries' laboratory.

Above: The upper floor of the North mill in 1968, littered with packaging materials for firelighters and a stack of firelighter moulds in the rear left hand corner.

Below: The remains of Mr Jeffries' laboratory following his move to Bradford-on-Avon.

Below: The 'Sharpes Super Centrifuge', used for the final purification of chlorophyll.

Above: In the background can be seen the asbestos shed that protected the chlorophyll factory's steam boiler, with its tall steel chimney projecting through the roof.
Below: Long after the flimsy boilerhouse collapsed,the boiler has been exposed to the elements.

Above: Seemingly timeless in its sylvan setting, this was Avoncliff fulling mill in August 2004. At that time it seemed as though the building would be allowed to gradually decay with dignity.

Opposite: Inside the tin shed, this is the primary chlorophyll centrifuge, with the asbestos-clad, steam heated extraction vessel and its loading platform in the background.

Above: Inside the tin shed; solvent vessels to the left and acetone recovery still to the right.

Below: The ground floor of the main building with the line-shafting prominent. The belt from the basement waterwheel gearing is missing but that from the auxiliary electric motor is in place. The large steel tank on the right is a benzine storage vessel.

Above: The upper floor of the mill in 2004. Much of the roof has collapsed and, with rainwater pouring in, the floor has largely rotted away.
Below: These two oval-section tanks in the basement were receivers for spent solvent from the centrifuges; one for acetone the other for either benzine or ethyl alcohol. Solvent from these tanks were periodically pumped to the stills in the tin shed for purification.

distillation and recovery of the various organic solvents used in the extraction process. These were expensive chemical agents and it was important that as much as possible was re-used. Distillation was done using steam-heated steel and copper retorts, the steam being provided from a small boiler-house positioned, as a fire precaution, at the far end of the mill yard near the railway crossing, as far from the main factory as possible. The boiler, which remains *in situ* although the wood and asbestos shed that contained it rotted away decades ago, is probably the most fascinating item of plant in the factory having once been a steam roller owned by Wiltshire County Council. Devoid of its cylinders and wheels it now sits rather forlornly amongst the undergrowth mounted on concrete supports. The tall steel chimney which replaced the original tapered, cast iron one fell down many years ago; all the gauges and fittings are long gone and someone has removed the smokebox door as some sort of trophy. I remember as a very young child seeing the same steam roller, obviously by then nearing the end of its useful life, parked-up with its living-van beside Ashley Road in Bradford-on-Avon when the lane to the Dog and Fox was widened and resurfaced.

By 1959 the chlorophyll craze was well and truly over and most of the claims for its near magical properties were utterly discredited. Demand fell away to its pre-war level and Avoncliff Mill was soon redundant. The mill was quickly sold to Ozonol Laboratories Ltd, makers of the once legendary 'Flights' firelighters, who installed mixing tanks on the top floor and packing equipment on the ground floor. Although no longer of any use, none of the chlorophyll plant was touched and Henry Jefferies continued to use the top floor of the nearby two-storey office and stores building as a private laboratory until he and my father built a new laboratory on land adjoining Mr Jefferies' house in Ashley Lane the following year. The firelighter business did not stay long, however, for less than a year after they began production at Avoncliff they were shocked to be told by their insurance company that fire cover could no longer be provided for the building. Obviously the pyrotechnic combination of a largely timber building impregnated with a decade's worth of highly inflammable solvents and filled with a couple of tons of equally inflammable firelighters was more than the underwriters could stomach. Production ceased immediately but L.M. Schoenfeld, the Managing Director of the company, was confident that the mill could be disposed of at a profit notwithstanding its incendiary nature. In a spirit of great optimism he wrote to the factory manager on 2nd January 1961 informing him that:

> 'This is to advise that we have written to important estate agents asking them to dispose of the works and, no doubt, some of them will contact you. Please offer them opportunities for inspection if so desired.

Above: Work under way in 2009 on the renovation of the roof of the mill.

Below: By 2010 the interior of the main mill building had been gutted and the entire roof removed. Here we see piles of rotten timber stacked in the mill yard.

Above: The interior of the tin shed with most of the chlorophyll plant cut up and removed. Only the main body of the primary centrifuge and the bottom tank of the ethyl alcohol still remain.

Below: The ground floor of the mill just prior to renovation showing the Sharpe's Super Centrifuge against the left hand wall. The large cupboard in the left background house River Authority water level recording and flood warning equipment.

Above: Renovation work well under way in the main building.

Above: The laboratory building cleared of undergrowth in preparation for redevelopment.

Below: Renovation of the mill building now almost complete, although some remnants of the framework of the tin shed are still in place.

If and when such inspection does take place, please report at once giving the names of the gentlemen inspecting and also of the name of the firm they are representing.'

Schoenfeld's optimism soon evaporated following a series of very disparaging reports from a number of agents who subsequently viewed the property. No buyer emerged and the mill gradually decayed. Fifteen years after the factory closed down it remained largely intact, a sign by the gate announced that it was the Avoncliff Chlorophyll and Derivatives Works', stacks of solvent drums stood untouched close to the boiler-house and an enormous, semi-buried tank half-full of acetone gradually rusted and evaporated away in the yard.

Then, in 1975, it was again advertised for sale, but this time as a potential residential development opportunity. The mill was purchased for the sum of £1,500 by a young man who intended to convert the mill into a house tor himself while living temporarily in the detached office block until the work was completed. Sadly this scheme never came to fruition, thwarted, I believe, by obstacles presented by British Railways over rights of access across their lines. Thirty years later, when the first edition of this book was published, the mill had fallen into extremely poor condition. Slipped tiles on the roof were left un-repaired and water was allowed to get into the rafters which resulted in a large section of the roof collapsing completely, thus exposing the floor timbers to the weather. Most of the attic floor had fallen through and the ground floor timbers were also in very poor condition. One of the main, eighteen-inch-square joists had collapsed into the basement and the floor above, which supports a number of heavy machines, was subsiding. All the major plant from the chlorophyll era remained *in situ* although anything of any value like the brass pressure gauges, stop valves, tachometers and brass-bound inspection portholes that once adorned the stills, was stolen long ago. The most remarkable surviving feature was the extensive system of pulleys and belting much of which, although modified for the Chlorophyll plant, must have been installed by William Selwyn in the 1870s.

When the first edition of this book was published in 2004 it seemed that the mill had descended into such a state of disrepair that, with the additional problem of access across the railway, it was beyond hope and its future would be one of progressive decay. In 2009, however, it was acquired by the Earl brothers, local builders from Westwood who had spent many frustrating years trying to discover the legitimate owners and negotiate the mill's purchase. At the time of writing restoration and adaptation to residential use is well under way and the result, a pleasing combination of the traditional and the thoroughly modern, is stunning. Access across the railway has been satisfactorily arranged, but plans for the incorporation of a micro-generation plant within the mill, a key part of the restoration plan, has been delayed by interminable and seemingly inexplicable bureaucratic obstacles created by the Environment Agency.

Below: The end result; to my mind a highly satisfactory blend of ancient and thoroughly modern, industrial and domestic architecture.

6

THE WORKHOUSE

Up until the 1750s the concept of the lower orders – agricultural labourers, for example, and the great mass of the working population – earning more than they needed for their immediate daily survival was utterly alien to the wealthy ruling minority. Subsistence level income was the universal norm and was generally considered as something to be applauded. As late as 1780 some of the nation's wealthier legislators were still arguing that to allow the working classes to earn more than a subsistence wage would mean that they might either accumulate wealth themselves or begin to consume luxury items. Both of these possibilities were seen as presaging the collapse of society as it then existed. The working man's role, they said, was to produce goods and provide services exclusively for the consumption of the wealthy; as soon as they were able to consume for themselves, then there would be the risk of a dilution of the luxury goods available for the upper echelons of society. Quite correctly, as was witnessed by the collective power of the Wiltshire shearmen at the turn of the eighteenth and nineteenth centuries, it was also argued that as soon as working men were able to accumulate capital as a result of being overpaid they would be in a position to demand even more rights and privileges by temporarily withdrawing their labour, with their standard of living cushioned by their savings. On the other hand, it was felt that there was a powerful moral obligation to ensure that the poor – or at least those who were loosely classified as the 'deserving poor' – should not be allowed to fall below the minimum subsistence level.

To ensure that the minimum levels should be maintained a range of private and parish-based charities gradually evolved to look after the interests of this particular group of poor people. Such arrangements were slowly codified during the sixteenth and seventeenth centuries into a system of parish relief under the aegis of the Justices of the Peace and funded by a rate charge. In pre-industrial England such charges on the parish were minimal, the 'deserving poor' were the old, the ill, cripples and lunatics and a tiny number who were temporarily out of work due to the vagaries of trade. Towards the middle of the seventeenth century, however, as the economy became more sophisticated and the first buds of industrialisation began to spring, the situation changed. Employment became more tenuous, industries tended to develop in the towns which led to a drift from the countryside, the wealthier parishes becoming magnets to a more mobile workforce. Consequently there developed a mass of unemployed labour seeking employment in the wealthier districts and if these people did not gain employment then they became a charge upon the rates which rapidly became unsustainable. To deter this drifting mass of unemployed transients, the Act of Settlement of 1662 gave the local Justices of the Peace the right to return any unemployed person to his previous parish of residence within forty days if they considered that he was likely to become a charge on the Poor Rate. This Act helped to relieve the burden on the wealthier parishes but also, unfortunately, had the effect of retarding economic development by preventing ambitious men from bettering themselves and also tended to hold down wage rates. In 1795 this Act was amended as the Act of Removal which subtly changed the condition for removal from 'if likely to become chargeable' to 'actually chargeable'.

Throughout this period aid was given to the deserving poor in the form of 'out-relief', that is, support to the needy in their own homes. In 1723 an Act was passed allowing (but not compelling) parishes to erect workhouses in which at least some of the parish paupers could be housed. These early workhouses, however, must be seen essentially as extensions of the benevolent system of out-relief and not as punitive establishments, although able-bodied inmates were expected to work for their keep and a failure to abide by the rules of the house could be sanctioned. By 1800 there were in excess of 4,000 of these parish workhouses in existence.

Bradford-on-Avon workhouse was established on one of the few plots of land in the town to have been completely wiped away by the construction of the Wilts, Somerset and Weymouth Railway in the 1840s. It stood on the west side of the Frome Road a little way to the south of the Three Horseshoes public house on the spot where the current railway station now stands. Before the deep cutting was made for the railway this plot sloped gently down through orchards to the River Avon. It was presumably built some time before Mr Rainey was appointed Overseer of the Poor in 1784. The regime of the Bradford Workhouse is described at some length by Sir Frederick Morton Eden in *The State of the Poor: A History of the Labouring Classes in England, with Parochial Reports*, which documented his tour of all the workhouses of England in 1797. Of Bradford, Eden writes:

> 'In 1784 an Act was passed enabling the parish to appoint a general overseer, with a salary of £100. Mr. Rainey, a gentleman of considerable property, has always filled the office, but he accepts only £60 a year. The Poor are relieved at home, or maintained and employed in a Workhouse, which though old has been much improved by him. The apartments are now exceedingly neat and comfortable; the Poor are kept clean and well fed, but are made to work or are punished. If the Out-Poor are idle or get drunk, otherwise misbehave, or refuse to send their children to service at a proper age, they are ordered into the house. Badging the Poor is

supposed to have reduced the rates. Mr. Rainey from his knowledge of law often prevents useless litigation; and, being well acquainted with the character and circumstances of every person who applies for relief, can discriminate very fairly between self-created and undeserved poverty.

Course of diet in the Workhouse: Breakfast – every day, onion broth made of water, onions, oatmeal and fat of meat broth; no meat broth used. Dinner – Sunday, Tuesday, Thursday, meat and vegetables; other days, bread and cheese. Supper – every day, bread and cheese. 2 lbs. of bread are allowed every day to those who work out of the house, and 1 lb. to those who spin. Children receive a quantity proportionate to their ages. The cheese is not weighed.'

This is a very different assessment than that made for the pre-1834 workhouse at Warminster, (now the Snooty Fox public house) which Eden described as 'a most grievous concentration of every species of vice'.

Of the few records of the Bradford-on-Avon workhouse that survive, those for 1820 are the most illuminating. By that time the gradual decay of the traditional woollen industry was pushing the old Poor Law system to its limits. In Bradford and the adjoining parishes of Winsley, Woolley, Holt, Atworth, South Wraxall and Limpley Stoke there were no less than 1,239 families in receipt of parish relief. Few of the trades of the principal members of these families are recorded, but of those that are recorded almost all are textile workers, as the table below shows:

The most striking fact is that a great many of these new paupers are from

	Shearmen	Weavers	Dyehouse Men	Spinners	Burlers Pickers Scribblers	Total on Relief
Bradford Union	42	52	16	4	9	636
Winsley	19	44	3		1	268
Woolley	4	26	1			156
Holt	11					64
Limpley Stoke						45
Wraxall						18
Atworth						52
Totals	76	122	20	4	10	1,239

the once elite ranks of the shearmen, the class of woollen worker most severely disadvantaged by the adoption of machinery by the Wiltshire clothiers. These 1,239 families represent a total pauper population of approximately 5,000 souls, only 151 of whom were accommodated in the workhouse.

The workhouse accounts for the year show that James Mitchell of Radstock supplied '48 score pairs of pigs at 10s/6d per score' and Isaac Batten supplied 2 cwt 2 qtrs 16 lb of cheese for £3/3s/0d. Other expenses included £2/14s/0d for second-hand clothes and a payment of 15s/0d to the clerk of the Parish of Atworth, 'for Bell and Grave'. In some cases the Overseer appeared to act in loco parentis, paying £7/6s/6d 'for the expenses of Sarah Cox's marriage'.

The Poor Law system of the 1820s was little changed in principle from that of two hundred years before and could not cope with the social and economic realities of the nineteenth century. Alterations to the administration of out-relief, springing from the decision of a group of beneficent Berkshire Justices of the Peace meeting in Speenhamland in 1795 that gave paupers allowance in aid of wages calculated upon the size of the family and the price of bread, led to the collapse of the existing structure of poor relief. By effectively guaranteeing a minimum wage the Speenhamland System absolutely ensured that no-one was ever paid more than that minimum. Unscrupulous employers systematically paid wages below subsistence levels, knowing that the shortfall would be made up at the expense of the better-off by way of the rates. The Speenhamland System, at a stroke, vastly inflated the cost of out-relief to the extent that it placed an intolerable burden on the Poor Law system as a whole.

The Central Government response to these problems was radical and took the form of the 1834 Poor Law Amendment Act which was a revolutionary piece of legislation designed to wipe out the iniquities of the past. The new law was very much based upon the presumption that the majority of paupers were no more than lazy idlers sponging on the more industrious members of society. Its aims were:

- To completely abolish the payment of out-relief to the able-bodied.
- To abolish the vague, subjective, parochial application of relief and impose nation-wide standards. This was achieved by doing away with Justices of the Peace as overseers of the poor and replacing them with an elected Board of Guardians who, it was supposed, would be more careful with the application of ratepayer's money. These guardians would, in turn, be regulated by a central government Poor Law Commission to ensure national uniformity.
- To compel individual parishes to group themselves into more efficient 'Poor Law Unions'. Each Union was to erect a strictly regulated workhouse in which the principle of 'Less Eligibility' would be maintained. 'Less eligibility' meant that paupers in the workhouse were never to be in a more comfortable situation than the poorest labourer not in receipt of relief.

The workhouse was no longer to be a welfare institution, the equivalent of an alms house, but was to become an abode of last resort. Henceforth, entry to the workhouse was, effectively, to be by way of a severe test. The workhouse would be strictly segregated with separate wings for able-bodied women, able-bodied men, children, the sick, infirm, lunatics, etc. Families would be automatically split up with the children accommodated in a separate wing under a separate superintendent in order that 'they might be educated by a person properly qualified to act as a schoolmaster.' The only chink of humanity in the 1834 Act seems to have been directed to the aged, who were again separated from other inmates in order that 'the old might enjoy their indulgences. Mothers of illegitimate children fared worst of all, the Commissioners ruling that: 'A bastard will be, what Providence appears to have ordained that it should be, a burden upon its mother, and where she cannot maintain it, on her parents.' No recourse was to be made to the child's father.

Originally it was intended that the workhouse should be largely self-sufficient growing or rearing its own food, for example, and making its own clothes and boots. It was immediately discovered, however, that to make boots or jerkin or jackets required a degree of skill and that most of the inmates were there because they were incapable of any worthwhile occupation. Such industrious activity in the house was quickly reduced to nothing more than rock breaking (to pave the parish roads), oakum picking (the unpicking of the fibres of old rope to produce a fibrous material for caulking) and the grinding of corn by hand.

The Act passed into law in 1834 and the newly formed Boards of Guardian were required to build the new Union Workhouses within two years. The Bradford-on-Avon Union was formed on 25th March 1835 by the combination of the parishes of Atworth, Bradford, Broughton Gifford, Great Chafield, Holt, Leigh and Woolley, Limpley Stoke, Little Chafield and Cottles, Monkton Farleigh, South Wraxall, the Tything of Trowle, Wingfield and Rowley, Winsley, and, intermittently, the Somerset parish of Freshford. The total population of the Union was 12,660 of which 3,352 lived in Bradford-on-Avon.

As we saw in a previous chapter, the Bradford Guardians exercised the option included in the 1834 Act to adapt an existing structure as a workhouse. The building selected was the former Moggridge and Joyce premises at Avoncliff built circa 1795, probably as an apprentice house. The building was purchased for £3,000 in 1836 and during the following year a further £1,986 was spent on its conversion to a workhouse to house 250 inmates. The work included the demolition of a number of internal walls to form larger dormitories. At that time curtain walls and an entrance block, complete with clock and bell tower, were built between the east and west wings to enclose the courtyard. An early two-storey extension to the rear of the central block contained a laundry and kitchen on the lower floor and dining room and chapel on the first floor. Two single storey wings with separate external entrances were added to provide male and female

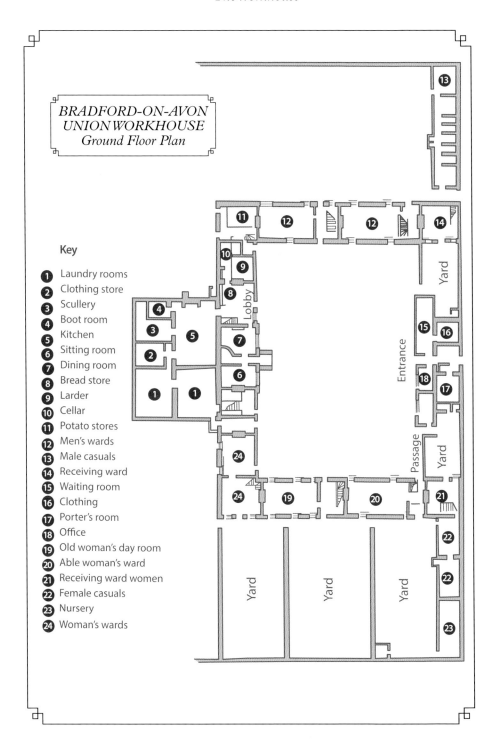

Key

1 Laundry rooms
2 Clothing store
3 Scullery
4 Boot room
5 Kitchen
6 Sitting room
7 Dining room
8 Bread store
9 Larder
10 Cellar
11 Potato stores
12 Men's wards
13 Male casuals
14 Receiving ward
15 Waiting room
16 Clothing
17 Porter's room
18 Office
19 Old woman's day room
20 Able woman's ward
21 Receiving ward women
22 Female casuals
23 Nursery
24 Woman's wards

BRADFORD-ON-AVON UNION WORKHOUSE
Ground Floor Plan

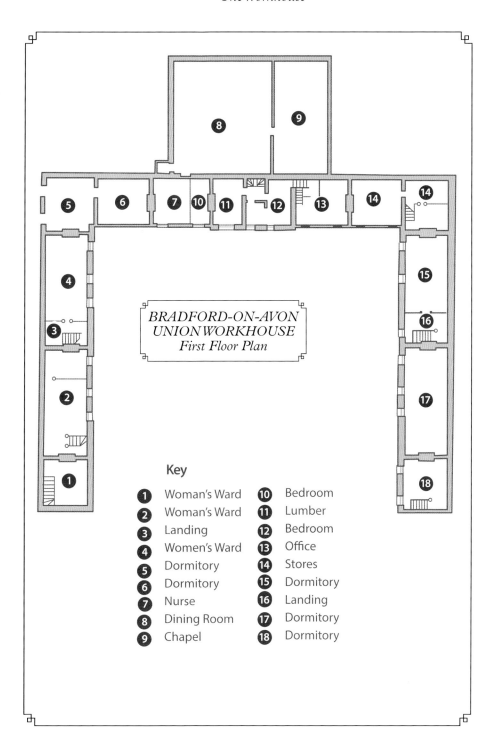

BRADFORD-ON-AVON
UNION WORKHOUSE
First Floor Plan

Key

1. Woman's Ward
2. Woman's Ward
3. Landing
4. Women's Ward
5. Dormitory
6. Dormitory
7. Nurse
8. Dining Room
9. Chapel
10. Bedroom
11. Lumber
12. Bedroom
13. Office
14. Stores
15. Dormitory
16. Landing
17. Dormitory
18. Dormitory

casual wards for vagrants. Later a school block was built at the southern end of the workhouse grounds. This building is difficult to date. Dealing with pauper children had always been a thorn in the side of the Poor Law Commissioners. Schools of a sort began to be constructed at workhouses in the metropolitan areas from the mid-1850s and the one at Avoncliff may date from then or possibly a few years earlier. Evidence for the earlier date can be deduced from the fact that in 1851 the workhouse held 107 pauper children and employed a school-master, William Sheppard, and a school-mistress, twenty-year-old Helen Brock. Alternatively, the school could date from the Education Act of 1870 which made the provision of elementary education for all children compulsory, in which case teaching during the earlier years must have been undertaken in the main building, which is unlikely. The general arrangement of accommodation within each wing of the main workhouse is indicated on the layout plan.

Sadly, the workhouse records for the most interesting period of its existence have been lost, the most complete coverage being only for the late 1890s and early twentieth century. It is possible to create a reasonably accurate picture of the poor of Bradford-on-Avon from the census returns from 1851 onwards. Unfortunately, the earlier returns, including that for 1841 which would have illustrated the blackest year in Bradford's industrial history, lack the detail of later records. What is evident from the census of 1851, though, is that the woollen industry was already a spent force. Whereas the workhouse returns for 1820 shows large numbers of unemployed weavers and shearmen they are no longer in evidence by 1851 despite the fact that many mills had closed in the woollen industry. We know that many of the mills had closed during the previous ten years and might have expected to see perhaps hundreds of unemployed cloth workers. The evidence, however, suggests that the labouring class had already, by 1851, drifted away from wool to other occupations. The following table shows the workhouse population broken down by previous employment:

Domestic servants	19
Agricultural labourers	28
Cloth workers	10
Laundresses	3
Seamstresses	3
Shoe makers	7
Weavers	3
Boatmen	1
Wool dyers	1
Old and sick	67
Children of school age	107

Throughout the rest of the century the workhouse population continued to decline, though this may be attributable as much to the humiliating conditions imposed by the concept of 'less eligibility' as to buoyant levels of employment.

	1831	1841	1851	1861	1871	1881	1891
Population of the Unions	11,994	12,341	10,734	9,764	9,927	10,120	10,245
Workhouse inmates			249	114	130	125	106

Those records that have survived from the late nineteenth and early twentieth centuries throw much more light on the workings of the Poor Law system in its declining years. The accounts for 1897 show total salaries for the workhouse officers as £79/1 1s/6d, plus a further £69/2s/9d for rations supplied to them by the Guardians. Day-to-day maintenance of the workhouse during the previous six months cost £30/6s/9d while blankets, sheets and bedding amounted to an expenditure of £21/15s/3d. Responsibility for the onerous task of collecting the Poor Rate from the ratepayers of Bradford-on-Avon lay with Percy Cockrom who, as an incentive to carry out his duty robustly, was paid in lieu of salary '£10 per cent on the amount collected'.

Perhaps the most interesting item in the accounts is a charge of £2/10s/0d for 'Right of Way over the Aqueduct'. Until some time after 1906 the canal towpath was not a public right of way and a grievous cause of contention. The Freeman Brothers, for example, who owned mills in Avoncliff, Freshford and Monkton Combe, were in frequent acrimonious dispute with the Great Western Railway because their workmen persisted in refusing to pay tolls when they used the towpath as a shortcut between factories. The principal reason for the ford remaining in use after the opening of the canal was that the canal company and its successor refused to allow pedestrians or vehicles across the aqueduct without paying a toll. It was not until the railway station was opened in 1906 that the Great Western realized it might be in their interests to encourage, rather than discourage, traffic from south of the river.

Despite the intention of the 1834 Act of reducing the level of out-relief, such disbursements continued to run at sums approximately double those paid out on the maintenance of inmates in the workhouse. Large sums, too, were paid to the county lunatic asylum for the upkeep of Bradford's forty-three insane. The table overleaf shows figures for 1897 rounded to the nearest pound.

The total costs of administering the Poor Law in the Bradford Union for the half-year ending Lady Day 1897 was £2,194, just under half of which was

In maintenance	£374
Out-relief	£641
Boarding out	£88
Non-resident reflief	£30
Paupers in institution	£20
Lunatics	£434
Extra medical fees	£7
Vacation fees	£28
Registration and office rent	£26

met by a County Council grant of £973. A further £1,127 was raised directly from the poor-rate, with a tiny balance generated by the labour of the inmates. This latter figure, as shown below, is a far cry from the Commissioners' original proposal that the new workhouses should be largely self-supporting.

Pig account	£15 5s 1d
Garden account	£16 6s 4d
Wood account	£4 15s 0d

Two years earlier, in 1895, new regulations had been agreed by the Board of Guardians in the hope of curbing the increasing levels of out-relief. As a general rule out-relief would not be granted in the following cases except under very exceptional circumstances:

- To non-residents of the Union.
- To wives deserted by their husbands.
- To wives or families of convicted criminals.
- To unmarried women with illegitimate children.
- To widows after the first six months of widowhood, when they would be expected to maintain themselves and one child.
- To wives or families of militiamen doing duty.
- To persons having relatives who are legally liable and capable of maintaining them.
- To a non-able-bodied widow or widower with an unmarried son at home earning full wages.
- To men who refuse to work at reduced wages, preferring out-relief.

This new robust regime obviously worked because by 1900 the number of paupers on out-relief numbered just 106, all of whom, except for twelve transient tramps, were old or ill. At that time there were only sixty-two workhouse inmates, forty-two males and twenty females including Amy, Ethel, Florence and Annie Stevens. One can only speculate as to what catastrophe had overtaken their family.

Tramps in tempory lodging	12
Illness	21
Old age	43
Out of work	1
Deaf and dumb	1
Blind	6
Bad Leg	1
Cripple	8
Imbecile	1
Wife in confinement	2
Widow with children	8
Funeral of child	2
Total	106

By 1917 the number of inmates at the Avoncliff workhouse had dwindled to just a handful and in that year the few that remained were transferred to the much larger institution at Warminster. That post-1834 workhouse was a spectacular hexagonal structure, one of a number of similar workhouses built to a model layout prepared by the Poor Law Commission's architect Sampson Kempthorne. The Bath Union workhouse, another fine example of Kempthorne's hexagonal design but adapted to meet local conditions by George Manners, the Bath City Architect, still survives in the form of St. Martin's hospital on Midford Road. The former Melksham and Trowbridge Union workhouse at Semington is an example of Kempthorne's alternative and more ubiquitous cruciform design.

There is a considerable body of folk memory that suggests that the regime at Semington workhouse was particularly severe. It is certain that tramps were required to break rocks as payment for a night's lodging in one of the workhouse's many vagrant cells, each of which was connected to a small workroom with a rock-breaking bench and a steel chute through which the night's production of crushed rocks would be tipped in to a skip. It is believed that this practice was continued after 1930 when the building became the Trowbridge Public Assistance Institution and only ceased to function in 1947. As a very old woman in the early 1960s my maternal grandmother, Rose Doel, lived in constant fear of being taken away to the workhouse. Whenever there was an unexpected visitor to her little house in Wine Street Terrace or a surprise knock on the door, she would turn quite white and shake with panic, shouting out 'Oh no, they're coming to take me to Semington, don't let them take me away.' Things were particularly bad if the knock came late in the afternoon, after she had had her daily bottle of Usher's Stout, brought up from the Seven Stars on Newtown. I never knew whether this stemmed from some dark and dreadful

Above: The workhouse before the First World War and before the fire that damaged part of the east wing. Note the chimney from the laundry behind the central block and the curtain wall, incorporating a lodge building, bell tower and clock, between the east and west wings.

Below: Red Cross nurses pose in the workhouse garden during the First World War. The bell tower and clock, now demolished, are clearly visible.

childhood memory or whether it was just a reaction to a kind of archetypal threat that constantly bore down on the lives of all late Victorian labourers and their families. The Doels were not a communicative family and I never dared ask.

Following its closure in 1917 Avoncliff workhouse was leased by the Red Cross which used it as a recuperation hospital for war-wounded soldiers. During that time the Red Cross barge '*Bittern*' was a common sight cruising the canal from Avoncliff to the Frome Road wharf in Bradford where the recovering men enjoyed the pleasures of the Canal Tavern.

In March 1923 the property was bought by two enterprising hoteliers, Walter Tyrell Morres and Harold Lyon Cuthell, and transformed into the Old Court Hotel, which they hoped would become an exclusive country retreat for the idle rich. Advertisements described it as:

'A dream hotel with lovely gardens where we could forget the servant problem, where our food was perfect and cooked to perfection without giving the least anxiety; where the furnishings were such as we would be pleased to call our own.

It is to give you the home of your dreams that 'Old Court' was created at Avoncliff near Bradford in Wiltshire – 'A gem in the Avon Valley'. Here you can spend a weekend, or a month or a whole year and enjoy every moment of your stay.

In the evening you may choose between dancing on a well-sprung floor or listening to Radio Paris or Barcelona on the wireless, or scoring off as fine a billiard table as you will ever meet.'

Skilfully avoiding any mention of the fact that the building was until recently an austere Union workhouse, the advertisement goes on:

'This fine old building is so very old that its early history has become dim and even antiquarians cannot give the exact date of its erection. It is certainly very beautiful.'

The lower floor of the chapel extension was made into a ballroom and dining room, tennis courts were laid our in the grounds nicely landscaped, but the hotel was never the success the proprietors had hoped for. During their tenure the two end bays of the east wing were badly damaged, possibly as a result of a fire, and were demolished, the truncated end of the building being subsequently rebuilt in a rather botched manner. When Walter Morres died in May 1928 the partners' dream had still not been realized; despite extensive advertising they had not succeeded in attracting the class of clientele they had hoped for, and furthermore they were involved in interminable litigation with the local authority over water rights, which rather took the edge off the venture. Walter Cuthell was probably relieved when the hotel was requisitioned by the Ministry of Works on behalf of the British Museum in the early years of the war when it became the Museum's temporary headquarters. Cuthell regained possession of the property after the war but was unable to make the hotel pay and in 1948 was put up for sale.

The former workhouse remained empty for four years until purchased in 1952 by the Dell family who converted it into flats. Over the next twenty years the building gradually deteriorated in the same slow-decaying way that the whole of Avoncliff seemed to run to seed in the 1950s and 60s, although again – like the hamlet as a whole – it still retained, with its peeling whitewash and unkempt trailing roses, a compelling rustic charm. It was during this period that the gatehouse and the stone portico at the front of the central elevation were removed, ostensibly because they had become unsafe. Eventually, in 1971, the building was rescued by Anthony Dunsdon who, in conjunction with the Architects Tim Organ and Hans Klaentschi and the builders PRC construction, has restored it to a very high standard as twelve individual private dwellings.

7

THE WATERWORKS

Bradford-on-Avon's domestic water supply, like many other north Wiltshire towns had long been dubious in both quantity and quality. Although the local authorities continued to make great strides to improve the situation after 1875, using the powers of the Public Health Act that came into force that year, it was not until the early years of the Second World War that supplies became anywhere near adequate. The vast influx of military personnel and dispersed industries into the Corsham area at the start of the war resulted in the construction of many new reservoirs and the sinking of numerous new wells and boreholes. All these new works were funded by central government and represented capital outlays that would, in peacetime, have been beyond the resources of the local water undertakings. Even after the war the essentially local nature of much of the water supply infrastructure, despite the wartime augmentations to the supply, led to many difficulties that were not fully resolved until the early 1980s.

During the 1870s the water supply in Bradford-on-Avon was amongst the most inadequate in the whole of Wiltshire and was suspected of being the cause of the town's high mortality rate. Most houses drew water from their own wells, the majority of which were contaminated, although there was a limited public supply taken from Ladywell at Newtown which fed a few roadside standpipes in the upper part of the town. In September 1877 a newly formed committee of the Bradford Town Improvement Commissioners sat to 'Consider the desirability of procuring a supply of pure water and the source from which it should be obtained.'

A few weeks later the committee was presented with the following report from the local Medical Officer of Health that highlighted the town's problem:

> 'Gentlemen, since our last meeting I am sorry to inform you there have been several cases of fever. I know of as many as twenty-three within this District and of six others who are supposed to have contracted their fever whilst staying in the town or following their occupation in it. In the majority of these cases the parties had been in the habit of drinking water from the public tap outside the Parish Church School or water which I believe comes from the same source.
>
> A sample of water which I understand is identical with this public tap has been through private agency analysed and condemned by

Mr Hoddart of Bristol and therefore I have had the tap closed. I would suggest that by careful examination it might be possible to find out where the impurities get into the springs in the locality and, by taking measures, secure its purity for the future.'

Attached to the report was a table showing the causes of death in Bradford-on-Avon for the quarter ending 30th June 1877:

Cause of Death	Under 5 years	Over 5 Years
Apoplexy	3	1
Measles	3	
Convulsions	3	
Typhus		1
Typhoid		1
Fever	1	
Hemipligia		1
Erysipelas		1
Old Age		2
Premature	2	
Drowning		1
Maranus	2	
Pruminion	1	
Pleurisy		1
Bronchitis	1	2
Injury (scalding)	1	
TOTAL	17	11

The total of 28 deaths gives an average of 22.992 per thousand of population.

The meeting was attended by the Reverend Canon Jones who lived at the Rectory and wished to complain about the foulness of his water supply, which originated at Ladywell, and which in his opinion was contaminated as it passed through the Chantry House. He stated that on one occasion he found putrefied fish in his water and on another it appeared to be impregnated with blood. Canon Jones pointed out that it was from a similar cause that the public tap near the school house had to be closed. One of his servants, whom the Canon had brought to the meeting as a witness, confirmed that on 24th June last 'the water looked like blood'.

A great deal of the committee's time in the early days of its existence was wasted in challenging the Trowbridge Water Company's attempt to become the statutory provider of water to Bradford-on-Avon. The argument ended in a hearing in the House of Lords in June 1877 which found in favour of the

Bradford Commissioners. The Bradford case was supported by Mr Robinson, a consulting engineer, who was subsequently to oversee the whole Bradford waterworks project over a six year period from 1877 until its completion in 1883.

Through the autumn of 1877 Robinson, in company with two local water diviners, toured the district around Bradford-on-Avon searching for suitable sources of supply and eventually identified two potential sites, an existing but never completed well on an allotment ground at Budbury and another on a plot of ground adjoining Wheeler's flock mill at Avoncliff. Robinson submitted his report on 10th January 1878 and as a result of his recommendations he was authorized by the committee to make further investigations and trial borings at both sites. Robinson was also asked to further examine the Ladywell spring in order to discover its origin and perhaps improve the quality of water flowing from it. During the following eighteen months nearly £2,000 was spent on the Ladywell scheme but no improvement in water quality was obtained and work there was abandoned.

WHEELER'S MILL

Acting upon Mr Robinson's advice the Town Commissioners had been in negotiation for some months with J.A. Wheeler at Avoncliff and had secured an option to purchase the mill and associated land and water rights for £2,028/2s/6d. The option ran until 25th December 1879. Once the site was secured Robinson prepared plans which were outlined in a report to the committee on 6th October:

> 'In accordance with your instructions to prepare a scheme for the water supply of the town by Utilizing Wheeler's Shoddy Mill at Avoncliff I have inspected the site and had the necessary observations taken to enable me to deposit with the Local Government Board plans and estimates of the cost of the works.
>
> I am of the opinion that a sufficient supply of water can be procured at this site and that by sinking deeper than the present sump or shaft and by excluding surface water by lining the shaft in the usual way for such works, a supply of underground water can be obtained free from the traces of organic impurity which appear on the samples that have been taken already.'

In a further letter to the Commissioners Robinson stressed the fact that he had been engaged by them as an engineer only and that his selection of Wheeler's Mill was based primarily upon the fact that it provided a convenient source of power to pump water to the proposed reservoir site near Winsley. In his letter he wrote:

> 'As soon as possible I advise a sample of water being sent from the proposed site at Wheeler's Mill in order that it may be analysed. It is important to note the proximity of the site to the canal, which is at a higher level, as the water may be derived from it. However, I presume the Commissioners have well considered this site before adopting it as of course I have not been asked whether the source is open to any objection.'

Having thus washed his hands of all responsibility for choosing Wheeler's Mill as a potential source of supply or of the quality of water to be found there, he then continued to extol the technical advantages of the site:

> 'In addition to the water power at the site there are a steam engine, boiler, centrifugal pumps, together with shafting, gearing and other plant. I propose to utilize the steam engine as a duplicate power to pump in case the turbine became stopped through floods and as the existing boiler is nearly worn out.

The water when collected in a sump or shaft will be pumped by the water power of the mill to a reservoir at Oakway Field where it will have an elevation sufficient to command the highest buildings in the town.

The turbine's power is beyond that required, and probably some arrangement can be made to utilize the excess with pecuniary advantage to the town.'

Meanwhile steps were being taken to acquire Oakway Field in Winsley, the property of Mr Wilkins, upon which it was intended to construct a 300,000 gallon covered reservoir. Simultaneously, rights were obtained from various landowners for the laying of a rising main from the proposed pump-house to the new reservoir and arrangements made to carry the pipes under the Great Western Railway and across the bed of the River Avon near Avoncliff ford.

These plans were seriously set back when the result of the first detailed water analysis was received, which stated that 'The amounts of un-oxidized, or only partially oxidized nitrogenous matter is sufficient to prevent me classing the water as nothing other than 'inferior' as regards absolute organic purity.

This adverse report, coupled with growing doubts about the water available at Wheeler's Mill, was sufficient to stop all further work there. Early in November the Commissioners wrote to the Local Government Board, which was providing loans to fund the project, that they had abandoned the scheme at Avoncliff and had decided to obtain their water instead from Budbury well in the town.

BUDBURY WELL

Early in 1880, acting on the advice of the eminent geologist, Mr George Bristow FRS, Robinson turned his attention to the well at Budbury which showed much apparent promise. The well was deepened to 140 feet and, with the aid of a £600 loan from the Local Government Board, horizontal adits were dug from the bottom of the shaft to intercept more underground springs, and Messrs. Waller and Company were contracted to 'erect temporary pumps and engines and other works to enable the Commissioners to decide upon the desirability of the new site'. The firm undertook to provide a pump capable of raising 18,000 gallons of water per hour from the well and agreed to operate the pump continuously for a period of four weeks for a fee of £140. Pumping began in April and was not immediately successful. During the summer the underground adits were further extended in the hope of tapping additional flows of water but with little success. Work at Budbury finally drew to a close on 29th September 1880. James Clark, the secretary to the Town Improvement Commissioners, noting in the committee minutes that 'they were unsuccessful in obtaining, a supply of water at Budbury well and have sunk a shaft at the north of Avoncliff on the other side of the river from Wheeler's Mill'.

The well at Budbury was immediately capped and abandoned and was soon forgotten about. When foundation work started on the private housing estate on the hillside between Budbury and the top of Wine Street in the 1960s there was consternation when the cap was unexpectedly broken through and the great well rediscovered. There was, of course, the usual rash of nonsense in the local press about secret tunnels to Farleigh Castle and the like, but amazingly, despite the fact that in 1880 the works at Sudbury represented a major civic undertaking and that it was completed just about within living memory, no reliable record of it could be found and no-one came forward to explain its history.

AVONCLIFF PUMPING STATION

In March 1880 the Commissioners once again turned their attention to the Avoncliff area which, based upon both engineering and geological reports as well as the results obtained by local dowsers, was generally considered the most likely location to find an adequate supply of water. Activity was concentrated north of the river near the ford where there were small springs that, according to local legend, never ceased flowing even in the most severe summers. C.W. Freeman, the owner of the former fulling mill on the north bank of the Avon at Avoncliff, was aware of the

Commissioner's unsuccessful efforts at Wheeler's Mill and had written to them on 19th August 1879 proposing his own mill instead:

> 'In the event of the Commissioners not having their water supply from the Westwood side of the Avon could you let me have a decision by Wednesday 27th inst whether or not they would feel disposed to purchase my property at Avoncliff for £1,200.'

At that time the Commissioners were not interested but six months later, in January 1880, they wrote to Freeman offering £800 for the mill. This offer was rejected but Freeman made a couple of counter-proposals during the following months offering to sell or rent a small part of his mill in which the Commissioners could erect their own pumping equipment. Neither proposal was acceptable and negotiations stalled throughout the summer. Freeman made a final offer on 18th October 1880 in which he stated that:

> 'I will take £1,000 for the whole of my property at Avoncliff or if the Commissioners desire I would let them have part of the mill with a plot of land... If necessary they could build out over the waterwheel. I should require them to put in a Turbine Water Wheel not to exceed 20 horsepower as I should retain the present wheel for my own use. They would have the first right to draw water from the head and a right of way across the railway line as I have at present. For this I should require the sum of £500.'

Freeman had assumed that the Commissioners would wish to sink a well on his land as the dowsers had been busy in a plot belonging to him that stretched parallel with the railway line from the mill towards the canal embankment. Water had been found in this area but the Commissioners were anxious to avoid negotiating with Mr Freeman, whom they found a difficult person to deal with, and hoped to trace the source of this water to other land adjoining. In this they were successful, the diviners locating a substantial flow beneath the bed of a large open quarry on the opposite side of the road from Freeman's mill. The quarry belonged to the Great Western Railway Company which had inherited it from the Kennet and Avon Canal Company, and it had been disused for over seventy years. Permission to sink an exploratory borehole was quickly obtained from the railway company and an option to purchase the quarry negotiated.

In the meantime Freeman's mill had been mysteriously gutted by fire and the owner, now in a rather less advantageous bargaining position, offered to sell the ruins to the Commissioners for the £800 that had been their initial offer.

The sinking of a substantial rectangular trial shaft in the quarry, nine-feet by six-feet, began in the spring of 1881 and was dug to a depth of approximately sixteen feet. From the bottom of the shaft a horizontal tunnel or adit was dug in a north-westerly direction for seventeen feet. This adit interrupted a number of underground springs and a flow of 80,000 gallons was recorded in twenty-four hours. A six-horsepower steam-powered pump was set up over the shaft to clear the water and the adit extended, by 16th November, to a length of eighty-four feet, by which time the daily flow had increased to 100,000 gallons. Mr Robinson, the consulting engineer, then ordered the excavation of a second adit heading due north for a distance of fifty-six feet, the entire length of which passed through water-bearing ground. By 25th November the well was producing 200,000 gallons of water per day and Robinson was sufficiently confident to report that:

'It will be considered that the works have been carried far enough to meet the requirements of the case as to quantity, and if this is so I would advise that the pumps be kept running for a day or two, after which samples should be taken for analysis.'

The subsequent analysis was not entirely satisfactory, the analyst, Dr Frankland, pronouncing that the specimen was 'by no means a first class water' but that it might be 'much improved by efficient sand filtration'. Nevertheless, the Commissioners decided to complete the scheme, a note in the committee minutes recording that:

'The problem that the newly formed Waterworks Committee sat to resolve on 18th April 1882 was essentially whether they should take up Freeman's offer and purchase the mill, which would be adapted to pump water to the reservoir, or whether to erect a completely new steam-driven pump-house at Avoncliff. Some consideration was given to a compromise scheme which would involve the mill being used to pump water under normal conditions, but with the addition of a steam pump to absorb the load at times of exceptionally high or low river level. The committee eventually decided to adopt the steam-powered option as recommended by Mr Robinson and on 4th May he was duly instructed to `carry out this scheme in accordance with the estimates already furnished'.

The quarry at Avoncliff was purchased from the Great Western Railway for £92 and tenders invited from selected contractors to build a pump-house and ancillary works on the site. The tender of £1,250 submitted by F.&W. Long Brothers of Bradford-on-Avon was accepted but only on the provision that the stone used in construction should come from Mr Godwin's quarry at Westwood.

This was the source of some difficulty for Long Brothers because they operated their own quarry in Bradford-on-Avon and their quote was based upon the presumption that they would be using Bradford stone. Foreseeing difficulties, the committee requested that Longs should provide two sureties to guarantee completion of the contract and also that they should give a written undertaking to use only Westwood stone. Such an undertaking was duly given but it came to the notice of the committee shortly after building work began that, with the apparent consent of Mr Robinson the engineer, Longs were in fact using Bradford stone. Both Robinson and the Long brothers were called to account over the matter and subsequently appeared before the committee. The younger Long brother's explanation is recorded in a committee minute which is quoted in full below:

> 'Mr Long junior attended the meeting and answered the questions asked of him. He said that Bradford stone was quite as good weather stone though not as fine grained as Westwood. He said that to use Westwood stone would increase his tender to £1,330/9s/4d. He also stated that the Town Hall, Saxon Church, Old Church and the White Hart Inn Coffee Tavern were all built of Bradford stone. He said that he was prepared to warrant that his stone would stand the weather.'

The committee chairman, Sir Charles Hobhouse, stated that he could give no opinion on the matter because he held the freehold of Long's quarry and thus had a vested interest. The majority decision of the committee, however, was that Long Brothers had not met the terms of their tender and the contract was withdrawn. Coincidentally, the meeting was also attended by Mr Griffith Griffiths, the builder who had won the contract to construct the 300,000 gallon underground reservoir at Winsley and who was also the unsuccessful under-bidder for the pump-house contract. Griffiths had put in a price of £1,388, using Westwood stone. He drew attention to the fact that he was excavating large amounts of what appeared to be good building stone at the reservoir site and offered to take over the pump-house contract for a fee of £1,300 if he could use this stone for the walls and Westwood stone for the quoins and dressings. After some debate it was established that the stone from the reservoir site was the property of the Commissioners, not Mr Griffiths, but it was agreed that if Griffiths was prepared to pay one shilling and sixpence per one-horse wagon load for the stone then the pump-house contract would be handed over to him, with the provision that the walling stone would be hammer-dressed instead of range work.

Construction was well under way when engineers appointed by the Local Government Board visited the site on a routine inspection and questioned the

Above: Bradford-on-Avon Waterworks pumphouse at Avoncliff. Built in 1883, it ceased to pump water in 1967 and was converted into a private dwelling in 1972.

Below: This rather out of focus photograph shows the pumphouse a couple of years after it fell into disuse. The circular building to the left is the breather from the adjacent underground reservoir which lay beneath what is now the garden of the house.

precautions that had been taken to protect the pump-house and well-head against the risk of flooding. On investigation it was revealed that during recent floods the river had risen to a level that would have been eleven inches above the floor of the engine-room and 3' 8' above the floor of the boiler-house. As a consequence all the works so far completed were reconstructed to ensure that even under the worst flood condition the floors were between one and two feet above high water level.

Problems emerged in March 1883 as the project neared completion. Both Mr Griffiths, contractor for the pump-house building, and Joseph Bennett who had the contract to lay the six-inch and eight-inch rising mains to the reservoir, advised the Waterworks Committee that without additional money they could not complete their contracts and would have to give them up. The exchange of strong words seems to have resolved Mr Griffiths' difficulties but Bennett was adamant that without an additional payment of £200 he could not proceed with the pipe-laying. Six weeks later, on 17 April, no progress had been made with the pipes and it was noted in the committee minutes that:

> 'Mr Bennett the Contractor for the pipe laying having neglected to proceed with due diligence with his works although he had received seven days notice to do so the Board have been obliged to advertise for fresh Tenders for the completion of his work which Tenders are to be considered today.'

Meanwhile Messrs Spencer and Gillett had nearly completed the erection of the two steam pumps and boilers which were expected to be ready for testing in a fortnight.

All the works were finally completed. George Batten of Rode was appointed first Engineman at a salary of thirty shillings per week, and the pumping station brought into use with little celebration on 3rd October 1883. Some members the Waterworks Committee were keen that there should be a public ceremony to mark the opening but others were less enthusiastic. Mr Hart said that understood that the Local Government Board, who held the purse strings, would be unable to bear any costs attending the celebration of the opening of waterworks but he felt sure that the feeling of the town was unanimous that the opening should be public.

Although the waterworks were now complete and distribution pipes were being laid throughout the town, revenue from the new service was somewhat lower than anticipated, as is illustrated by the first report of the Waterworks Committee which was published in April 1884:

> 'Since the time when the Water Works were opened to the public in

Above: The small opening ceremony outside the town hall in Bradford-on-Avon to celebrate the opening of the waterworks. The ornamental fountain was a temporary affair and was removed soon afterwards.

October last, no less than 190 buildings of various descriptions have had water laid on and whilst the income from sale of water to 25 March last amounted to £43/13s/2d the working expenditure has been £57/2s/8d.

After a few initial teething troubles the steam plant settled into a reliable routine with just the occasional stoppage due either to wear of the pump piston rings or to the ingress of grit via the suction strainer. The most persistent problem seems to have been that of pilferage of coal from the boiler-house, a nuisance that became so rife that a police watch was kept and eventually a man named Norris and a lad were apprehended in the act and duly prosecuted.

INTO THE TWENTIETH CENTURY

Some time before the First World War the steam pumps and boilers were ripped out and replaced by a pair of Campbell gas engines and a producer-gas plant. At the time producer gas, which is chiefly a mixture of carbon monoxide and nitrogen, was becoming widely used in industry as a cheap and efficient fuel for early designs of internal combustion engines. It also had the advantage of being easily produced locally and in small volumes which made it an ideal fuel for use in remote locations where no mains fuel supplies were otherwise available. The gas is made in a producer plant that consists, in its simplest form, of an enclosed furnace with a thick bed of coal or coke through which air is passed at high velocity. Although coal or coke fuel is still required it is consumed much more economically than in a steam boiler of similar nominal power. The main engine at Avoncliff was a 47 hp Campbell machine with a large flywheel and horizontal cylinder driving a three-throw plunger pump in the well. The standby plant was a similar but smaller 32 hp machine which for some reason was replaced by a 40 hp oil engine at a later date.

THE SECOND WORLD WAR

Although Avoncliff well provided water to the greater part of Bradford-on-Avon there were certain areas of the town, including parts of Trowbridge Road, some sections of Tory and most of the Bearfield, Bath Road and Ashley Lane areas, where the supply was very unreliable. The situation quickly deteriorated during the early years of the war and the consultant George Parker-Pearson was recruited to look into the problem. Parker Pearson's report highlighted the rapid increase in the town's population as the main factor, writing that:

'The estimated peacetime population of the District is 4,750, but owing to the influx of persons billeted under the Government Evacuation Scheme and the occupation of several large houses by government departments, the present estimate is 7,000.'

He recommended that additional water sources should be found to meet the shortfall and in August councillor Guy Underwood and Mr Mullins, a well known Bradford water diviner, began the search. Guy Underwood lived in Belcombe House near Belcombe Court and, as well as being a popular town councillor was also a well respected barrister. It was not until his death in 1964 that the huge breadth of his accomplishments became generally known. He was a great naturalist and collector, a competent draughtsman, amateur archaeologist, a talented artist, glassblower and sculptor and a writer whose interests extended from history to mysticism. His great passion, though, was for dowsing, and not just for water. He held a belief, that virtually dominated all other aspects of his life, that there is a series of naturally occurring patterns and 'lines of influence' in the landscape which may be discovered by dowsing. These patterns, which he described as the 'Geodetic System', he thought determined, amongst other things, the routes of ancient tracks and the locations of holy sites. The influences of these lines of force, he suggested, determined the most minute aspects of life on earth, regulating, for instance, even phenomena like the paths that cattle always took when crossing fields. In 1959 he wrote a book that is now quite rare and much sought after entitled *Patterns of the Past* which encapsulated all his theories but, knowing the controversy it would arouse, arranged to have it published five years after his death in order that it would not influence people's opinion of his current work.

After his death all of his personal possessions were heaped on the lawn of Belcombe Court and sold by auction. I had known Guy Underwood as a child and attended the auction in order, hopefully, to buy some sort of little memento. I was rather taken by a useful-looking box of sable-haired watercolour brushes but the auctioneer would not take a bid from me because I was too young. Luckily for me Mrs Jefferies (the wife of my father's accomplished friend Henry Jefferies) was also at the sale and she bought the brushes for me for ten shillings.

Guy Underwood and Mr Mullins started by making a further attempt to locate the source of Ladywell. The search proved fruitless but they did locate three new underground watercourses nearby, the most powerful of which was estimated to yield 6,000 gallons per hour and flowed at a depth of twenty feet below No.6 Newtown. It was not considered feasible to tap any of these underground streams and, anyway, further analysis of water from Ladywell, which was presumed to come from the same source and was still used to supply the Chantry House and the Public Baths, proved that it was badly polluted.

They then turned their attention to the Avoncliff area where in early August 1941 they discovered a very powerful flow of water beside the lane from Belcombe to Avoncliff approximately sixty yards from the junction with the road to Turleigh. Over the following winter a test bore proved the quantity of water and, following a satisfactory analysis, work began on sinking the well which was eventually dug to a depth of thirty-five feet and lined with four-foot diameter concrete tubes. The site of this well, known as the Belcombe Sub-Station, is marked by a small, flat-roofed square building in a vaguely art-deco design, carrying the engraved date '1943' above its door and enclosed by a wire mesh fence. Initially a single Lee-Howl electric pump was installed and, using this, test pumping over a period of three days resulted in a lowering of the water level in the well by six feet, leaving a depth of nine feet. Calculations indicated that the Sub-Station could provide an average of 700,750 gallons per week to supplement the main Avoncliff station's 1,240,000 gallons. The new well was connected via the existing rising main to the reservoir and pumping began on August 1943. A second Lee-Howl pump was fitted as a standby in October.

By 1949, after six years of minimum wartime maintenance and subsequent peacetime shortages, the plant in the old pump-house at Avoncliff was nearing the end of its life. The pumps were worn out, the gas producer plant was becoming increasingly difficult to maintain and the standby oil engine was described as 'virtually derelict'. In March that year all the old plant was taken out of use and a new electric pump installed by the Stanley Engineering Company of Bath. The following year work began on the construction of a second reservoir at Winsley.

Shortly after this work began doubts arose as to the purity of the water from all the sources at Avoncliff. It was suggested that because the wells and adits were so close to the river they were becoming contaminated by river water polluted with sewage which was entering the river from the treatment plant on the opposite bank. Measurements were taken which proved that the water level in the new Belcombe Sub-Station was twenty-five feet above normal river level and that the rest level of the well in the main pump-house was nine feet below river level. These findings made the probability that the river was the cause of the contamination unlikely because if the wells and river were linked then the levels in all of them would be much the same. Nothing could be done is at this time to improve the situation, which was to be a continuing cause of concern for another fifteen years.

Three years earlier, in the spring of 1947, the erection of a small estate of prefabricated bungalows at Ashley Close near the Dog and Fox inn on Ashley Road was the catalyst for the solution to one of the most niggling of Bradford's water problems. An erratic water supply had been a feature of the Bearfield and Ashley Road area ever since the waterworks were first commissioned in 1883, but it was a poor area and residents there, mainly private tenants, just had to put up with it. The Ashley Close prefabs, however, were council houses and the local authority felt it had a moral obligation to provide a decent water supply to its tenants. A short while earlier work had started on a new project known as the Bradford High Level Water Scheme, which involved the construction of two booster stations — one at the top of Wine Street and one in Sladebrook – designed to increase the pressure in the mains at the top of town. The Sladebrook booster was completely underground while the one at Wine Street was housed in an awfully ominous semi-underground building that looked very much like some sort of windowless military bunker. This 'bunker' was something of a children-magnet. It had a number of large iron trapdoors on top through which equipment could be lowered and which amused very young children no end on account of the reverberant echoes that could be produced by jumping up and down on them. Slightly older children were rather in awe of the gurgling and roaring noises that seemed to emanate from it from time to time. On one occasion a maintenance engineer must have left one of the trapdoors unlocked because we were able to climb inside where, in the gloom, we were rather terrified by the network of huge pipes and stop-valves that seemed to emerge from the floor and wind their way pointlessly around the chamber before disappearing underground again. Then one of the automatic electric pumps started up with a deafening roar that nearly frightened us to death.

The Wine Street booster was only partially successful and in 1954 a more robust alternative was proposed. By that time the pumps at Wine Street had been running continuously for seven years and were worn out and in need of replacement. Central to the new scheme was a small holding tank and a booster pump-house erected beside the Bath Road just north of its junction with Ashley Road. Very similar in construction to the Belcombe Sub-Station, it housed a 6 hp, electrically driven Worthington Simpson centrifugal pump. The new pumps came on-line in December 1957 and the improvement was immediately noticeable. It was soon discovered that there was a major drawback to the scheme. Due to some fault in the design of control gear for the electric pump, every time it started up there was widespread interference with television reception in the Bath Road, Bearfield and Ashley Lane areas. The problem was not resolved until March 1959 by which time the plant was rapidly approaching redundancy following the connection of the Bradford urban water supply to the much more reliable Rural District supply at Fairfield.

A rash of new housing developments in the town, especially the new council estate at Elmfield which was completed in 1959, had put additional demands on the water system which it had been hoped could be solved by finding an additional source in Avoncliff. In July 1957 two dowsers, Mr Fry and S.J. Harvey, were paid £8/16s/0d to search for new borehole locations on land belonging to Miss Davis at Avoncliff. Meanwhile, John Wallis Titt, a Warminster-based firm of well-sinkers, was asked to quote for making two new wells, one to a depth of sixteen feet and one of forty feet. Test bores for the new supply made in September failed, but by that time the Local Government Board was sceptical about the whole Avoncliff supply situation and it was because of this that connection was made to the Rural District main at Fairfield in Bradford Leigh.

A report produced in July 1964 drew attention to the overall inadequacy of the Avoncliff source and it was decided, with a view to eventually closing down the plant there, that when the plant attendant retired in November he would not be replaced. The following year the plant attendant's cottage, (formerly 'Mill House'), on the opposite side of the road from the pump-house was offered for sale for £750. The quality of water from the main well continued to deteriorate and the Water Board's report for 1966 noted that:

'The Bradford sources are still in need of supplementation from outside sources and the supplies from Avoncliff springs are a constant source of concern both relative to quantity and quality.'

During 1967 the situation continued to deteriorate and the decision was taken to close down the main well. That year the Water Board reported that:

> 'This shallow well source, because of repeated pollution, has been taken out of use and only the well at Belcombe station is used by Bradford.'

Used for a while for rough storage, the Victorian pump-house was sold in 1972 and subsequently converted into a house. Two years earlier, in 1970, a major new water main was laid via South Wraxall to the Winsley reservoirs from a new borehole at Holt and the Belcombe well was retained only as a reserve supply. Today, the pumping equipment is still *in situ* but disconnected and in very poor condition.

THE WESTWOOD PROBLEM

Although the new waterworks had an immediate effect upon Bradford's urban water supply problem nothing had been done to alleviate the difficulties in the rural areas. This was particularly true of Westwood where the hardships of the inhabitants were exacerbated by the knowledge that copious amounts of water flowing from just a few yards from their homes was being siphoned-off to Bradford.

There were a number of wells in the village and efforts had been made by the Tugwell family in the latter part of the nineteenth century to provide a limited public supply in Upper Westwood from the Cuffley spring. Earlier in the century it had been agreed that water from Cuffley spring should be collected in a reservoir to supply the workhouse, but that any excess above the requirements of the workhouse should be made available to the village. Shortly before the First World War some rather ineffective improvements were made to the Westwood supply. In 1910, a small pump-house was built over a well on the Belcombe to Avoncliff lane within sixty yards of the site of the wartime Belcombe sub-station. Pipes were laid from there to Westwood village but the well failed and the whole enterprise was a disaster. The pump-house building was demolished in 1944, the site having become a dangerous playground for children who threw broken tiles from the roof at the insulators on the nearby railway telegraph lines, and no trace of it now remains. For many years some of the telegraph poles beside the railway at Avoncliff sported small, red and white enamel signs that read, 'Throwing Stones at the Telegraphs is Prohibited' - is it possible to think of a notice more likely to incite young children to do just that! In 1912 new pumps were installed at the Cuffley spring although the main beneficiary of this was the workhouse rather than the village.

Following the closure of the workhouse in 1917, when the remaining inmates were transferred to Warminster, the building was taken over, temporarily, as a recuperation hospital for injured soldiers during the latter stages of the First World War. It was then, as we have seen, purchased in March 1923 by the partnership of Walter Tyrell Morres and Harold Lyon Cuthell, who refurbished the building and subsequently ran it as the 'Old Court Hotel'. In the interim, by a tacit agreement with the Tugwell family, the local authority diverted the bulk of the output of the Cuffley spring to the benefit of the villagers.

The situation continued in a fairly equitable fashion for the next five or six years; the people of Westwood resigned themselves to an erratic supply of dubious water and the proprietors of the Old Court Hotel made do, grudgingly, with their reduced portion from the Cuffley spring. Then, during the summer of 1929, there occurred one of the longest droughts in living memory and the Cuffley spring dried to a dribble. The following winter, too, was abnormally dry and things were becoming desperate, especially for the Old Court Hotel which found that virtually the whole of its meagre water supply was being diverted by the local authority to the village of Westwood. Morres and Cuthell probed through the dusty documents inherited when they purchased the old workhouse. They discovered an agreement between Mr Tugwell and the Poor Law Guardians under which the workhouse proprietors agreed to allow water to be pumped to the village only after the workhouse reservoir was full. The partners then promptly sued the local authority, complaining that, deprived of their rightful supply of fresh spring water, they were compelled to abstract water from the river, and that 'Residents do not like the idea of using river water and are curtailing their visits for that reason.'

Ultimately the hotel proprietors lost the case on the grounds that the agreement referred to was only between Mr Tugwell and the Poor Law Guardians and that after the building ceased to be a workhouse it ceased to have validity. It was recognized, however, that the hotel owners had some right to the water from Cuffley spring and it was agreed that the village should be supplied with water from that source only between the hours of 11am and 3pm. The most significant outcome of the case, though, was that it, together with the recent drought, highlighted the plight of the village and steps were taken in 1930 to ameliorate its difficulty. A survey undertaken that year showed that:

> 'There are 466 persons in the Parish of Westwood but not all are supplied with water. Taking, however, an estimated population of 500 at 20 gallons per head, the demand would be 10,000 gallons, and there is the possibility that the Old Court Hotel might require a further amount of water than that which is obtained from the Cuffley spring.'

The water authority looked again at the trial shaft that had been sunk on the premises of Wheeler's Mill in 1879 and calculated that it could supply a

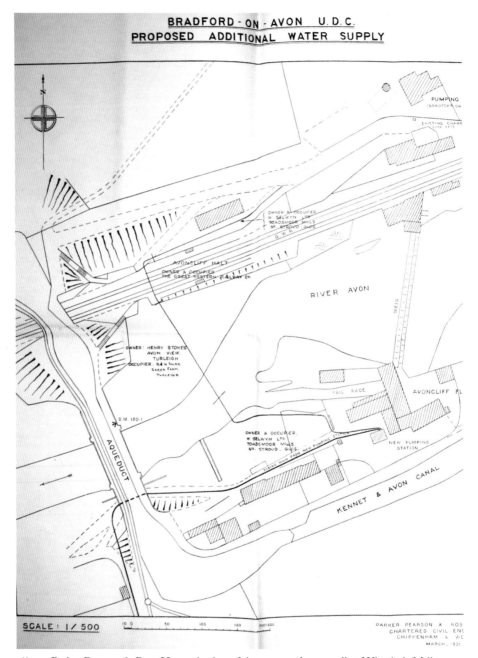

Above: Parker Pearson & Ross Hooper's plan of the proposed new well at Wheeler's Mill at Avoncliff. To the top right of the plan can be seen the existing Bradford-on-Avon Waterworks Co's pumphouse with its adjacent reservoir, (indicated by a dotted outline), and its associated circular breather tower as seen on page 191.

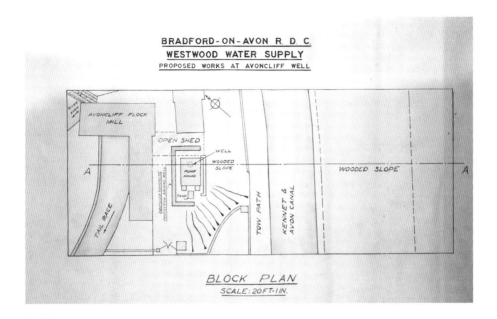

BRADFORD-ON-AVON R. D. C.
WESTWOOD WATER SUPPLY
PROPOSED WORKS AT AVONCLIFF WELL

BLOCK PLAN
SCALE: 20FT·1IN.

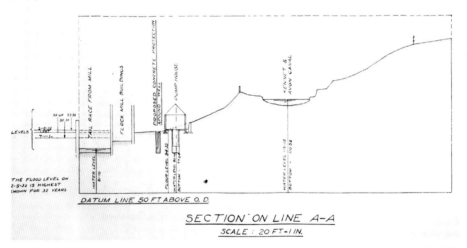

SECTION ON LINE A-A
SCALE : 20 FT·1 IN.

Above: Detailed plans and sections of the proposed new well and pumphouse at Wheeler's Mill.

minimum of 70,000 gallons of water per day. In that year, due to the drought conditions, it was feared that there would be a shortfall in the Bradford urban area of some 50,000 gallons per day over the most critical three month period and it was quickly realised that the well at Wheeler's Mill could meet this shortfall and also supply the 10,000 gallons required at Westwood. In March 1931 the Chippenham firm of Parker Pearson and Ross Hooper started work on refurbishing the well and building a new pump-house. A 3' 6" diameter shaft was dug to a depth of 16' 9" to intercept the underground watercourse that was known to exist there and the well immediately filled to a depth of five feet. A triple-throw ram pump driven by a 6 hp oil engine was set up over the shaft and it was found that this equipment could deliver a continuous flow of 2,500 gallons per hour without reducing the level of water in the well. Two pipelines were connected to the new pumping station. One of these followed the route proposed in 1879, across the river bed and under the railway embankment to join the Winsley rising main at the old pumping station. The second pipe was buried beneath the road under the aqueduct and then travelled up the hillside to a new reservoir with a head of 275 feet on the northern edge of Westwood village.

Everything seemed satisfactory until the spring of 1932 when a prolonged period of torrential rain resulted in the highest river levels of the century on 2nd May. The river was within inches of flooding the well shaft but then slowly receded. It seemed that the works had escaped unscathed but analysis of the water over the next few days showed serious pollution. A prolonged investigation proved that river water was percolating into the shaft through fissures in the rock stratum approximately twelve feet below ground level. It was imperative that this ingress of polluted water should be prevented, so Parker Pearson and Ross Hooper were called in again to devise a solution. Their plan was to excavate a three-foot wide trench around the well at least as deep as the shaft and, if necessary, somewhat deeper, then fill this with concrete to form a sort of subterranean coffer dam around the well. Eventually, however, it was decided that the scheme would not be cost-effective and the well was abandoned.

Above: The wartime pumphouse at Belcombe, bricked-up and abandoned in 2010

8

PILLBOXES

Probably the most exciting discoveries my friends and I made as young children in the mid-1950s were the clusters of rather sinister, but hugely exciting, red-brick pillboxes hidden away in secret corners all through the Avon valley from Bradford to Avoncliff and beyond. Although, by 1955, the Second World War was already ten years in the past its aftermath pervaded much of Britain. North Wiltshire remained a hive of military bases, (many of them, unknown to the general public at the time, being rapidly reactivated as the threat of the Cold War intensified), and men in uniform were everywhere. In Bath, Tommy Best's ramshackle warehouse in Avon Street was overflowing with army surplus gear still arriving daily from wartime depots around the world a decade after hostilities ended. There you could buy almost anything from crate loads of Whitworth spanners, tank radios, uniforms and inflatable boats to clipboards, cooking utensils and left boots by the score, and all marked with the War Office broad arrow. Strangely, though, apart from knowing that we had 'licked the Jerries' in 1945, most of us didn't really know what the war had been about, though there was a vague perception that we actually lived in the middle of a battlefield and that the pillboxes that we found were just some of its scattered relics.

Many of the pillboxes were positioned on the edge of rising ground and over the years of disuse earth had gradually fallen into the narrow entrances blocking the means of access. We avidly dug all of these out, certain that in one of them we would eventually find some forgotten, un-recovered relic – perhaps a Vickers machine gun (with a belt of ammunition) still trained on the southern approach to Avoncliff aqueduct, or maybe a handy box of Mills grenades – but, of course, we never did.

Due to the enormous weight of reinforced concrete used in their construction and the fact that the majority were built in spectacularly inaccessible locations, the wartime pillboxes have proved to be remarkably resilient despite the fact that they had an active life of just a few months. When Sir Charles Hobhouse tried in the 1980s to remove a pillbox that was pugnaciously squatting on valuable agricultural land in the middle of one of his fields at Monkton Farleigh using copious amounts of gelignite he discovered just how intransigent a pillbox can be. The high explosive charges simply shattered the concrete structure into a dozen or so unmanageable five-ton chunks and spread them over a half acre of meadow, effectively sterilizing most of the field.

The pillboxes were built as a response to the imminent risk of invasion that faced Britain in the spring of 1940. During the first few months of the war it had been presumed that this conflict, like the last, would be slogged-out across fixed battle-lines in the heart of Europe and that the British mainland had little to worry about. The rapid and unexpected collapse of France in the spring of 1940 changed all that and Britain suddenly found herself exposed, devoid of military allies and, following the loss of virtually all her artillery at Dunkirk, practically defenceless. Conventional military thinking, backed up by intelligence reports, made it increasingly likely that, with Germany in control of the French ports, invasion and a subsequent German occupation was inevitable. On 22th May General Sir Edmund Ironside was appointed General Officer Commanding Home Forces and was asked to put in place measures to thwart the expected invasion. This invasion was expected to take the form of a massive cross-Channel assault together with parachutists and glider-borne troops who would take over key inland positions, often taking advantage of the many partly completed and unguarded airfields in south-central England. Colerne airfield was singled out as being particularly likely to figure in the German invasion plan and for this reason a number of pillboxes in the Corsham area faced north to the airfield rather than south to the coast, as might be expected. Ironside's scheme, which was accepted by the Chiefs of Staff on 25th June, was intended to protect London and the industrial Midlands. The scheme consisted of a forward coastal defence manned by regular troops using the few weapons that still remained after Dunkirk, reinforced by road blocks at natural defiles and at nodal points inland, manned by the Home Guard. Further inland there was to be a strong defensive line of anti-tank ditches and pillboxes, known as the GHQ line, running from Highbridge in Somerset to Reading and then skirting around the south of London before running up the east coast towards Newcastle. In the southern areas further Command, Corps and Divisional defence lines ran south from the GHQ line to the coast dividing the region into small defensive boxes.

The Avoncliff and Freshford area was of immense importance in this plan as it was the point at which three major elements of the GHQ line and an important Command stop-line met. The west-east defences consisted of two lines of pillboxes approximately twenty miles apart. The northern line, designated the 'Red Line', stretched for sixty-eight miles from Freshford then skirted north of Corsham through Great Somerford to Tilehurst near Reading and was intended to have 186 pillboxes, eleven anti-tank emplacements and seventeen miles of anti-tank ditch. The most important southern or 'Blue Line' was fifty-eight miles in length and stretched from Freshford through Avoncliff and Bradford-on-Avon to Tilehurst. It was intended to include 170 pillboxes, fifteen anti-tank emplacements and five miles of ditch. For much of its length it followed the course of the Kennet and Avon Canal which itself presented an admirable anti-tank obstacle. The Bristol Outer Defence Line or 'Green Line' ran roughly north-east from Highbridge to Freshford and then on via Stroud to the southern outskirts of Gloucester. This line, which was ninety-one miles long, was to consist of no less than 319 pillboxes although many of those on the northern reaches remained un-built when the plan was abandoned in 1941. The fourth line of pillboxes that terminated at Freshford was the north end of the only partially completed Salisbury stop-line, which drove northwards through Frome and Hinton Charterhouse. Nearby, the underground ammunition depots at Corsham and Monkton Farleigh, together with their associated railway loading yards, were provided with dedicated clusters of pillboxes for their own local defence.

A contract for the construction of all the defences on the Blue Line was let to the Devizes building firm of Chivers – one of the many such companies that did well out of the war – on 19th September 1940, several weeks after work had commenced on other elements of the defences. Most of the pillboxes were completed by the end of the following February when the War Office peremptorily called a halt to the programme, but very little progress had been made on the proposed anti-tank ditches which were proving to be much more difficult to excavate than at first envisaged.

Almost as soon as work started on construction of the defence lines many members of the War Cabinet and of the Chiefs of Staff Committee voiced the opinion that the current plan was unsatisfactory. They felt that Ironside, who was a veteran of the First World War, was applying the discredited static defence strategies of that earlier conflict to the fast-moving, blitzkrieg tactics of the present war. Some members, too, considered the pillbox to be a death-trap for the soldiers condemned to man them. The majority opinion was that what was required was a more dynamic system of mobile defence able to react quickly to the enemy's every move. The upshot was that General Ironside was made Field Marshall, given a peerage and put out to grass. He was replaced on 16th July 1940 by the younger and more forward thinking General Alan Brooke. General Brooke, later Lord Alanbrooke, was in agreement with the majority opinion, noting in his diary on 22nd July, after a tour of inspection of the works in hand that:

> 'Much work and energy was being expended on an extensive system of rear defence, comprising anti-tank ditches and pillboxes, running roughly parallel to the coast and situated well inland. This static rear defence did not fall in with my conception of the defence of the country.
>
> To my mind our defences should be of a far more mobile and offensive nature. I visualize a light defence along the beaches, to hamper and delay landings to the maximum, and in the rear highly mobile forces trained to immediate aggressive action intended to concentrate and attack any

landings before they had time to become too well established. I was also relying on heavy air attacks on the point of landing, and had every intention of using sprayed mustard gas on the beaches.'

Brooke argued throughout the autumn and winter against the existing fixed defence lines, commenting, after a visit to the highly vulnerable eastern defences on 29th January that:

'Guy Williams has been commanding this large front from the beginning, but I was not entirely happy about his methods. Being an Engineer, his mind naturally turned to the construction of defensive lines. Such lines might have been alright if we had troops to man them, but we have not. What little troops we had as reserves I did not want to lock up in defensive systems. I wanted to retain them for a mobile role of an offensive defence, ready to strike rapidly at any enemy that gained a foothold on our beaches.'

Eventually, as we have seen, Brooke got his way. At the end of February all pillbox construction stopped and local commanders were urged not to use those that were finished as the primary means of defence. It was recommended that simple trenches and earthworks should be dug both close to the pillbox locations and elsewhere for use instead. The fact that Ironside's pillbox programme was prematurely terminated explains, to some extent at least, their apparently haphazard distribution, and more importantly, the haphazard distribution of the supporting works such as anti-tank ditches and anti-tank obstacles.

DESIGN AND CONSTRUCTION

At least fourteen different 'standard' designs for pillboxes were produced by the Directorate of Fortifications and Works, as well as numerous one-off specials for specific locations. By far the most numerous in the Avoncliff area were the large and small hexagonal pattern (Types 22 and 24) and the small square Type 26, though there were others which are described below. Slightly further afield there are a number of massive Type FW3/28 pillboxes for the 2-pounder anti-tank gun at Semington and a massively constructed pillbox for a Vickers machine gun at Monkton Farleigh. It is easy to be fooled into thinking that the majority of pillboxes are built of brick, but this would be erroneous as they are in fact made of reinforced concrete up to 3' 6" in thickness. Removable timber panels were used for the interior shuttering but brick shuttering was used externally and was usually left in place after the concrete had set.

In extraordinarily difficult locations where site conditions would have made conventional building techniques impossible the War Office resorted to the use of prefabricated concrete pillboxes. These consisted of pre-cast concrete interior and exterior panels that were bolted together and then the space between filled with poured concrete. Throughout the country only an extremely small number of these were built and two are at Avoncliff. They are very rare survivors and should be, but are not, scheduled for preservation. The first of these is between Belcombe and Avoncliff, sandwiched on a very narrow strip of land at the bottom of a steep embankment between the river and railway at a point opposite the little Belcombe pumping station. The second can be found by going underneath the canal aqueduct on the north bank of the river and following the footpath through the quaintly-named Melancholy Walk towards Murhill. One first stumbles upon a standard octagonal pillbox, again sandwiched between the river and railway near the outfall adit from one of the canal siphons. Passing this pillbox, continue until the path passes under the Freshford railway viaduct. The pre-cast pillbox stands high on the embankment by the south abutment of the viaduct, partially concealed by trees. On the opposite bank of the river there is a conventional pillbox hidden beneath the railway arch.

LOCATIONS

Taking the east side of Bradford-on-Avon as an arbitrary starting point we can follow the defence line through the Avon valley. From the east the route has followed the railway line from Bradford Junction with three pillboxes guarding the bridge over the River Biss. Near Bridge Street in Bradford-on-Avon there is a particularly fine square concrete example concealed on the embankment west of the line and north of the river in the grounds of the Hall, just before the line crosses the railway bridge. During the 1950s this pillbox was still disguised as a railway platelayers hut, clad in old railway sleepers with a false pitched roof and covered in ivy. The cladding has now all fallen away but the building is still difficult to locate as it is now submerged in dense undergrowth. It is unusual in that it retains a heavy iron door securing its entrance. The next example is hidden below the railway bridge and faces the weir at Greenland Mill.

Until recently there was a line of three pillboxes along the towpath of the Kennet and Avon Canal between Trowbridge Road and Frome Road bridges but two of these were rather pointlessly destroyed during the restoration of the canal and the third, as we have seen in a previous chapter, collapsed into the Frome Road clay pit in the 1960s. Two conventional octagonal pillboxes covered the river bridge at Barton Farm where one still stands on its little promontory almost surrounded by water. Its twin on the opposite bank near the railway bridge was very effectively disguised as a summerhouse, complete with ornate tiled roof, but was demolished by the Royal Engineers in the 1950s.

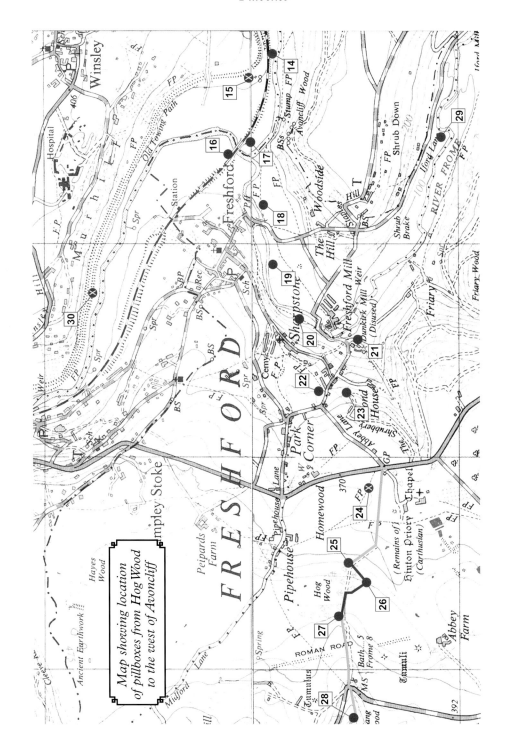

Map showing location
of pillboxes from Hog Wood
to the west of Avoncliff

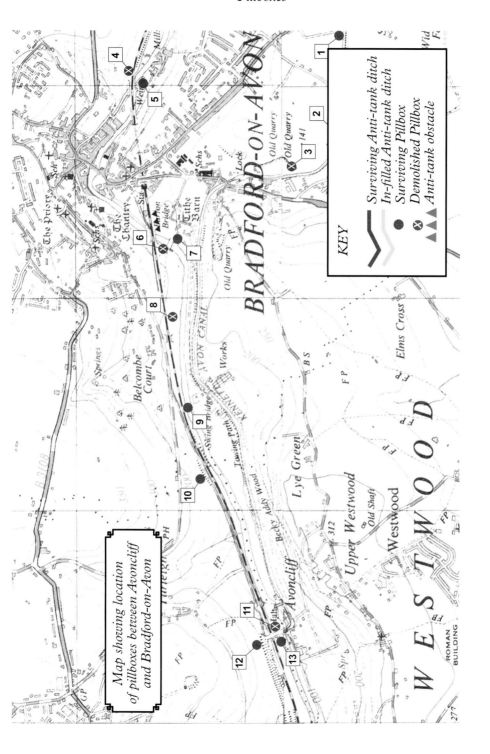

Map showing location of pillboxes between Avoncliff and Bradford-on-Avon

KEY

Surviving Anti-tank ditch
In-filled Anti-tank ditch
Surviving Pillbox
Demolished Pillbox
Anti-tank obstacle

The area immediately east of the railway bridge was considered a weak point in the defences where enemy armoured vehicles, unhampered by the river, might find a route northwards. The gap was obstructed by a line of conical concrete tank-traps extending from Bradford-on-Avon signalbox to the parapet of the bridge. The signalbox was demolished in 1966 but the concrete 'pimples' remain. Just how effective these tank traps would have been is debatable because they were built in such small numbers. At Bradford-on-Avon, for example, it would have been just as easy for a German tank to have steered around the other side of the signalbox which was completely unprotected. Elsewhere in the near neighbourhood there are other groups of equally ineffective tank traps. At Semington there are several rather impressive sets of cylindrical concrete traps on the canal towpath both east and west of the village and one supposes they were designed to force enemy tanks into the fields of fire of the three massive 2-pounder pillboxes nearby. There is a similar arrangement beside a small bridge over the Semington Brook near Whaddon Grove Farm. At that point it seems that the military planners hoped to hamper the enemy at the bridge in order to bring them within range of a further group of 2-pounder pillboxes nearby. The low-lying land in the Semington area was thought to be the most vulnerable point on the whole GHQ line and was designated an 'Anti-Tank Island' and heavily fortified. For those interested in our wartime defences the area is well worth a visit. A further group of apparently ineffective anti-tank blocks, built to a pyramidal design, still survive at Shoscombe Bottom near Radstock while a little further afield, at Dinder in Somerset, there is a very impressive line of rectangular blocks and other defences that would have much more successfully protected a natural defile there.

Between Bradford-on-Avon and Belcombe the natural topography the precipitous slope of Grip Wood with the canal and river below – offered such a difficult terrain that no additional defences were necessary and it is not until we come to the eastern edge of Avoncliff that more pillboxes are encountered. Due to the numerous approaches to the hamlet from the south and west and to the shallow river crossing and the presence of the canal aqueduct, Avoncliff was thought to be another very vulnerable location. The threat here, though, was believed to come from highly mobile infantry, light artillery and motor transport units rather than heavy armoured vehicles and in consequence there are no anti-tank pillboxes. Instead, the canal crossing and the broad riverside meadow to the south were swept by a large number of infantry pillboxes, arranged very loosely in mutually defensive groups of three.

The first pillbox to be encountered as one approaches from Belcombe is the riverside pre-cast example described above. This was supported by a semi-buried octagonal red brick pillbox built on the crest of what was until recently a steep grassy bank that rises to the north of the lane to Avoncliff approximately

100 yards west of Belcombe pumping station. This slope used to be known as 'Adder Bank' because on hot summer days it was alive with snakes basking in the sun but it is now very heavily overgrown and almost impenetrable. The pillbox, which had a broad arc of fire extending from Bradford sewage works to the aqueduct, is still just accessible from the field above although it is now well hidden amongst the undergrowth. The third pillbox in this group was spectacularly sited on the aqueduct although, sadly, there is no trace of it now. It stood on the precipitous promontory between the north end of the aqueduct and the top of the steps from the railway station. It commanded a field of fire across the weir to the water meadow and also covered both north and south approaches to the aqueduct. Supporting fire across the aqueduct was provided by a square pillbox positioned on the north bank of the canal where it turns towards Murhill. This also protected the long straight section of the towpath westwards towards Winsley sewage works. From there the chain was continued by the first of three octagonal pillboxes carefully positioned at curves on the towpath to cover the entire length of the canal from Murhill Bridge to Limpley Stoke Bridge. These were all destroyed during the restoration of the canal.

Perhaps the best-concealed of all the pillboxes in Avoncliff, and the one which eludes all but the most determined investigator, is built into the abutment of the railway bridge facing towards Freshford. It is buried in the embankment between the aqueduct and railway bridge close up against the wing wall of the bridge and is now completely enshrouded in brambles. Fire from this location, supported by the octagonal pillbox in Melancholy Walk already described, would sweep the railway line and both banks of the river.

On the east side of Rowley Lane, the narrow road that descends from Westwood to Farleigh Hungerford, almost opposite Rowley Manor (reputedly the only surviving building of the lost village of Rowley), near the point where it joins the main road, there is a most unusual pillbox buried in the bank. It is one of the few pillboxes completed at the north end of the Salisbury-Freshford stop line and was built to house a 6pdr Hotchkiss gun, which, for its time, was a pretty formidable weapon. A small square structure, the whole building is buried in earth except for a short entrance tunnel from the roadside and a large rectangular loophole at the front overlooking the valley. The loophole does not appear to be well protected but there may once have been an armoured shield. In the floor directly in front of the loophole is a ring of very sturdy holdfast bolts set in concrete to mount the gun.

Beyond the pre-fabricated pillbox at Freshford viaduct the Green Line heads off along the River Frome through Freshford where two octagonal pillboxes protect the bridge by the New Inn with another pair covering the small bridge behind Freshford Mill. The line then climbs through the woods parallel to but to the south-west of Rosemary Lane to Hinton Charterhouse which is really the extremity of our area of interest. There though, hidden in Hog Wood near Pipehouse (and luckily accessible by public footpath) is a remarkable survival. In the interest of speed and economy it was planned from the start that the GHQ line would take the greatest possible advantage of natural obstacles like canals, rivers, high railway embankments and deep cuttings along its route, but, where no such obstacles existed, artificial anti-tank ditches were to be built. Until work began on sections of these ditches it was not appreciated how much time and labour would be absorbed in them and as a consequence very little was completed before the linear defence scheme as a whole was abandoned. In Hogg Wood, however, there is a 300 metre length of completed ditch skirting the edge of the wood, together with three pillboxes (one at each change of angle) and several dug-out infantry gun pits. Isolated and completely useless as a defensive measure, the ditch, some twenty feet wide and twelve feet deep – big enough, indeed, to drive a lorry through without being seen from the surrounding fields, though that was not its purpose – is a quite extraordinary sight. The ditch continued down across the hillside to Midford Brook to the west and to the top of the steep-sided valley leading down to Dunkirk on the east, but much of this was infilled at the end of the war. Around the pillboxes in Hog Wood a number of complex, zig-zag infantry trenches also still survive.

Below: This pillbox on the edge of Hog Wood gives covering fire across the point where the anti-tank ditch (seen in the foreground) turns at an acute angle.

Note: The locations of the various pillboxes illustrated on this page and those that follow can be found by referencing the numbers on each photograph against the maps on pages 208 and 209.

Below: Just beyond the boundary of the maps, this unusual and very well concealed pillbox housed a powerful 6 pdr Hotchkiss gun which ranged over the twin bridges, an effective 'squeeze point' for invading forces, in the valley at Farleigh Hungerford.

Above: Further afield, this is one of a series of 2 pdr anti-tank pillboxes at Semington which formed a formidable 'anti-tank island' at a nodal point on the GHQ 'Blue' stop-line.

Below: Near Whaddon Marsh Farm, these anti-tank 'pimples', overlooked by a further series of 2 pdr anti-tank pillboxes, protect a vulnerable crossing point on the Semington Brook.

9

HOUSES: PUBLIC AND PRIVATE

In the introduction to this book I mentioned that Avoncliff today is not quite what it seems, and it is now time to explain what I meant. A few years before the coming of the canal Avoncliff consisted of no more than half a dozen houses, three mills, a public house and what we can pretty safely assume was an apprentice house. By the mid-1850s the equation was little changed – one mill and five houses had gone but six new houses had been built and the apprentice accommodation was now the Union Workhouse. At the start of the twentieth century (even, indeed, at the start of the Second World War) things were still much the same except for the addition of the local authority waterworks in 1883.

At first glance things still look much the same today until you realize that, almost without exception, the industrial buildings have metamorphosed into private houses: both the Main and South Mills on the Westwood bank are private dwellings; the old workhouse is now a rather attractive group of private homes, the waterworks pump-house has been a domestic dwelling since 1972, the stables that once belonged to Freeman's Mill have been converted into a house and even the barges moored on the canal are more homes than boats. Plans were prepared long ago to turn Freeman's Mill, until recently the only surviving bastion of dereliction, into a house and, despite several setbacks, work is now in hand to turn those plans into reality. Most astonishingly of all, the underground reservoir that once provided water to the workhouse is now the setting for a most spectacular underground house. The only commercial building to remain in trade (though hardly unchanged) throughout this entire period is the Cross Guns.

Amongst the earliest buildings in Avoncliff, the deeds of the Cross Guns (known until about 1822 as the Carpenter's Arms), date from 1712 but make reference to a public house at the same location a century earlier. The only older building that we can be certain of is the fulling mill on the north bank but, of course, with the passage of time many earlier buildings may have come and gone; little, for example, is known of the provenance of the row of five dwellings known as Ford Cottages which were demolished in the 1850s. The oldest part of the public house is the central block with two prominent gables; the extensions to east and west probably date from the early nineteenth century. The odd-shaped extension to the western end conforms to the road layout that resulted from the construction of the aqueduct which implies it was built some

Above: This photograph was taken just after the First World War, but the building remained virtually unchanged until the 1970s when the attic space was extended.

time after 1805. Inside the building two internal windows in the west wall of what was until the 1970s the public bar and is now the larger dining room were originally external windows of the seventeenth century structure. When the canal was built the embankment was brought up close to the rear of the public house, necessitating the blocking-up of the rear ground floor windows in the original building; the western extension, which post-dates the canal, was built without rear windows. It might be argued (although without any supporting evidence) that the pub was enlarged as a result of the increased trade brought by the canal.

The clothing firm of Moggridge and Joyce are reputed to have held either the freehold or a lease of the public house during the early years of the nineteenth century which was a period when they were firmly entrenched at Avoncliff. The firm is known to have issued pay tokens from both its Avoncliff and Dunkirk factories so it is reasonable to assume that they possessed establishments where these could be exchanged. The issuing of such pay tokens or private currency is often equated with the disreputable 'truck' system, whereby labourers were paid in tokens which could only be spent or exchanged at company-owned pubs or shops where prices were greatly inflated. Although the iniquitous practice of 'truck' was rife, this was not always the reason for payment in company tokens as in many instances they were issued because there was, particularly during the latter part of the eighteenth century, a chronic shortage of small coinage.

It is most likely that the Carpenters Arms became the Cross Guns in recognition of the Bradford Division of the Volunteer Yeomanry who established a rifle range near the site of the present-day sewage works beside the canal some time after 1794. This locally recruited, unpaid county defence force under the command of Richard Long, the High Sheriff of Wiltshire, was formed in 1794 in response to a call by Pitt the younger for 'Volunteer companies and bodies of Yeoman Cavalry' to defend the country against a French invasion following the declaration of war in 1793. After the defeat of the French Army the volunteers remained in existence as a paramilitary police force which, in the event of civil disturbance, could be 'Called out ... by the Sheriff of the County for the suppression of riots or tumults within their own or adjacent counties, or by Royal Warrant in case of invasion.'

The Yeomanry were called upon to put down rioting agricultural labourers in Warminster, Trowbridge and Bradford-on-Avon in 1822. It is quite possible that the change of the pub's name to the Cross Guns was meant as a salutary reminder to potential rioters that retribution was close at hand.

By the mid-nineteenth century the relevance of the Volunteer Yeomanry had waned, but in 1859 a wave of groundless central government paranoia in response to Napoleon III's European sabre-rattling led to a resurgence of interest. Hugely expensive coastal defences were thrown up around Britain's sea approaches and a call went out for the formation of local Volunteer Rifle Corps. The 9th (Bradford-on-Avon) Battalion of the Wiltshire Rifle Volunteers was formed in 1860 and the canal-side rifle range was resurrected. Nearby, various Battalions of the Somerset Rifle Volunteers either built or renewed ranges at Box, Warleigh and Claverton Down. Ranges were generally 1,000 yards long with firing points at 100 yard intervals. The targets, or 'butts', near Avoncliff were in a natural hollow in the field immediately to the west of the sewage works. Because of the difficult lie of the land, the shooting position for the 1,000 yard range was on the far side of the valley on the hillside below Turleigh, which meant that the bullets flew across Avoncliff Lane, the Great Western Railway line and the Kennet and Avon Canal and its towpath. In a contemporary history of the Corps, written in 1888, Major Robert Dwarris Gibney commented on this, writing that the line of fire:

> '... extends across sundry footpaths, a canal and a railroad. That there were no accidents is attributable more to good luck than good guidance. The shorter ranges across the canal were tolerably secure. A red flag, much shouting and an occasional despatch of one of the squad to the dangerous point to stay man, woman or child from running into danger or to inform the cursing bargee of his being cared for would suffice. The Great Western Railway Company evidently for very many years troubled themselves not about such trifles as bullets through their carriages.'

The Avoncliff range continued to see constant use for training by the Duke of Edinburgh's Wiltshire Regiment throughout the Boer War and the First

World War. During the Second World War the shorter ranges only (from the south side of the canal) were used by the Home Guard and, apparently, by American units stationed at Camp Field in Westwood. My grandmother recalled seeing soldiers 'at the butts' during both World Wars and took me to see the remains of the targets and the shooting positions, which were still quite intact, in the early 1950s. The latter consisted of a row of rectangular positions from which the soldiers would fire in a prone position, marked out by semi-buried railway sleepers. Nothing remains to be seen now at the firing point, but scraping away the soil behind the easily identifiable target positions will unearth large numbers of Snider and Enfield bullets along with 9mm Sten gun rounds. These short-range weapons were fired from a trench that can still just be identified fifty yards in front of the target.

In 1840, and probably for several years before, the Cross Guns was the property of G & T Spencer, Bradford-on-Avon's biggest brewer with a brewery in Whitehead's Lane, a malthouse on the Frome Road and numerous public houses in the district. At the height of their success in 1884 the Spencer brothers built a new, prison-like ale and porter store on the south side of Silver Street which still stands today. In the early years of the twentieth century Spencer's bought up a large number of individual public houses and small breweries from as far afield as Berkshire, Bristol and Taunton. For some time the Board of Directors were mystified as to why the managing director, Mr A.D. Hatch, insisted on securing the freeholds of most of the brewery's public houses in his own name on behalf of the brewery, but for some reason they seemed to acquiesce.

A lease of the Cross Guns prepared by A.D. Hatch on 30 March 1889 has an inventory attached which makes it clear that the building had changed little by 1947 when plans were first made to bring the sanitation into the twentieth century. It is possible to identify most of the ground-floor rooms mentioned in the 1889 inventory on the drawings prepared in 1947 and, indeed, the few people who visited the pub in the 1960s would have noticed that the layout was still virtually unaltered.

1889 - INVENTORY OF THE CROSS GUNS
PARLOUR: 36-inch register grate and a painted corner cupboard with two doors.
TAP ROOM: Four-foot oven range and boiler and a settle with backing. A forty-foot glazed partition with four iron fence rods in the partition.
BAR: Painted and glazed partition with glazed door and counter with two cupboards each 10' x 7". Seven painted shelves attached to the wall.
KITCHEN: 32-inch hob grate. Painted dresser with two cupboards and four drawers, 8' 6" wide with shelves above and a painted shelf in the window.

SITTING ROOM: 36-inch register grate. Painted partition and door to divide the room. Also a 17' 8" canvas and paper partition.
BEDROOM ADJOINING SITTING ROOM: Two painted doors and frames to form a wardrobe 4' 4" x 6' 2".
NEXT BEDROOM: 18-inch hob grate.
CLUB ROOM: 36-inch hob grate.
CELLAR: Eighteen-foot run of double housing for casks. A similar seven-foot run.
BREWHOUSE: Baking oven as fixed.
STABLE: Hay rack and manger for three stalls.
FRONT OF HOUSE: Thirty-six yard run of railings as fixed, with eighteen posts and two rails.

The years immediately before and after the First World War were times of great change in the brewing industry. Before the war many smaller breweries were taken over by larger firms who wanted, not the manufacturing capacity of the smaller firms, which were often inefficient and archaic, but the tied public houses that went with them.

The post-war closures were often a more tragic tale. During the latter part of the nineteenth century German beer had gained an unassailable reputation for excellence among British working men and was the beverage of choice for all who could afford it. To take advantage of this reputation a number of brewery companies were formed in Britain with names that implied a German connection where no such connection actually existed – they were wholly British owned and brewed fairly traditional British beer, although the bottle labels at first glance may have suggested otherwise. Amongst these were the Anglo-Bavarian Brewery at Shepton Mallet and its sister brewery on the London Road in Bath, near its junction with Cleveland Bridge Road, both of which grew very rich indeed in this way. Anglo Terrace', a row of ugly late Victorian houses on the north side of London Road was built to house employees of the brewery, access to which was gained through an archway between the houses now known as Burdall's Yard.

Fallout from the First World War proved to be the company's downfall. Anti-German feelings ran high during the war and its aftermath, and Englishmen resolutely refused to purchase anything, even the best beer in the world, that smacked of the Teutonic. The Anglo-Bavarian and a host of other quasi-Germanic breweries were quickly reduced to bankruptcy, despite their squeals of innocence, and the market never recovered.

The closure of Wilkins and Hudson's brewery, whose monolithic brew-house towers over Bradford-on-Avon from its prominent position at the bottom of Wine Street, was also brought about by the First World War. Throughout the

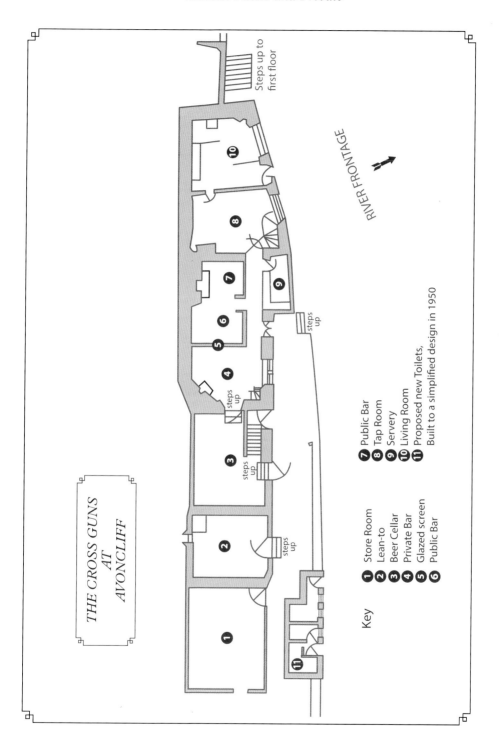

THE CROSS GUNS
AT
AVONCLIFF

RIVER FRONTAGE

Steps up to first floor

steps up

steps up

steps up

steps up

Key

1 Store Room
2 Lean-to
3 Beer Cellar
4 Private Bar
5 Glazed screen
6 Public Bar

7 Public Bar
8 Tap Room
9 Servery
10 Living Room
11 Proposed new Toilets,
Built to a simplified design in 1950

early years of the twentieth century and right through the Great War the brewery maintained its pre-war prosperity, the minutes of the company's twenty-first annual general meeting in July 1918 noting that 'Under all the difficulties, we propose the payment of the very handsome dividend of ten percent on the Ordinary Shares, same to be free of Income Tax.'

There was a warning, however, that such prosperity might not continue. After noting with regret that the Chairman of the Company remained absent due to his continuing military duty, the Deputy Chairman remarked that as a result of the war 'The Company has lost the services of the secretary, two Brewers and many other members of staff and under the circumstances it was difficult to carry on the business.'

Despite the payment in the following year of a similar ten percent dividend plus an additional tax-free bonus of ten percent, it was becoming obvious that with a depleted staff and facing stiff competition from the bigger brewers, Wilkins and Hudson were facing an uncertain future. The end came at 12:15 on the afternoon of Friday 6th February 1920 at an Extraordinary General Meeting of the Company at 13 Queen Square in Bath. Negotiations had been going on for a while with Usher's of Trowbridge and at the EGM it was resolved '...that the Company be wound up voluntarily and that the draft agreement with Usher's Wiltshire Brewery be approved.'

Just over a month later, on 9 March, a creditors' meeting was held at Queen Square, the last entry in the Company minute book recording simply that 'No creditors appearing, our business was terminated.'

The demise of Spencer's brewery, owners of the Cross Guns, was an altogether different affair. During 1909/10 there had been something of a scandal at the Brewery when it was discovered that the Managing Director of the Company, Mr A.D. (Andrew) Hatch had been falsifying the alcohol duty accounts. Spencer's were prosecuted and a substantial fine was imposed. A problem arose in that Andrew Hatch and other members of his family were substantial shareholders in the brewery and that if he were asked to sever his connections the financial consequences for the brewery could be dire. Also, it was considered that in the straight-jacketed moral climate of the time the inevitable public disclosure would reflect badly on the company's standing in the county. So Andrew Hatch remained as Managing Director and accepted liability for payment of the fine. Unwilling to actually part with the money, he used his shareholder power to arrange that the sum was simply entered as a debit against him in the company accounts.

Following the death of Andrew Hatch in 1911, his son A.B. (Basil) Hatch became Chairman and Managing Director and initially agreed to accept liability for his father's misdemeanours. Meanwhile there were rumblings of further irregularities on the part of young Basil Hatch sufficient for the Secretary to warn him, in a memo of 10th November 1911, that 'No monies of the Company must be used for any purpose other than the Company's business.'

Early in 1914 Basil Hatch went back on his agreement with the Company regarding his father's liability for the Excise fine and threatened to bring an action against the company to nullify the debt. Hatch's claim was dismissed by the Board as the following extract from the Company minute book explains:

> 'The Secretary reminds the Board that when the accounts were presented for the year 1909/10 the question arose as to a fine that the Company had to pay in consequence of False Entries made in the Excise Books with the knowledge of the Managing Director, and that he had declined to treat such payment as a liability of the Company and it remained to the debit of Mr Basil Hatch.
>
> Mr Hatch now takes exception to the debit and alleges that the directors had condoned the matter. The views of the Secretary are now confirmed that it is a proper charge against the late Managing Director.'

Basil Hatch appears to have inherited his father's penchant for constructive accountancy, which was to lead to the ultimate ruin of the company. In May 1913 scrutiny of the accounts revealed disquieting irregularities which were revealed to the Board of Directors at a special meeting on 12th June when the Company Secretary informed them that:

> 'I regret to have to report to the Board upon certain matters that have come to light upon making up the accounts to 31 March. When the accounts were made up last September it was evident that monies received by the Managing Director were not being paid into the bank when received and the following Minute was passed on November 11th 1912: 'That all monies be paid into the Bank as and when received.'
>
> This has not been done.
>
> In making up the accounts to 31st March some of the accounts which in the past had been regularly paid showed, on examination, that in the latter half of the year settlements were most irregular and on examination of the accounts, and visits to some of the houses, these irregularities are confirmed.
>
> Mr Hatch says that some of the monies received have been paid in since 31st March. I cannot say that all deficiencies have been accounted for. Mr Basil Hatch does not admit any beyond those he has been challenged with, and in some cases disputes the amount to be accounted for.'

A week later the Directors met again and resolved,

> 'That Mr A.B. Hatch be suspended from the office of Managing Director and that the Secretary inform Mr A.B. Hatch of his suspension and that the meeting be adjourned until this day week with a view to him supplying the Secretary with full information as to cash transactions which have not already been explained, and, if such a statement is furnished the Directors will at the adjourned meeting favourably consider the question of accepting the Managing Director's resignation, if tendered, instead of passing a resolution removing him from office.
>
> The Secretary was instructed to inform the Capital and Counties Bank, Bradford-on-Avon that until further notice cheques will be signed by the Secretary alone.'

The situation for the Company now became serious due to the fact that Basil Hatch, though now suspended as Managing Director, was still a major shareholder and a member of the family who, through the medium of the Hatch Trust, controlled much of the capital of the company in the form of debentures. Over the years the Directors had allowed the personal finances of both Andrew and Basil Hatch to become too deeply integrated into those of the company and, in the acrimony that resulted from the exposure of Basil Hatch's dubious dealings, the whole edifice was on the point of collapse. On 10th July Basil Hatch sought unsuccessfully to placate the Directors, the Company Secretary noting that:

> 'Mr A.B. Hatch's letter of this date was read and it was felt that no good would result from an adjournment though the directors would be pleased to have all accounts cleared up at the earliest time and regret that they must consider their decision as to his suspension at the last meeting as final.
>
> They also required an undertaking from him not to collect any monies or visit any of the Company's houses, or to go to the Brewery except on the Secretary's request to clear up any matters.'

Later that day the Board accepted Hatch's letter of resignation. With the company finances in turmoil it was unlikely that it could continue to trade. Faced with the prospect of family disgrace the Trustees of the Hatch Trust called for the liquidation of the company and on 16th July a provisional agreement was made with Usher's Wiltshire Brewery of Trowbridge for the takeover of the assets and stock of the business. Five days later the financial situation became critical, the Board Minutes recording that:

'The Secretary also reported that it was absolutely necessary to arrange for financial help to carry through the week and after considerable discussion it was agreed that he should put the matter before Mr Usher and explain the position and ascertain whether it would make any difference to him carrying out the scheme if the Company suspended payment.'

A temporary loan was raised to keep the business going until a proper resolution could be found. Finally, on 2nd August, the Directors unanimously agreed that the company should be voluntarily wound up and that Stephen Tryon of Albion Chambers, Bristol, should be appointed liquidator. Hatch had already disposed of the malthouse and some of the public houses a year or two earlier to raise additional revenue.

All the company's assets were purchased for the sum of £56,000 by Ushers of Trowbridge who promptly put the Brewery and other property in Bradford--on-Avon up for sale by auction, retaining only the portfolio of public houses. Included in the sales particulars for the auction, which took place at the Swan Hotel on 28th July 1914, were the main brewery buildings in Whitehead's Lane (complete with 18 horsepower horizontal steam engine and boiler by Spencer and Gillett of Melksham), the two-storey ale and porter store on Silver Street (the upper floor of which had, until recently, been used as the Volunteers Drill Hall), the manager's house adjoining the brewery and various shops and premises in St. Margaret's Street. The auction was not a success and the plant and premises at Bradford-on-Avon were later disposed of in a piecemeal fashion.

Thus, in 1914, the Cross Guns became an Usher's pub. At that time there would still have been a reasonable trade; the canal was still commercially active, both mills were hard at work under William Selwyn's ownership and, although the quarries had closed a decade earlier, there was still a sizeable workforce of thirsty masons employed at the stone yard. In the immediate post-war years, too, the inmates of the Red Cross hospital also contributed to the coffers of Usher's Wiltshire Brewery.

The large influx of museum and engineering personnel into the area during the Second World War must have maintained trade sufficiently to induce Usher's to make some improvements to the premises in 1949. These improvements were, by modern standards, fairly minimal, amounting to the installation of mains water to the building and the replacement of an earth closet in the garden and an earth urinal beside the lane in front of the pub by a purpose-built toilet block (draining into the river). The proposed facilities were rather more luxurious than those that were actually built and which still stand today.

By the early 1960s trade had dwindled away. The mills were derelict, the canal was dry, the wartime immigrants had drifted away and the stone yard was long gone. Most of the public rooms, including the tap room and the private bar, were shut up, leaving only the public bar, devoid of its glazed partitions, open for trade. Through 1967 and 1968 my friend Geoff and I frequently walked to Avoncliff for a drink and, night after night, we would be the only patrons of the Cross Guns with its old-fashioned wooden settles beside the fire and its walls and ceiling covered in ancient and curiously embossed zinc sheet coated in layer upon layer of yellowy-brown paint. The public bar seemed always to be in a state of dingy semi-darkness, lit by a single forty-watt lamp, which gave the place an air of claustrophobic gloom or romantic intimacy, depending upon one's company. For a while at the end of the decade the Cross Guns experienced a brief renaissance as it became popular with the relatively affluent and newly mobile sixties generation (particularly sixth-formers from Fitzmaurice Grammar School). The private bar reopened to cope with the growing clientele and the outside brightened-up with the addition of a few coloured lights and a coat of hideous blue paint, but the resurgence did not last. Notoriously fickle, the tight-knit group of revellers soon transferred their allegiance to the Three Horseshoes in Bradford-on-Avon and then to the Canal Tavern.

Suddenly tastes changed. Country pubs like the Cross Guns were perceived as old-fashioned, the haunts of old men drinking old-fashioned beverages like

Below: A typical busy summer Sunday at the Cross Guns in July 2014.

mild and bitter and Oatmeal Stout, and trade fell away sharply. Around this time the Cross Guns, like a number of Usher's other nine hundred or so pubs, was seen as commercially unviable and sold to a private landlord. Fortunes did not revive until the cultural revolution of the 1980s when such pubs transformed themselves into country restaurants and also started to sell the new lagers that suited the younger taste.

The last twenty-five years have seen enormous changes. The small living room at the west end of the building has become a kitchen and the former tap room, public bar, private bar and beer cellar have all been knocked into one large dining area with a bar at the east end. Externally there have been changes too, with a rear extension to the attic of the newer block at the west end of the building which has rather spoilt the symmetry of the end elevation. This work has also included the addition of three new dormers in the front of the roof and a new asymmetrical window in the front elevation. The once-overgrown garden that sloped down to the river has been terraced in concrete to provide an alfresco riverside dining area. Until very recently, when under new ownership the pub underwent a radical modernisation (which included indoor toilets), the sanitary contrivances remained much as they always were.

ANCLIFF DOWN

By 1971, when it was offered for sale, the former workhouse had fallen into a sorry state. The gatehouse and entrance block with its bell tower and turret clock, the pillared portico on the principal frontage and the mid-Victorian range of school buildings at the south end of the workhouse garden had all been demolished, ostensibly because they had fallen into a dangerous condition. The property was eventually purchased by Anthony Dunsdon who had been searching for some time for an old property of character that he could renovate as a home for his growing family. The Dunsdons moved into the 1830s chapel block at the rear of the main eighteenth century range of buildings in 1972 while the latter were let out to tenants at modest rents and restored on a limited budget as they fell vacant. By the mid-1980s Mr Dunsdon came to the conclusion that to restore the whole building to the condition in which he would have liked to see it would require resources well beyond those he had anticipated and reluctantly accepted that the property might have to be sold.

Aghast at the horrible schemes proposed by some of the property developers who expressed interest in the site, Anthony Dunsdon reappraised the situation and decided that to ensure the character of the building was not irretrievably ruined he would, after all, have to oversee its professional restoration himself. In this he was aided by the relative ease with which finance for such schemes could be raised at that time. The architects Tim Organ and Hans Klaentschi were commissioned to prepare plans for the restoration of the building which involved a great deal of sympathetic alteration to the interior without materially affecting the façade. Building work, which took two years to complete, was undertaken by PRC construction.

The interiors of the resultant ten houses in the main three-sided block that surrounds the courtyard have a gentle Mackintosh influence. The chapel extension which had been the Dunsdons' home was converted into two additional houses.

The architects had hoped to rebuild the east wing of the workhouse to its original form by replacing the two bays that had been lost in the 1930s, but were thwarted by the County Council Planning Department who saw this proposal as new construction rather than restoration. After much wrangling the council partially relented and, as a rather unsatisfactory compromise, allowed one of the two missing houses to be replaced. Close inspection of the stonework will reveal the extent of the rebuilding, which is pretty well in harmony with the older structure. As the reconstruction neared completion Anthony Dunsdon looked to build himself a new home in the three acre plot that had once been the workhouse garden. Aware that an application to the local authority for planning permission to build a conventional house would inevitably be refused, Tim Organ and Hans Klaentschi came up with a highly imaginative and radical plan to build an underground house on the site of the workhouse reservoir. Initially turned down by the Planning Department in 1993 on the grounds that whilst the house might well be underground the road approaching it and the cars parked outside certainly would not be, the scheme was subjected to a public enquiry and referral to the Secretary of State who eventually recommended its acceptance in February 1995.

The next problem was to find a building firm prepared to take on the rather difficult task of building the house. The nature of the job put it beyond the capabilities of the traditional small house-builders, yet it was too small a job for most of the larger contractors who might have both the expertise and specialist equipment to see it through to completion. In any case, the prices quoted by those larger firms who could be persuaded to tender were prohibitive on account of their bloated overhead costs. A contract to build the house was eventually awarded in April 1995 to the local building firm of Shellard and Winter who completed the work in August 1997.

The house is not actually built in the underground reservoir but around three sides of it, leaving the original floor of the chamber, re-laid with reclaimed engineering bricks, as a sunken courtyard. On the fourth side, to the west, the courtyard is bounded by a massive retaining wall. The most difficult stage of the construction programme was the excavation of the hundreds of tons of earth and clay from around the perimeter of the reservoir to a depth of some fifteen

Above: 'Ancliff Down', the underground house built within the reservoir of the former workhouse.

Below: A view looking north across the grass covered roof of Ancliff Down.

feet to provide the space in which to build the house. Beds of clay, much deeper than expected, were discovered on the sloping site and as excavation advanced on the south side of the reservoir the clay was found to be sliding downhill into the void, putting the entire project in jeopardy. Only the employment of a massive earthmoving machine – difficult to manoeuvre onto the site around Avoncliff's narrow lanes – saved the situation.

What strikes one immediately upon coming across the house is its pleasant lack of pretension. It would have been easy, given the location, to have built something grossly ostentatious but the house, named Ancliff Down, is instead discreet and in harmony with its surroundings. The structure, which is covered with earth flush with the surrounding landscape, is of standard industrial concrete elements faced with original Westwood ashlar blocks recovered from the reservoir and from the debris of the workhouse school building that was unearthed during the excavation. Internally the concrete beams that support the roof and floor panels are exposed without decoration and protrude through the front wall of the building. These projections, like angular corbels, together with the tall narrow windows, give the whole building a pleasant Mackintosh-with-a-hint-of-deco atmosphere, which was the architects' intention. Throughout the house and grounds much use has been made of reclaimed material, particularly paving that once formed the floor of the old workhouse and slabs from the bottom of the reservoir, all of which seem to make the house snugly integral with its surroundings.

10

CONCLUSION

So, that was Avoncliff where, it might seem, the current of the Avon has swept along the industrial detritus of the eighteenth and nineteenth centuries from the whole of England and deposited key elements of each upon its banks where the valley narrows. In part this little history may have appeared a little too personal and nostalgic, but it is my interpretation, based upon sixty years of intimate association, of the forces and influences that have battered Avoncliff into the shape it is today.

In my lifetime I have been privileged to have seen so many changes at Avoncliff carried through from start to finish, though it would be foolish, of course, to presume that those changes have reached an immutable maturity, for in sixty years time the hamlet will be as different then for some new historian as it was sixty years ago for me. Over the last six decades I've seen the last bow-hauled barge and the first modern, diesel-powered pleasure boat creep across the canal aqueduct; with the demise of the Chlorophyll and Derivatives factory I've seen the end of industry in Avoncliff and, in moments of melancholy while I scratched the names of lost loves and absent friends in the stonework of the railway bridge I've witnessed the passage of the last steam engines en route for Barry scrap yard and the first of the Western Region Hymek diesel hydraulic locomotives making their maiden journeys from Swindon works to St Phillip's Marsh engine shed in Bristol, resplendent in experimental colour schemes of desert sand, maroon and two-tone green. The scrap trains were truly tragic sights; one of the few remaining serviceable steam locomotives, gasping and wheezing after years of indifferent maintenance, would haul six or seven more condemned locomotives – devoid of coupling rods and piston rods to reduce their rolling resistance – clanking and groaning from Swindon to Woodham's scrap yard in South Wales. Dai Woodham, though, refused to cut them up and over the next twenty years many, though not all, were purchased by a plethora of preservation societies and restored to running order.

Perhaps with a subconscious reference to my first trip to Avoncliff as a child with my Aunty Molly, in the winter of 1979 my wife and I took our twelve month old son, Alistair, for a frosty walk along the canal bank from Limpley Stoke, where we lived for a time, to view the preparations for the final restoration of the aqueduct at Avoncliff. Maybe, in sixty years time, he will stand in the same place and recount to his son how he saw the last pleasure craft cross the aqueduct before the Health and Safety Executive ordered the closure of the canal on account of the risk to public health posed by its stagnant waters, and how he saw the last electric locomotive flash past below the railway bridge before the tracks were lifted and the alignment transformed into the north Wiltshire inter-urban cycleway. *Sic transit gloria mundi*, I suppose, but Avoncliff's moment of true glory is perhaps debatable.

Below: In 1948 this rather wonderful Great Western Railway oil lamp still survived at the top of the steps leading to the down platform at Avoncliff Halt.